SNAPE

A DEFINITIVE READING

LORRIE KIM

STORY SPRING PUBLISHING
PEKIN, IL

Story Spring Publishing, LLC
3420 Veterans Drive, #325
Pekin, Illinois 61554
www.storyspringpublishing.com

Cover Design: Liz Mattison Copyright ©2016
Photo Credits: Back cover photo by Kyle Cassidy. Photo on Page 307 by Elizabeth Wu.

Ordering Information:
Quantity sales. Special discounts are available on quantity purchases by corporations, associations, and others. For details, contact the publisher at orders@storyspringpublishing.com.

SNAPE/Kim, Lorrie.—1st ed.
ISBN: 978-1-940699-13-4
Library of Congress Control Number: 2016944924

CONTENTS

Dedication iii

Acknowledgements v

Abbreviations vii

Introduction: The Magnificence of Severus Snape 1

Severus Snape And the Sorcerer's Stone...5
    Overview: Snape, Year by Year 6

Severus Snape And the Chamber of Secrets..25

Severus Snape And the Prisoner of Azkaban 43
    Plot: Spoilers Ahead...43
    Snape's Year in Overview 47
    Slytherin, Gryffindor, Grudges, and Dumbledore...............................51
    The Return of the Marauders 55
    Snape's Assignment 58
    The Nature of Life Debts 62
    Snape's Flashback and Trauma 73

Severus Snape And the Goblet of Fire 85
    Snape's Year in Overview 86
    Puberty, Time Travel, and Second Chances 90

Severus Snape And the Order of the Phoenix 109
    Plot: Learning from Snape.. 110
    Snape's Year in Overview 113
    Occlumency.. 118

Severus Snape And the Half-Blood Prince 157
    Snape's Year in Overview 159
    Spinner's End... 165
    The Chosen One's Broken Nose... 176
    Snape's Defense Against the Dark Arts Classroom 177
    The Half-Blood Prince: Potions 181
    The Half-Blood Prince: Invented Spells... 184

Severus Snape And the Deathly Hallows, Part 1......................................215
  Plot...215
  Snape's Year in Overview...217
  Severus Snape and the Deathly Hallows......................................219
  Defense Against the Dark Arts: Lessons Snape Taught Harry........220
  The Snape-Shaped Hole...239
  "Look . . . at . . . me. . . ."..242

Severus Snape And the Deathly Hallows, Part 2......................................247
  Snape's Memories..249
  The Forest Again..288
  King's Cross: Master of Death..289
  The Flaw in the Plan: Invisible to Voldemort..............................292
  Epilogue...295

Works Cited..297

Index..299

About the Author..305

for Dominus

ACKNOWLEDGEMENTS

Thank you to Mark Dominus for supporting the writing of *SNAPE*. You are the clever, grumpy, magical love of my life.

Thank you to Diane Tarbuck and Chris Hagberg of Story Spring Publishing for your faith in this project and this subject and for your years of kindness to me. Diane, you were the first person ever to affirm that it would be worthwhile for me to write something about Snape. You made this book happen.

Thank you to Michele Combs of Carpe Indexum for cheering the writing of this book the whole way then standing ready to do a Hermione-quick indexing job at just the right moment.

Grace Gordon, thank you for the constant support and unerring knowledge of the world of books.

Professors Karen Wendling and Patrick McCauley are the open-minded, open-hearted founders of the Harry Potter Conference at Chestnut Hill College in Philadelphia, Pennsylvania. It has been a marvel to experience the powerful, joyous growth of your multidisciplinary event every year.

Some of the most incisive commentary and rousing debate I've ever enjoyed has come courtesy of the members of Potterdelphia, especially Grace Gordon, Madeleine Lifsey, and Skott Stotland.

With my whole being, I am thankful for the critical thinking and encouragement from my writerly friends: Emma Grant, Victoria McManus, Logospilgrim, Fox Estacado, Lisa Nicholas, Hilary K. Justice, Mara T. Stein, Alyse Leung, Satis, Libby Weber, and Wendy Worthington.

Thank you, always, to the creators of Snapecast, especially Rachael Vaughn and Shannon Sauro. You taught me so much and still do.

To everyone who has ever volunteered to organize a *Harry Potter* academic convention, you have my awe and gratitude.

Most of all, thank you to the wise scholars of the fifth grade reading groups: Iris, Grace, Sofia, Sophie, Khari, and Finn. It was a pleasure learning from you while serving Fudge Flies and Sorcerer's Scones. And thank you to Lily, Slytherin potioneer, who has been teaching me about Snape for years.

ABBREVIATIONS

HP/SS   Harry Potter and the Sorcerer's Stone

HP/CoS   Harry Potter and the Chamber of Secrets

HP/PoA   Harry Potter and the Prisoner of Azkaban

HP/GoF   Harry Potter and the Goblet of Fire

HP/OotP   Harry Potter and the Order of the Phoenix

HP/HBP   Harry Potter and the Half-Blood Prince

HP/DH   Harry Potter and the Deathly Hallows

All *HP* page numbers given are found in the Scholastic Trade Editions. Please see the "Works Cited" section on Page 297 for more information.

INTRODUCTION:
THE MAGNIFICENCE OF
SEVERUS SNAPE

The *Harry Potter* series may be named after the Boy Who Lived, but if you want to know the story, keep your eyes fixed on Snape. This hook-nosed, greasy-haired, grumpy character is one of J.K. Rowling's enduring gifts to English literature. He's the archetypal ill-tempered teacher: acerbic, yet horribly, deliciously funny. When he's in a scene, you can't take your eyes off him. Snape is always the story.

In Snape, Rowling created a character of almost perfect ambiguity, a double agent who rose to become the right-hand man of both generals on opposing sides of a war. He's at once self-controlled and seething with bitterness. Every sentence, every action has at least two possible and contradictory interpretations. The question of Snape's true loyalties is at the heart of the books' mysteries. Is it possible, ever, to know what lies underneath his façade?

It is. With a close look at each of the books, everything about Snape becomes knowable.

Is he a classroom bully? Without a doubt. He can be unfair, petty, mocking, prone to blatant favoritism—many of the traits that schoolchildren most loathe. But underneath his scathing surface is someone who cares desperately, enough to devote his adult life to protecting everyone in his world, even those whom he dislikes. And he does this all undercover, pretending to be evil, accepting that he will live and die without the chance to defend himself and clear his name.

Do his accomplishments cancel out the cruel things he's done? Not at all, and that is part of the power of this character. He is often unlovable, immature, unattractive, not even kind—but he made something of himself. His story tells us that hope and greatness are for everybody, not only for those who have always been good. When we learn all the harm he did in his youth, we learn how to understand without excusing, how to give ourselves and others a second chance.

With all his ugly qualities, what makes this character a favorite with so many readers?

He's smart. He's competent. His sarcasm is funny and his bitterness can be bracing. He always knows what to do. He's always there when you need him. There are things that only Snape can do. A wizard who has done evil and then felt remorse knows how to *undo* evil magic in a way that those who have always been good cannot know.

He's hideous, bless him, and sensitive to indignities. He loathes being mocked, especially by children; everyone sees him seething. But in all things, he does as much as he can with what he has and no more. As an adult, he becomes, not attractive, but *something*. Potent. Magnetic. He commands attention. When he is brave, he is almost beautiful.

He is kind to mothers, even if not to their children. He risks his life to help them. He knows how it feels to be powerless or unwanted. As vicious as he can be, when lives are at stake, there is nothing he won't do to protect others.

For a close reader, the character of Snape is endlessly rewarding. Some mysteries are easily explained; some fizzle out. But the more you read Snape, the more you learn of him, the more thrilling he becomes.

Working for Dumbledore, he learns how to atone. He chooses what is right, never what is easy. He assumes a thankless life that guarantees he will be universally hated, universally mistaken for evil, and resists the human urge to protest his innocence. He withstands these tests, even when people cry out to him at their moment of death, because his commitment is to something greater. He forgoes recognition, forgoes adult love, turns his formidable gifts to pulling off the unspeakable under conditions that are unthinkable—accepting that his achievements will never be known. He will never claim the role of hero. Against all instinct, he wills himself to do what must be done. And we, the readers, are his witnesses. Of his many sacrifices, we see that the costliest was the renunciation of his human right to show his true self. He keeps his truths tightly hidden until his dying breath, when he is finally free to command the books' hero: "Look at me."

J.K. Rowling took an enormous risk, gambling the climax of her epic series on her ability to build Snape's ambiguity to the breaking point and then show us his true self at the end. And what do we see when all is revealed? A vision of love so white-hot that it dazzles. This recognition of Snape is what brings completion to the series. And it brings the story back to Snape again and again.

SEVERUS SNAPE
AND THE SORCERER'S STONE

A seething brew of bitterness, spite, and lilting genius: from his first searing look into Harry Potter's eyes to his last, Severus Snape commands attention. This character is one of J.K. Rowling's master creations, a deadly man of contradictory extremes who may be profoundly good, profoundly evil, neither, and both. His impenetrable eyes are "cold and empty and made you think of dark tunnels." (*HP/SS*, 136) In this series about dark tunnels that lead always to revelation, the struggle to discover what—if anything—lies beneath Snape's façade of perfect ambiguity yields endless rewards for the reader.

Of all the people important to Harry's first year, Snape is the one he encounters last, a good four-tenths into the novel. By then, he's met or heard of Hagrid, Dumbledore, Voldemort, Quirrell, Malfoy, the Weasleys, Hermione, and McGonagall. He's been lulled by the excellent Welcoming Feast, found his place, seen one marvel after another—until this chilling moment.

> Professor Quirrell, in his absurd turban, was talking to a teacher with greasy black hair, a hooked nose, and sallow skin.
>
> It happened very suddenly. The hook-nosed teacher looked past Quirrell's turban straight into Harry's eyes—and a sharp, hot pain shot across the scar on Harry's forehead. (*HP/SS*, 126)

Harry has never felt this pain before.

> The pain had gone as quickly as it had come. Harder to shake off was the feeling Harry had gotten from the teacher's look—a feeling that he didn't like Harry at all.
>
> "Who's that teacher talking to Professor Quirrell?" he asked Percy.

"Oh, you know Quirrell already, do you? No wonder he's looking so nervous, that's Professor Snape. He teaches Potions, but he doesn't want to—everyone knows he's after Quirrell's job. Knows an awful lot about the Dark Arts, Snape." (*HP/SS*, 126)

Harry, and the reader, learn six things about Snape from this indelible first impression. He is ugly in a way that frightens children. He has some connection with Harry's childhood trauma. He is close to evil. He's perennially discontented: "everyone knows" he covets the Defense Against the Dark Arts job. And he doesn't like Harry Potter.

Overview: Snape, Year by Year

Snape's dislike of Harry is one of four elements that remain noteworthy about him through the seven years that Harry knows him. The others are: Snape's hostility toward other teachers who hold the Defense Against the Dark Arts position, Snape's reputation, and the mystery of Snape's true motives. Taken together, a consideration of these four elements yields a good overview of Snape's life at any point in the story.

Snape's personal dislike of Harry

After that first eye contact, Harry finds Snape's hostility even harder to shake off than his damage from Voldemort. Any child would be sensitive to inexplicable dislike from an adult in a position of power. But for an abused, orphaned survivor of violent crime, it is a nightmare come to life, fodder for Harry's terrifying dream that night about Quirrell's turban, Malfoy, and Snape. (*HP/SS*, 130)

The first day of Potions class cements Harry's understanding: "Snape didn't dislike Harry—he hated him." (*HP/SS*, 136) In all the ensuing mysteries about Snape's true motives, Snape's loathing of Harry is one of the few givens, constant and absolute. For seven books, readers may never be certain why Snape does anything, but one thing is for sure: it's not for love of Harry.

Snape targets Harry for bullying from the first time he calls roll in Potions class.

"Ah, yes," he said softly, "Harry Potter. Our new—*celebrity.*"

Draco Malfoy and his friends Crabbe and Goyle sniggered behind their hands. (*HP/SS*, 136)

Snape, as the Head of Slytherin House, has mocked Harry's heroic reputation to his first-years already, and they follow his lead to gang up on Harry. By this time in the story, we have seen that the rest of the school hates Slytherin. Hagrid even tells Harry, "There's not a single witch or wizard who went bad who wasn't in Slytherin" (*HP/SS*, 80), an assertion that goes unrefuted for almost three volumes. Slytherin, under Snape's leadership, has won the House Championship for the past six years. There is a narrative to be read here about the Slytherin teacher who zealously safeguards the morale of his first-year students, who walk into a school that sees them as villains. But it is obliterated by the appalling spectacle of an adult singling out one child and teaching the other students to mock him.

This passage introduces another constant: Snape's baseless conviction that Harry enjoys the notoriety that comes of his traumas. Nowhere in *Sorcerer's Stone* do we see where Snape gets this idea, so the reader, like Harry, experiences it as arbitrary and bewildering.

But then, Snape casts a magic spell.

> "You are here to learn the subtle science and exact art of potion-making," he began. He spoke in barely more than a whisper, but they caught every word—like Professor McGonagall, Snape had the gift of keeping a class silent without effort. "As there is little foolish wand-waving here, many of you will hardly believe this is magic. I don't expect you will really understand the beauty of the softly simmering cauldron with its shimmering fumes, the delicate power of liquids that creep through human veins, bewitching the mind, ensnaring the senses. . . . I can teach you how to bottle fame, brew glory, even stopper death—if you aren't as big a bunch of dunderheads as I usually have to teach." (*HP/SS*, 136-7)

With that rapturous ode to magic, this character reveals what is sacred to him. "Subtle science and exact art": he wants the children to know that mindset and discipline matter in magic. "Foolish wand-waving" is the first indication in the series that Snape's magical signature is self-sufficiency, magic not dependent on wands or incantations or anything outside the power of the solitary mind.

There are barbs embedded throughout his teaching, petulance and resentment in every sentence: "Foolish." "I don't expect you will really understand." "As big a bunch of dunderheads as I usually have to teach." He is insulting children who haven't even done anything, punishing them for the shortcomings of others. We can't tell yet if he truly covets the Defense Against the Dark Arts position, but it seems true enough that he's teaching Potions against his will—he's being compelled to, and he considers it too good for most of them.

But even the barbs hint at one of Rowling's more buried themes: the loneliness of the gifted. "Foolish wand-waving" sounds like the retort of a child whose own passions have been denigrated. "I don't expect you will really understand" conveys the melancholy of long disappointment. "Dunderheads": a cry of frustration from the prodigy mismatched with students whose minds work very differently. Rather touchingly, despite his rage, he seems unable to give up hope that he can convey a bit of the wonder of magic to these unpromising initiates.

"The beauty of the softly simmering cauldron with its shimmering fumes." This is a magical image for what we Muggles would call a *flow state*, the quietly sustained ecstasy of full absorption in creative activity. It is a state of enjoyment in one's own powers, a self-sufficient form of vital happiness. Bitterness, loneliness, and hostility fall away. For the rest of the series, when we see Snape endure unspeakable pressures, we can remember that he revealed his secret in this first speech: as long as he could sustain a soft simmer, whether in a cauldron or in his own mind, he had a limitless source of joy.

"The delicate power of liquids that creep through human veins." Every ghoulishly funny hint of this character's spookiness comes through in this phrase. He's talking about blood; is he being sinister? Why "creep"—could he not say "flow"? Is stealth part of the beauty for him? Is he talking about good or about poison? Does he enjoy unnerving people, or does he even realize he's doing it?

But while she distracts us with this creepy humor, Rowling quietly tucks into this phrase the first hint to foreshadow the eventual grand message of her series. In subsequent volumes, Harry will learn that when his mother died to save him, her sacrifice invoked an "ancient blood magic" that protected Harry, and eventually even Voldemort, against Dark Magic. Snape, too, will learn more about how this magic works— love, the magical term for what we Muggles call oxytocin, the hormone that flows in our blood to increase empathy—and he will come to use that knowledge to stopper death.

But both Harry and Snape are years away from such mastery here. Snape's first-year Potions speech is about the excitement of *promise*. It is

Rowling's most real demonstration of magic in this book, casting a spell on the reader—deliberately chosen words that create an intentional change—to transform this classroom bully into a figure of fascination.

Harry and Ron receive Snape's speech in silence, but it has an incendiary effect on Hermione, establishing the curiously fraught dynamic between Snape and Hermione that could fill a separate book in itself. She is dying to talk to Snape, with an urgency that ramps up in four uncontrollable surges that eventually lift her straight out of her seat. She receives every one of his communications here and always will. And repeatedly, through his attempts to ignore her, Snape telegraphs: *I am not speaking to you. You are not the story.*

> Hermione Granger was on the edge of her seat and looked desperate to start proving that she wasn't a dunderhead.
>
> "Potter!" said Snape suddenly. "What would I get if I added powdered root of asphodel to an infusion of wormwood?"
>
> *Powdered root of what to an infusion of what?* Harry glanced at Ron, who looked as stumped as he was; Hermione's hand had shot into the air.
>
> "I don't know, sir," said Harry.
>
> Snape's lips curled into a sneer.
>
> "Tut, tut—fame clearly isn't everything." (*HP/SS*, 137)

Fame isn't everything? Putting aside, for a moment, the fact that fame means nothing at all to Harry: then what is?

> He ignored Hermione's hand.
>
> "Let's try again. Potter, where would you look if I told you to find me a bezoar?"
>
> Hermione stretched her hand as high into the air as it would go without her leaving her seat, but Harry didn't have the faintest idea what a bezoar was. (*HP/SS*, 137)

Does Snape's choice of questions mean anything in particular?

> He tried not to look at Malfoy, Crabbe, and Goyle, who were shaking with laughter.

"I don't know, sir."

"Thought you wouldn't open a book before coming, eh, Potter?" Harry forced himself to keep looking straight into those cold eyes.

He *had* looked through his books at the Dursleys', but did Snape expect him to remember everything in *One Thousand Magical Herbs and Fungi*? (*HP/SS*, 137-8)

Did Snape, in fact, expect this? No, he couldn't have; surely, Malfoy, Crabbe, and Goyle had not memorized their textbooks. Surely, "opening a book" is not the same as memorizing the contents before school even begins. Is Snape inventing reasons to harass this child? Is he, as adults sometimes do, re-engaging in an old fight of which Harry, and the reader, know nothing?

Snape was still ignoring Hermione's quivering hand.

"What is the difference, Potter, between monkshood and wolfsbane?"

At this, Hermione stood up, her hand stretching toward the dungeon ceiling.

"I don't know," said Harry quietly. "I think Hermione does, though, why don't you try her?" (*HP/SS*, 138)

The one student who *has* memorized their textbooks is the Muggle-born who did not take her place at Hogwarts for granted, the one driven to teach herself all the magic she could, as soon as she could, because to her, magical education is a privilege and a dream come true. Perhaps she reminds Snape of himself at that age, and he is not in the mood for cozy reminiscences or self-awareness. Perhaps he is not ready to be done with long-ago resentment of students who coasted, assuming that they belonged, that the world owed them this privilege and they need not show appreciation. Perhaps these details about Potions were things he had taught himself before entering school.

Snape snaps out the answers to his sudden questions, adding, "And a point will be taken from Gryffindor House for your cheek, Potter." (*HP/SS*, 138)

And the stand-off is over. Snape asserts his dominance over his class and Harry loses a point, but it's only a point. His time with the Dursleys has trained him well: he doesn't back down, Snape has no reply to his succinct comment about Hermione, and he deflects Snape's focus back to the class at large, where it belongs. Harry is a formidable opponent. Snape commences teaching more or less normally, no more unpleasant than the average miserable wretch of a teacher.

> He was just telling everyone to look at the perfect way Malfoy had stewed his horned slugs when clouds of acid green smoke and a loud hissing filled the dungeon. Neville had somehow managed to melt Seamus's cauldron into a twisted blob, and their potion was seeping across the stone floor, burning holes in people's shoes. . . .
>
> "Idiot boy!" snarled Snape, clearing the spilled potion away with one wave of his wand. (*HP/SS*, 139)

Some elements of this scene are notable, even sound. His praise of Malfoy is delightfully technical: that's one thing that counts more than fame for him, apparently. At this point, appropriate priorities from this teacher come as a surprise and a relief. He seems to like Malfoy, not just favor him; maybe he's human. His name-calling of Neville is the beginning of a long and shameful enmity, but it makes pure sense based on his nature as an impatient prodigy who should not be teaching an entry-level class. Many readers have speculated that Snape has complicated reasons for disliking Neville, but given Snape's intolerance, Neville's class performance is surely sufficient.

> Neville whimpered as boils started to pop up all over his nose.
>
> "Take him up to the hospital wing," Snape spat at Seamus. Then he rounded on Harry and Ron, who had been working next to Neville.
>
> "You—Potter—why didn't you tell him not to add the quills? Thought he'd make you look good if he got it wrong, did you? That's another point you've lost for Gryffindor." (*HP/SS*, 139)

This display of twistedness assures Snape of a place in the literary pantheon of bad teachers. Improvising unspoken rules, scolding select children for not following them, ascribing absurd motives to children, silencing objections with capriciously applied penalties—in every way, Snape violates the standards of fairness that are especially crucial to children.

> This was so unfair that Harry opened his mouth to argue, but Ron kicked him behind their cauldron.
>
> "Don't push it," he muttered, "I've heard Snape can turn very nasty." (*HP/SS*, 139)

Ron and Harry have learned the rules of engagement with Snape, and it's just the first day.

There must be an alternate universe somewhere in which Severus Snape is put on probation for his classroom behavior. In this universe, he would apologize to his Slytherins for teaching them to bully and find ways to raise Slytherin morale that don't involve cruelty. He would apologize to Harry. He would apologize to Hermione and learn to call on her fairly. Dumbledore would speak to him about his name-calling of Neville. He may be essential to the larger plan, but that is not how to treat children.

But this is Hogwarts as Rowling created it, and it is also, sometimes, the real world. Some teachers really do run their classrooms by the rule of petty tyranny, and headmasters do not always know or care what goes on in the classroom, and many readers recognize this bullying dynamic from their own experience. We don't know yet what has made this teacher so despicable. We don't even know, in the story, that he is only 31 years old. We can only look into his "cold and empty" eyes and wonder, *What happened to you?*

> Harry told Hagrid about Snape's lesson. Hagrid, like Ron, told Harry not to worry about it, that Snape liked hardly any of the students.
>
> "But he seemed to really *hate* me."
>
> "Rubbish!" said Hagrid. "Why should he?"
>
> Yet Harry couldn't help thinking that Hagrid didn't quite meet his eyes when he said that. (*HP/SS*, 141)

Some of the most trusted adults in Harry's life seem to recognize Snape's tyranny but permit it to go unchecked. They appear, even, to respect Snape. In typical adult fashion, they seem to know more about Snape than they are willing to divulge to a child, even though it directly affects Harry's life. Understanding Snape, then, will have something to do with understanding adulthood. Not maturity; goodness knows that Snape has demonstrated less maturity than some of the children he teaches. But perhaps there is something about his story that adults feel would be more than most children could understand, even children who have lost as much innocence as Harry.

Professor McGonagall seems not only to respect Snape but to actively enjoy working with him. The two of them exhibit a seamless partnership when they, and Quirrell, track the troll to the girls' bathroom. As though by wordless agreement, Snape handles the troll, McGonagall the students. Snape says nothing, although "Snape gave Harry a swift, piercing look" (*HP/SS*, 177)–the first, unnamed instance of Legilimency in the series, one of many adult skills the children have never dreamed of.

Why is Snape present at the scene of an emergency with McGonagall and Quirrell? It is not because he's a Head of House, like McGonagall, or Flitwick and Sprout would be there, too. McGonagall is there as Deputy Headmistress. Quirrell is there as Defense Against the Dark Arts professor, but he is useless; he whimpers and clutches his heart. This is an early instance of Snape stepping in and performing the duties of the Defense teacher without the title, but on a different level, it functions also as a signal to the reader: Snape is always where the story is.

Harry's next confrontation with Snape occurs a few days later when a mysteriously limping Snape confiscates a library book from him, citing a rule he may or may not have made up on the spot. Reasoning, "Why should he be afraid of Snape?", an irritated Harry heads to the staffroom to ask for his book back, on the chance that "Snape wouldn't refuse if there were other teachers listening."

> He pushed the door ajar and peered inside—and a horrible scene met his eyes.
>
> Snape and Filch were inside, alone. Snape was holding his robes above his knees. One of his legs was bloody and mangled. Filch was handing Snape bandages. (*HP/SS*, 182)

A horrible scene. Everything about this tableau captures the revulsion that students feel when they learn too much about their teachers: the queasy intimacy. The shabbiness. The indignity of Snape's undress. This is what happens when we look underneath Snape's defenses. His shame is too grotesque to look upon.

"Blasted thing," Snape was saying. "How are you supposed to keep your eyes on all three heads at once?"

Harry tried to shut the door quietly, but—

"POTTER!"

Snape's face was twisted with fury as he dropped his robes quickly to hide his leg. Harry gulped.

"I just wondered if I could have my book back."

"GET OUT! *OUT!*" (*HP/SS*, 182-3)

Harry escapes with his life and tells Ron and Hermione he thinks Snape is trying to steal what the three-headed dog is guarding.

Hermione's eyes were wide.

"No—he wouldn't," she said. "I know he's not very nice, but he wouldn't try and steal something Dumbledore was keeping safe." (*HP/SS*, 183)

With two notable exceptions, this will remain Hermione's assessment of Snape throughout the series: not nice, but trustworthy. She joins Hagrid and McGonagall in judging Snape to be essentially good and always on Dumbledore's side.

The first exception occurs during the following day's Quidditch match when Hermione believes Snape is the one trying to kill Harry by jinxing his broom. She tries to interrupt the jinx by setting Snape's clothes on fire.

The afternoon's events certainly seemed to have changed her mind about Snape.

"I know a jinx when I see one, Hagrid, I've read all about them! You've got to keep eye contact, and Snape wasn't blinking at all, I saw him!"

"I'm tellin' yeh, yer wrong!" said Hagrid hotly. "I don't know why Harry's broom acted like that, but Snape wouldn' try an' kill a student!" (*HP/SS*, 192-3)

Hermione never again jumps to that kind of half-informed conclusion about Snape; the second exception does not occur until the end of the sixth book and Snape does everything in his power to lead her to it. But perhaps her conscience didn't bother her overmuch about setting fire to the robes of the teacher who treats her as though she were invisible. The fire didn't hurt him, after all. We never do learn whether he figures out who set it. Either he truly didn't see her or he didn't acknowledge her, but either way, she's learned a use for invisibility.

For their next Quidditch game, the Gryffindor team gets a nasty surprise: Snape insists on being the referee, although he has never refereed before. In the absence of evidence to the contrary, Harry draws the reasonable conclusion that Snape intends to kill him, or at least to prevent other teams from overtaking Slytherin in the rankings. Certainly, he has been noticing an unwelcome increase in the incidence of Snape in his life.

> Harry didn't know whether he was imagining it or not, but he seemed to keep running into Snape wherever he went. At times, he even wondered whether Snape was following him, trying to catch him on his own. Potions lessons were turning into a sort of weekly torture, Snape was so horrible to Harry. Could Snape possibly know they'd found out about the Sorcerer's Stone? Harry didn't see how he could—yet he sometimes had the horrible feeling that Snape could read minds. (*HP/SS*, 221)

Rowling seeds her writing about Snape with ambiguous motives and contradictory possible interpretations. Snape has stepped up surveillance on Harry: Why? For his own reasons, or on orders? Is he trying to catch Harry on his own or trying to make sure others do not, or both? Would he be horrible to Harry in Potions anyway, or is he under stress and taking it out on Harry? Is Snape performing what we later learn is Legilimency, or does Harry just have a guilty conscience?

To Harry's relief, Dumbledore attends the Quidditch match, as well.

> There was simply no way that Snape would dare to try to hurt him if Dumbledore was watching.
>
> Perhaps that was why Snape was looking so angry as the teams marched onto the field, something that Ron noticed, too. (*HP/SS*, 222)

Snape's mood worsens during the game. Gryffindor George Weasley hits a Bludger at him, unprovoked. Snape awards Hufflepuff a penalty for that and then, a few minutes later, "another penalty for no reason at all." (*HP/SS*, 223)

Bias? Petulance? Or something else?

Harry misses Snape "by inches" when he dives for the Snitch, leaving Snape "white-faced and tight-lipped." (*HP/SS*, 224) Harry catches the Snitch and everyone lands amid cheers.

Almost everyone, that is.

> Snape spat bitterly on the ground. (*HP/SS*, 224)

A teacher did *what*? In front of Dumbledore. In front of his students.

It hurt no one that he spat, but the degree of bitterness is remarkable. Even readers familiar with Snape's entire story can look back on this scene, way back in Harry's first year, and be startled to revisit this moment.

Snape's hostility to the Defense Against the Dark Arts (Defense) teacher

But Harry has little time to ponder Snape's shocking display. Minutes later, he recognizes Snape, hidden under hooded robes, running to a secret meeting with Quirrell in the Forbidden Forest. He overhears Snape threatening Quirrell about the Sorcerer's Stone: "You don't want me as your enemy, Quirrell." (*HP/SS*, 226)

You don't want me as your enemy. Occasionally, a sentence about Snape stands out in high relief against all the ambiguity because it is universally true, no matter what a character or reader believes about him. From every angle, this unreadable man is formidable, a terror as an enemy.

Convinced that Snape is going to steal the Sorcerer's Stone, Harry, Ron, and Hermione plot to stop him. Unfortunately for them, they run straight into the good cop-bad cop team of McGonagall and Snape.

> "What are you three doing inside?"
>
> It was Professor McGonagall, carrying a large pile of books.
> (*HP/SS*, 267)

She drops the books in shock when Harry tells her they think someone will steal the Stone.

> "I don't know how you found out about the Stone, but rest assured, no one can possibly steal it, it's too well protected."

"But Professor—"

"Potter, I know what I'm talking about," she said shortly. She bent down and gathered up the fallen books. "I suggest you all go back outside and enjoy the sunshine." (*HP/SS*, 268)

The kids are plotting to disobey her when . . .

Hermione gasped. Harry and Ron wheeled round.

Snape was standing there.

"Good afternoon," he said smoothly. (*HP/SS*, 268)

He never disappoints.

"You shouldn't be inside on a day like this," he said, with an odd, twisted smile.

"We were—" Harry began, without any idea what he was going to say.

"You want to be more careful," said Snape. "Hanging around like this, people will think you're up to something. And Gryffindor really can't afford to lose any more points, can it?" (*HP/SS*, 268-9)

Snape's "odd, twisted smile" tells the reader that he's up to something, himself. "You want to be more careful" is a classic teacher's line to let students know they're being transparent. In this case, though, it's also a genuine teaching moment from an experienced adult who knows what these children are fighting. With a couple of subtle clues, Rowling shows that Snape has spoken to McGonagall and come to reinforce her warning with his own. His mention of being "inside" echoes McGonagall's words, and the taunt about Gryffindor's points, in addition to the great benefit of annoying the students, recalls McGonagall's and Snape's friendly rivalry. (*HP/SS*, 152)

After Snape leaves, Harry assigns Hermione to keep an eye on Snape, making tactical use of Snape's tendency to treat Hermione as invisible. This time, though, Hermione reports that it didn't work: "Snape came out and asked me what I was doing, so I said I was waiting for Flitwick, and Snape went to get him, and I've only just got away, I don't know where Snape went." (*HP/SS*, 270) Apparently, Snape is perfectly capable of seeing this child and calling her bluff when it suits him.

When Harry and his friends pass through several enchantments guarding the Sorcerer's Stone, Snape's is the last protection before Harry gets to the Mirror of Erised, in which Dumbledore has hidden the Sorcerer's Stone. It takes very little guidance for young readers to recognize that the protections set by Sprout, Flitwick, McGonagall, Quirrell, and Snape were designed specifically for Harry and his friends to solve. Only Dumbledore's protection, the Mirror of Erised, was foolproof against theft, which explains why McGonagall was so certain that the Stone was impossible to steal. She was surely aware that she and her colleagues deliberately set all the other challenges at an appropriate level of difficulty for a group of first-year students.

Following the timeline of events, we can see that it must have been sometime after Christmas that Dumbledore asked the other teachers to set up their protections, a sort of practical final exam for Harry and friends. By then, McGonagall had the opportunity to observe Ron's skill at chess, Flitwick had already commented on Harry's flying (*HP/SS*, 165), and Quirrell knew the three students could knock out a troll. Sprout's protection, as writer Clare Moseley has pointed out, indicates that when the teachers planned the protections, they were not sure which friends would end up accompanying Harry: the Devil's Snare was meant for Neville. (Clare Moseley 2015)

In contrast to the bluntness of Quirrell's protection and the simplicity of Dumbledore's, Snape's is intricately designed to challenge the puzzle solver on several skills with the charming addition of potentially lethal consequences for incorrect guesses; perhaps they were Snape's idea of a personal touch. He has brewed potions and poisons. He has presented them in seven bottles, that magic number, to make the allegorical point that the treasure under guard is about human dreams and choices. He has provided limited quantities to indicate that there is a correct strategy to taking the potions: if the potions are wasted, there will be no more. He has tucked the clues into verse form, eight rhyming couplets, to heighten the sense of occasion. (*HP/SS*, 285)

This is what it looks like when Snape finally calls on Miss Granger. This final clue is written in text and logic, the language of her power.

> Hermione let out a great sigh and Harry, amazed, saw that she was smiling, the very last thing he felt like doing.
>
> *"Brilliant,"* said Hermione. "This isn't magic—it's logic—a puzzle. A lot of the greatest wizards haven't got an ounce of logic, they'd

be stuck in here forever."

"But so will we, won't we?"

"Of course not," said Hermione. "Everything we need is here on this paper." (*HP/SS*, 285-6)

They're in mortal danger, but she's *relieved*. She's even *smiling*. She can't help it. This is the child who understands the beauty of the softly simmering cauldron, needing nothing more than what's in her own mind. This clue was designed for her alone. He foresaw that she would be here.

Hermione works out which potion was meant for Harry. It brings him to the chamber containing the Mirror of Erised, where Quirrell is already trying to extract the Sorcerer's Stone. Quirrell confirms to Harry that Snape hasn't been plotting against Harry after all. With this early plot twist, J.K. Rowling establishes that in the magical world she's created, it's always worthwhile to read beyond surface appearances.

"But I thought—Snape—"

"Severus?" Quirrell laughed, and it wasn't his usual quivering treble, either, but cold and sharp. "Yes, Severus does seem the type, doesn't he? So useful to have him swooping around like an overgrown bat. Next to him, who would suspect p-p-poor, st-stuttering P-Professor Quirrell?" (*HP/SS*, 288)

Those looking to decode Rowling's mysteries see that in her stories, ill temper, even bullying, do not necessarily signify evil.

"But Snape tried to kill me!"

"No, no, no. *I* tried to kill you. Your friend Miss Granger accidentally knocked me over as she rushed to set fire to Snape at that Quidditch match. She broke my eye contact with you. Another few seconds and I'd have got you off that broom. I'd have managed it before then if Snape hadn't been muttering a countercurse, trying to save you." (*HP/SS*, 288-9)

Hagrid had been right and Hermione wrong: when trying to understand what Snape is doing and why, it is not enough to "read all about" jinxes. We will see in future volumes that when Hermione makes mistakes, especially regarding any sort of defense against the Dark Arts, she never lets herself forget them. It is easy to imagine her responding this way when she eventually hears about this encounter from Harry. She won't make this mistake again.

> "Snape was trying to *save* me?"
>
> "Of course," said Quirrell coolly. "Why do you think he wanted to referee your next match? He was trying to make sure I didn't do it again. Funny, really . . . he needn't have bothered. I couldn't do anything with Dumbledore watching. All the other teachers thought Snape was trying to stop Gryffindor from winning, he *did* make himself unpopular. . . (HP/SS, 289)

Snape's reputation

What Quirrell says is not enough to allow the reader to untangle all the complications that went into Snape's motives when he insisted upon playing Quidditch referee. *We don't have the full picture.*

Did Snape really want to referee? Or did someone order him to insist upon it? Did he truly want to stop Quirrell from killing Harry? Or did he have to pretend as much because Dumbledore was watching? Did "all the other teachers" really think he was just trying to stop Gryffindor from winning? It was certainly the most believable explanation about this teacher who has done everything in his power to help his students secure the House Championship for the past six years. Likely, at least some, perhaps all, the other teachers did think he was trying to cheat; it would not have been feasible for Dumbledore to have taken every teacher but Quirrell into his confidence.

Snape was in a position, either voluntarily or under orders, to present a cover story that would attract active dislike from his colleagues. He was unable to defend himself by explaining his true motive, which involves doing work he sometimes dreads in order to protect a boy he can't stand. For the man who is all about modes of defense, to be unable to defend himself, to be *not seen* for his true self, must have been almost unbearable.

The mystery of Snape's true motives

Does he truly want to prevent Harry's death? We have the clue that he looked angry before the match and spat upon the ground after: he was not trying to hide from Dumbledore that he loathed the experience, so we can guess that at least he was not actively hoping for Harry's death and hiding it from his boss, or he would have presented a smoother face. He was "white-faced and tight-lipped" by the end of the game; perhaps he didn't want to be in the midst of Quidditch play and he looked angry because Dumbledore required him to join the game. Perhaps he just despised the clumsiness of the cover story: if Snape has no prior history of involvement in Quidditch, nobody would believe that he would want to referee unless he were driven by some ulterior motive. Contributing inexorably to the worsening of one's own reputation cannot be fun for anyone. The themes in the terms of Snape's employment begin to take shape for the reader.

> "But Snape always seemed to hate me so much."
>
> "Oh, he does," said Quirrell casually, "heavens, yes. He was at Hogwarts with your father, didn't you know? They loathed each other. But he never wanted you *dead*." (*HP/SS*, 290)

Snape knew Harry's father? How could the adults in Harry's life have kept this information from him? They loathed each other? This brings to mind one of the few details anyone has given Harry about James: McGonagall telling Harry that James, "an excellent Quidditch player himself," would have been proud of Harry's skills. (*HP/SS*, 152)

The reader doesn't know yet that James, like Harry, had played Seeker. We can't guess yet that Snape has probably had literal nightmares of Seeker Potter flying at him on an expensive broom. At the moment he spat upon the ground, psychologically speaking, Snape was probably back in his school days as a scrawny teen. He did not want to referee, got no credit for doing so anyway, angered his colleagues, dodged a Bludger attack from George Weasley, and could not defend himself by explaining. The only outlets for his feelings were the second penalty he awarded Hufflepuff "for no reason at all" and his freedom to spit on the ground when it was all over. The one perverse mercy was that it was a phenomenally short game, thanks to Harry's skill—not a consideration to move Snape to gratitude.

Hagrid was right: Snape never wanted Harry *dead*. We are meant to take Quirrell's word on this one. The servant of Voldemort could surely sense Snape's feelings about this, and he has no reason to lie, since he thinks Harry won't survive much longer. Another series theme takes shape: the line between hating your enemies and believing they deserve to die.

Dumbledore tells Harry that James and Snape detested each other, but James saved Snape's life. He didn't believe Snape deserved to die.

> "Professor Snape couldn't bear being in your father's debt. . . . I do believe he worked so hard to protect you this year because he felt that would make him and your father even. Then he could go back to hating your father's memory in peace. . . ."

> Harry tried to understand this but it made his head pound, so he stopped. (*HP/SS*, 300)

Again, we don't have enough clues to understand what Dumbledore means. Any full reading of the *Harry Potter* series must include awareness that Rowling published this first installment without any guarantee that she would be able to publish another, let alone her grandiose dream of an entire seven-volume arc. The revelations at the end of *Sorcerer's Stone* are designed to be sufficient to close out the story but provocative enough to support subsequent investigation.

But on another level, the reader's experience of seeing fragmented explanations for Snape's erratic, unpleasant behavior, the mystery of how trustworthy adults can work with him despite his violations of common decency, is a potent reminder that this is how it feels to be a child in a world run by incomprehensible adults. Why do adults do anything? The literary experience of deciphering Severus Snape is the experience of maturing from childish to adult understanding.

By the end of *Harry Potter and the Sorcerer's Stone*, the triumph of three first-years over Voldemort and Quirrell has quite reasonably won the House Cup for Gryffindor.

> "Which means," Dumbledore called over the storm of applause, for even Ravenclaw and Hufflepuff were celebrating the downfall of Slytherin, "we need a little change of decoration."

> He clapped his hands. In an instant, the green hangings became scarlet and the silver became gold; the huge Slytherin serpent vanished and a towering Gryffindor lion took its place. (*HP/SS*, 306)

This decision of Rowling's has been unpopular with many readers, who object to the cruelty of announcing the last-minute reversal by staging a victory for the Slytherin children and then taking it away publicly, in front of competitors who wish them ill. It could have been done without this dramatic switch. While "even Ravenclaw and

Hufflepuff were celebrating the downfall of Slytherin," Draco Malfoy looks "stunned and horrified" (*HP/SS*, 306) and surely cannot be the only one to feel betrayed that the headmaster is leading three-quarters of the school to cheer against the remaining quarter. Disturbingly, the author presents the scene without any hint of sympathy for the Slytherins. Readers must either join in the cheers—which may not be a stretch for those who have endured bullying from classist, cowardly, cheating bullies like Draco—or, if this disturbs them, they must step back from the story and set themselves in opposition to the author, who has condemned this kind of inter-group hostility so clearly when it comes from Slytherin characters.

In this light, Slytherin's six-year streak of winning the House Championship comes into focus as a campaign of pride and rebellion. The House Cup simply meant more to Slytherins than it did to other students. Snape had reason to grub for House points. We don't know yet that he was only 24 years old when the winning streak started, but it has been a remarkable achievement for a very young teacher. With everyone from the fellow students to the headmaster set against his Slytherin charges, we see that his snickering and bullying—still absolutely wrong, still shameful from a teacher—might seem to him, and his students, to be petty retaliation in the overpowering context of a school that will not protect them.

Slytherin would have taken the loss of the House Championship hard under any circumstances, but with the emotional momentum of the last-minute switch and the cheering that ensued, Dumbledore has just guaranteed that Snape will be leading a lengthy, rageful group counseling session in the Slytherin common room. Retaliations will be forthcoming, and Snape will not be able to keep tabs on them all. It would be superhuman of the Slytherins not to take out their resentment of the Gryffindor headmaster on Gryffindor students, especially those who won the extra points. Harry may have defeated his mortal enemy at the end of his first year, but Snape's enmity is, by far, the greater part of his story.

SEVERUS SNAPE
AND THE CHAMBER OF SECRETS

As the second book in the series, *Harry Potter and the Chamber of Secrets* begins by reintroducing the main characters via their most typical traits. Snape, we are reminded, is "cruel, sarcastic, and disliked by everyone except the students from his own House . . ." (*HP/CoS*, 77) He makes a memorable entrance, catching Harry and Ron as they speak ill of him.

> Harry spun around. There, his black robes rippling in a cold breeze, stood Severus Snape. He was a thin man with sallow skin, a hooked nose, and greasy, shoulder-length black hair, and at this moment, he was smiling in a way that told Harry he and Ron were in very deep trouble. (*HP/CoS*, 78)

This reintroduction shows Snape at his most iconic, with his unpleasant appearance and his preternatural ability to detect Harry's misdeeds.

Snape's personal dislike of Harry

Harry and Ron start out the school year with a serious infraction, violating decrees against secrecy and underage magic by arriving at Hogwarts via flying car. Snape looks "happier than ever" (*HP/CoS*, 80) to see them get in trouble and crestfallen when he learns that they will not be expelled. He will have to put up with Harry's presence after all. But he will soon have greater irritants, including the buffoon who is the newest teacher at Hogwarts.

Snape's hostility to the new Defense teacher

We find that Snape has been denied the Defense Against the Dark Arts position once again, this time in favor of a monstrously incompetent narcissist named Gilderoy Lockhart.

25

Lockhart is the opposite of Snape in just about every way. He is all surface, no substance. He appears benevolent but reveals himself, in the end, to be evil and remorseless. When his spells fail in public, he is not even abashed. He produces nothing of value but steals credit for the work of others. He is even the opposite of Snape in looks, matinée-idol handsome with wavy blond hair and pastel robes.

In *Sorcerer's Stone*, it is unclear at what point Dumbledore knows that Voldemort lives in Quirrell's head. The deliberate lack of evidence permits a range of disturbing readings. Did Dumbledore know all along and permit a mass murderer in his classrooms? Did Dumbledore suspect nothing until after Voldemort's presence killed a teacher and nearly killed a student?

With *Chamber of Secrets*, Rowling provides a bit more evidence that Dumbledore brings dangerous people into the school knowingly, and his staff must treat these criminals as colleagues. Hagrid explains that Dumbledore considered no other candidates for the position: "Gettin' very difficult ter find anyone fer the Dark Arts job. People aren't too keen ter take it on, see. They're startin' ter think it's jinxed. No one's lasted long fer a while now." (*HP/CoS*, 115)

Perhaps Rowling found that she had been too subtle about Dumbledore's intentions or that readers did not read her clues correctly because they found it too difficult to believe that Dumbledore would hire a dangerous criminal to teach his students. In 2013, 15 years after the publication of *Chamber of Secrets*, Rowling confirmed that Dumbledore knew what he was doing when he hired Lockhart.

> Many staff were baffled as to the reason that Albus Dumbledore chose to invite Gilderoy Lockhart back to Hogwarts as Defence Against the Dark Arts teacher. While it was true that it had become almost impossible to persuade anybody else to take the job (the rumour that it was cursed was gathering strength both inside and outside Hogwarts), many teachers remembered Lockhart as thoroughly obnoxious, whatever his later achievements.
>
> Albus Dumbledore's plans, however, ran deep. He happened to have known two of the wizards for whose life's work Gilderoy Lockhart had taken credit, and was one of the only people in the world who thought he knew what Lockhart was up to. Dumbledore was convinced that Lockhart needed only to be put back into an ordinary school setting to be revealed as a charlatan and a fraud.

Professor McGonagall, who had never liked Lockhart, asked Dumbledore what he thought students would learn from such a vain, celebrity-hungry man. Dumbledore replied that 'there is plenty to be learned even from a bad teacher: what not to do, how not to be.' (J.K. Rowling, 2013)

In *Sorcerer's Stone*, Snape's job regarding Defense Against the Dark Arts was to keep tabs on Quirrell until the curse helped rid the school of him. For *Chamber of Secrets*, the game is a bit more complex. Dumbledore again uses the terms of the curse to set an outside limit on how long Lockhart will plague the school. But Lockhart does not have an agenda to kill Harry, so Snape is not posted on guard duty over him. Instead, Lockhart serves as filler. As long as this unqualified man holds the Defense post and absorbs the one-year curse on it, that post is essentially empty. Unknowingly, he provides a cover for Snape to be the true Defense teacher that year. Rowling has Snape reveal this covert agenda during one moment only, when he must block Lockhart's false claims from interfering with true defense against the Dark Arts. Several beings have been Petrified and can only be saved with a potion.

"I'll make it," Lockhart butted in. "I must have done it a hundred times. I could whip up a Mandrake Restorative Draught in my sleep—"

"Excuse me," said Snape icily. "But I believe I am the Potions master at this school."

There was a very awkward pause. (*HP/CoS*, 144)

Someone or something within Hogwarts has declared a mysterious "Chamber of Secrets" to be open. They are threatening "Enemies of the Heir"—the Heir of Slytherin, that is, who wanted to exclude Muggle-borns from Hogwarts. Draco takes the opportunity to further his own prejudices. At the first incident, when Filch's cat is Petrified, Draco shouts, "Enemies of the Heir, beware! You'll be next, Mudbloods!" (*HP/CoS*, 139) "Mudblood" is an offensive term for Muggle-born witches and wizards, such as Hermione, who come from entirely non-magical backgrounds. Draco's cry declares a campaign of terror and potential hate crimes.

Hermione is determined to find out what Draco knows about the attacks by impersonating Slytherins whom he trusts.

> "All we'd need would be some Polyjuice Potion."
>
> "What's that?" said Ron and Harry together.
>
> "Snape mentioned it in class a few weeks ago—"
>
> "D'you think we've got nothing better to do in Potions than listen to Snape?" muttered Ron. (*HP/CoS*, 159)

As usual, Hermione is memorizing everything Snape says. She may have an easier time paying attention to him because of the certainty that he will never look at her or acknowledge her, whereas most students, including Harry and Ron, find it preferable to avoid Snape's eye whenever possible. She wills Harry and Ron into brewing Polyjuice Potion with her.

> Unfortunately, the potion was only half finished. They still needed the bicorn horn and the boomslang skin, and the only place they were going to get them was from Snape's private stores. Harry privately felt he'd rather face Slytherin's legendary monster than let Snape catch him robbing his office. (*HP/CoS*, 185-6)

Once again, Rowling makes the point that to an abused child, great but distant evil may not be as frightening as petty tyranny in daily life.

Hermione proposes that the boys create a diversion in Potions class so she can steal what they need from Snape's private stores. Accordingly, Harry throws a firecracker into Goyle's cauldron.

> Goyle's potion exploded, showering the whole class. People shrieked as splashes of the Swelling Solution hit them. Malfoy got a faceful and his nose began to swell like a balloon; Goyle blundered around, his hands over his eyes, which had expanded to the size of a dinner plate—Snape was trying to restore calm and find out what had happened. Through the confusion, Harry saw Hermione slip quietly into Snape's office. (*HP/CoS*, 187)

True to form, Hermione gets away with stealing right under Snape's nose while Snape is preoccupied with his ill will toward Harry.

> "If I ever find out who threw this," Snape whispered, "I shall *make sure* that person is expelled."

Harry arranged his face into what he hoped was a puzzled expression. Snape was looking right at him, and the bell that rang ten minutes later could not have been more welcome. (*HP/CoS*, 188)

Then follows one of Rowling's cleverest, most subtle storytelling moments. At two points in *Chamber of Secrets*, she employs strategies of wordlessness or omission to plant clues about what Snape is really thinking.

"Snape can't prove it was you," said Ron reassuringly to Harry. "What can he do?"

"Knowing Snape, something foul," said Harry as the potion frothed and bubbled.

A week later, Harry, Ron, and Hermione were walking across the entrance hall when they saw a small knot of people gathered around the notice board, reading a piece of parchment that had just been pinned up. Seamus Finnigan and Dean Thomas beckoned them over, looking excited.

"They're starting a Dueling Club!" said Seamus. "First meeting tonight! I wouldn't mind dueling lessons; they might come in handy one of these days. . . ." (*HP/CoS*, 188)

The two conversations are separated by a double-spaced line break, a week in time, and a change of scene, but they occur consecutively: Dueling Club is the direct answer to Ron's rhetorical question. What can Snape do? Tensions between opposing groups of students are so volatile that someone has created an actual explosion in his class, causing physical harm. He can't know Harry was only trying to create a diversion. He probably thinks Harry wanted to hurt Goyle; any teacher would think that. Dumbledore is no closer to finding the culprit, but Snape must defend against the Dark Arts—he must teach the children to resist the suspicion and hostility that increase in atmospheres of heightened fear. Or, if they cannot resist, he must program defenses into them before the fighting escalates further.

What would a person do if they wanted to teach de-escalation without revealing that they personally oppose certain aggressive movements? If they work with Gilderoy Lockhart, they might mention the idea of a workshop, suggest that they have personal expertise in the subject, then sit back and let Lockhart's nature take its course.

> "Now, Professor Dumbledore has granted me permission to start this little dueling club, to train you all in case you ever need to defend yourselves as I myself have done on countless occasions— for full details, see my published works.

> "Let me introduce my assistant, Professor Snape," said Lockhart, flashing a wide smile. "He tells me he knows a tiny little bit about dueling himself and has sportingly agreed to help me with a short demonstration before we begin." (*HP/CoS* 189)

Sometimes readers, especially young readers who are accustomed to trusting adults, are uncertain who suggested the dueling club. Lockhart says it was his idea and nobody contradicts him. Could he have been telling the truth, this one time? It is a fun exercise to point readers to clues that Rowling has scattered around this book. Lockhart is remarkably consistent, and even the most resilient teachers can't hide their annoyance.

Lockhart ruffles Professor Sprout:

> "Just been showing Professor Sprout the right way to doctor a Whomping Willow! But I don't want you running away with the idea that I'm better at Herbology than she is! I just happen to have met several of these exotic plants on my travels. . ."

> "Greenhouse three today, chaps!" said Professor Sprout, who was looking distinctly disgruntled, not at all her usual cheerful self. (*HP/CoS*, 90)

. . . disgusts Hagrid:

> "Givin' me advice on gettin' kelpies out of a well," growled Hagrid, moving a half-plucked rooster off his scrubbed table and setting down the teapot. "Like I don' know. An' bangin' on about some banshee he banished. If one word of it was true, I'll eat my kettle." (*HP/CoS*, 114-5)

. . . doesn't seem to care that he is completely ignorant about healing spells:

"Doesn't know what he's saying," said Lockhart loudly to the anxious crowd of Gryffindors pressing around them. "Not to worry, Harry. I'm about to fix your arm."

"No!" said Harry. "I'll keep it like this, thanks. . . ." (*HP/CoS*, 172)

. . . and seems to be saying he is an international-level athlete:

"Tomorrow's the first Quidditch match of the season, I believe? Gryffindor against Slytherin, is it not? I hear you're a useful player. I was a Seeker, too. I was asked to try for the National Squad, but preferred to dedicate my life to the eradication of the Dark Forces. Still, if ever you feel the need for a little private training, don't hesitate to ask. Always happy to pass on my expertise to less able players. . . ." (*HP/CoS*, 163)

Readers can see, from these examples and others, that Rowling has crafted a portrait of a man with a compulsion to claim others' ideas and abilities for his own, impervious to resistance. It is a near certainty that Lockhart will appropriate any good idea, unwittingly providing cover if anyone wants to advance a surreptitious agenda of their own.

Lockhart and his less gifted assistant take their positions to duel. Ron whispers to Harry, "Wouldn't it be good if they finished each other off?" (*HP/CoS*, 189) At this point, Snape is just as worthless as Lockhart to them. Lockhart doesn't seem to have a plan about which spells to teach.

Both of them swung their wands above their heads and pointed them at their opponent; Snape cried: *"Expelliarmus!"* There was a dazzling flash of scarlet light and Lockhart was blasted off his feet: He flew backward off the stage, smashed into the wall, and slid down it to sprawl on the floor. (*HP/CoS*, 190)

Snape's defensive magic is powerful enough to knock down an opponent: disarmament can overpower attack without introducing further aggression. An unsettled Lockhart decides the students will pair up for the next exercise.

Harry moved automatically toward Hermione.

> "I don't think so," said Snape, smiling coldly. "Mr. Malfoy, come
> over here. Let's see what you make of the famous Potter. And you,
> Miss Granger—you can partner Miss Bulstrode."
>
> Malfoy strutted over, smirking. Behind him walked a Slytherin girl
> who reminded Harry of a picture he'd seen in *Holidays with Hags*.
> (*HP/CoS*, 191)

Why is Snape pairing up students who would like nothing better
than to hurt one another? Is he hoping his Slytherins will teach some
Gryffindors a lesson?

> "Wands at the ready!" shouted Lockhart. "When I count to three,
> cast your charms to Disarm your opponents—*only* to disarm
> them—we don't want any accidents—one . . . two . . . three—"
>
> Harry swung his wand high, but Malfoy had already started on
> "two": His spell hit Harry so hard he felt as though he'd been hit
> over the head with a saucepan. (*HP/CoS*, 192)

Overcome by animosity, Harry and Draco forget about disarming
and simply attack one another.

> "Stop! Stop!" screamed Lockhart, but Snape took charge.
>
> "*Finite Incantatem!*" he shouted; Harry's feet stopped dancing,
> Malfoy stopped laughing, and they were able to look up.
>
> A haze of greenish smoke was hovering over the scene. Both
> Neville and Justin were lying on the floor, panting; Ron was
> holding up an ashen-faced Seamus, apologizing for whatever his
> broken wand had done; but Hermione and Millicent Bulstrode were
> still moving; Millicent had Hermione in a headlock and Hermione
> was whimpering in pain; both their wands lay forgotten on the
> floor. (*HP/CoS*, 191-2)

Lockhart and Snape are teaching two different lessons. The friendly
pairs are gaining introductory experience with supportive peers. Their
energies are moderately elevated and they are in a receptive state for
learning. The enemies paired up by Snape are undergoing a different
experience entirely. They are flooded by such enmity that they forget
they are in a lesson and should follow instructions. It seems likely that

Hermione disarmed Millicent, as instructed, but once Millicent attacked, even Hermione forgot about her wand.

The state of true combat bypasses reason and engages a different set of responses. Lockhart is teaching a gentlemanly sport, a parlor game; Snape is reproducing the life-threatening tensions currently disrupting the school and tailoring the lesson to take that combative mindset into account. In sport, one hexes according to rules of etiquette; in fighting, such thinking will be a disadvantage. The skills learned under casual conditions may not transfer to true danger, but the reflexes and drilling learned from combat training can—if they are well managed—transfer successfully to any situation. Untrained fighters do not know how they will react under strain; they may panic, default to unsuitable techniques, overreact, or freeze. Snape is teaching the students some default options if they find themselves in true conflict. So far, he has taught them *Expelliarmus*, to disarm an enemy, and *Finite Incantatem*, to end a hex. He has demonstrated de-escalation only.

Even Lockhart is beginning to catch on.

> "I think I'd better teach you how to *block* unfriendly spells," said Lockhart, standing flustered in the midst of the hall. He glanced at Snape, whose black eyes glinted, and looked quickly away. "Let's have a volunteer pair—Longbottom and Finch-Fletchley, how about you—"
>
> "A bad idea, Professor Lockhart," said Snape, gliding over like a large and malevolent bat. "Longbottom causes devastation with the simplest spells. We'll be sending what's left of Finch-Fletchley up to the hospital wing in a matchbox." Neville's round, pink face went pinker. "How about Malfoy and Potter?" said Snape with a twisted smile. (*HP/CoS*, 193)

The "twisted smile" here is the same as the "twisted smile" from *Sorcerer's Stone* (*HP/SS*, 268-9) when Snape is indirectly warning the kids to draw less attention to themselves: Snape has an agenda he will not divulge. He, and the author, will distract from this, especially from the possibility that it is a *good* agenda, by adding a touch of nastiness: readers can be so disturbed by his disgraceful undermining of Neville that they might assume his motives for teaming up Draco and Harry are equally unpleasant.

Snape whispers a suggestion to Draco and both Slytherins smirk. Maybe he does enjoy the thought of Slytherins showing up Gryffindors.

He thinks he has this under control.

> Malfoy raised his wand quickly and bellowed, *"Serpensortia!"*
>
> The end of his wand exploded. Harry watched, aghast, as a long black snake shot out of it, fell heavily onto the floor between them, and raised itself, ready to strike. There were screams as the crowd backed swiftly away, clearing the floor.
>
> "Don't move, Potter," said Snape lazily, clearly enjoying the sight of Harry standing motionless, eye to eye with the angry snake. "I'll get rid of it. . . ." (*HP/CoS*, 194)

Snape does vanish the snake, but not before Harry shocks everybody by revealing himself to be a Parselmouth.

> Snape, too, was looking at Harry in an unexpected way: It was a shrewd and calculating look, and Harry didn't like it. (*HP/CoS*, 195)

"Shrewd" and "calculating" tell us that this information means something to Snape, something unfrightening but tricky, new, and well beyond the scope of Lockhart's understanding. We don't learn anything more specific about his thoughts. But clearly, he had not expected Harry to demonstrate more facility with snakes than students from Slytherin's own house. Whatever other motives he had for his many actions during Dueling Club, it seems likely that he suggested *Serpensortia* to Draco as a display of Slytherin pride, not an opportunity for Harry to upstage everyone.

Slytherins have not forgotten the previous year's ignominious loss of the House Championship to Gryffindor, especially the taunting way the Gryffindor headmaster announced a victory for Slytherin and then staged an ostentatious reversal, to cheers. We know from Lucius Malfoy's reprimand in Borgin and Burkes (*HP/CoS*, 50) that Draco was brooding on favoritism all summer. As the Gryffindor Quidditch team discovers, Lucius has been paying attention to his child's grievances, and he's been in touch with Snape about them.

The Gryffindors are about to start a practice session when the Slytherin team kicks them off the pitch. They are armed with a note from Snape, a new Seeker, and seven gleaming Nimbus Two Thousand and One brooms, courtesy of that new Seeker's father. (*HP/CoS*, 111)

Seven expensive brooms, better than Harry's Nimbus Two

Thousand? Isn't that a bit excessive of Lucius Malfoy? Is that even fair?

This extravagance may seem a disproportionate response to a school grudge. But if we reconsider events from *Sorcerer's Stone*, we can start to see that from a Slytherin perspective, the story can look quite different. It's worthwhile to refresh our memories with a few questions:

- Are first-years allowed their own broomsticks? *(HP/SS, 67)*
- Why did Harry have one as a first-year? (*HP/SS*, 151-2)
- Are first-years allowed on the Quidditch teams?
- Why was Harry? (*HP/SS*, 152)
- Who usually pays for student brooms? (*HP/SS*, 165)
- Who paid for Harry's? (*HP/SS*, 164)
- Did Harry need help paying for a broom? (*HP/SS*, 75)
- How did the rest of the school react when Slytherin lost the House Cup at the Leaving Feast? (*HP/SS*, 306)

It may be that from a Slytherin perspective, Hogwarts under Dumbledore has demonstrated such entrenched institutional bias that it would be impossible for Slytherins to win anything fairly, even when they deserve it. Perhaps the best they can hope for is to offset the bias themselves, from a position of relative weakness. If Dumbledore's favorite gets a school-funded broom, a private donor can provide Slytherins with top-quality brooms, at least, even if fairness is out of reach.

Draco knows his father has gone to this expense, which is more than would be expected of any school parent. He doesn't know that when his father was drumming his fingers in Borgin and Burkes, appearing to dismiss Draco's complaints about favoritism, Lucius was actually anxious to begin a revenge campaign to destabilize Dumbledore's administration by unleashing Slytherin's monster to kill Muggle-borns. As Harry and Ron learn when they impersonate Crabbe and Goyle, Draco doesn't know who's unleashing the monster. (*HP/CoS*, 223)

Lucius has shielded his child from his doings, preserving Draco's innocence and deniability: "Father says to keep my head down and let the Heir of Slytherin get on with it. He says the school needs ridding of all the Mudblood filth, but not to get mixed up in it." (*HP/CoS*, 224) His campaign of destabilization creates an atmosphere of suspicion that only leads the rest of the students to marginalize Slytherins further.

"That's two Gryffindors down, not counting a Gryffindor ghost, one Ravenclaw, and one Hufflepuff," said the Weasley twins' friend Lee Jordan, counting on his fingers. "Haven't *any* of the teachers noticed that the Slytherins are all safe? Isn't it *obvious* all this stuff's coming from Slytherin? The *Heir* of Slytherin, the *monster* of Slytherin—why don't they just chuck all the Slytherins out?" he roared, to nods and scattered applause. (*HP/CoS*, 258)

Lee Jordan's reaction is the same kind of fear that led to Slytherin's rift with the other Founders in the first place. According to Professor Binns, Salazar Slytherin thought Hogwarts would be safer if they could just "purge" the school of all Muggle-borns. (*HP/CoS*, 151)

This entire volume is about the danger of dormant resentments that can be awakened in an atmosphere of suspicion. Slytherins' reaction to Dumbledore's public humiliation of them at the *Sorcerer's Stone* Leaving Feast may have contributed directly to Lucius Malfoy's retaliatory attacks on Muggle-borns.

Snape's reputation

What does Snape think about all this? We know he works to advocate for the interests of Slytherin students within the school, above all; that is a constant. He loathes Harry personally, although he doesn't wish Harry dead; that is also a constant. He may be feigning opposition to the attacks in order to fool Dumbledore and his colleagues. He may be feigning surreptitious support for the attacks, underneath a cover of neutrality, in order to escape suspicion from Voldemort sympathizers. At this point, the readers know nothing about Snape's family background and how he might feel about purebloods and Muggle-borns. Is he egging on Draco's outspoken threats? Is he in sympathy with Lucius's anti-Muggle-born agenda? Is he pleased that Lucius has gotten the board of governors to suspend Dumbledore?

Through a masterfully infinitesimal fissure in her narrative, using silence rather than words, Rowling makes it just possible to discern a hint of Snape's feelings about the attacks on Muggle-borns. Blink and you'll miss it; it's too early in the game for Rowling to surrender more than a glimpse of Snape's true self.

Hermione is absent from Potions class because she's in the Hospital Wing, Petrified: "Snape swept past Harry, making no comment about Hermione's empty seat and cauldron." (*HP/CoS*, 267) By now, we know that when Snape is conscious of Hermione, he makes no acknowledgment.

> "I'm quite surprised the Mudbloods haven't all packed their bags by now," Malfoy went on. "Bet you five Galleons the next one dies. Pity it wasn't Granger—"
>
> The bell rang at that moment, which was lucky; at Malfoy's last words, Ron had leapt off his stool, and in the scramble to collect bags and books, his attempts to reach Malfoy went unnoticed.
>
> "Let me at him," Ron growled as Harry and Dean hung onto his arms. "I don't care, I don't need my wand, I'm going to kill him with my bare hands—"
>
> "Hurry up, I've got to take you all to Herbology," barked Snape over the class's heads, and off they marched, with Harry, Ron, and Dean bringing up the rear, Ron still trying to get loose. (*HP/CoS*, 267)

Hypervigilant Snape has an uncanny ability to sense and punish Gryffindor aggression against any Slytherin, especially Draco. But here, Ron spends several minutes under Snape's supervision lunging at Draco, growling death threats, forcibly restrained by two other Gryffindors. Snape might miss the occasional moment, but not a struggle that lasts for the entire walk to the castle doors. Through careful use of the passive voice—"his attempts to reach Malfoy *went unnoticed*" [italics mine]— Rowling hints that Snape saw Ron's anger but let it pass unremarked. We don't know yet that Snape has any history around Slytherin boys wishing death on Muggle-born girls. We only know that something about Draco's comment overrides Snape's usual eagerness to take Draco's side against Gryffindors, the only instance such a thing happens in the series.

The mystery of Snape's true motives

Like all the other proper teachers at Hogwarts, when it comes to life and death matters, Snape's protectiveness extends even to the students he dislikes. When Snape initiates a thoroughly enjoyable ouster of Lockhart from the staff room, it's the first time Rowling presents Snape's powers in an unambiguously positive light, a source of glee uniting all characters and readers who side with Hogwarts and against Lockhart. He may be a git, but he's *our* git, and we savor the sight of him giving Lockhart what he deserves.

Snape stepped forward.

"Just the man," he said. "The very man. A girl has been snatched by the monster, Lockhart. Taken into the Chamber of Secrets itself. Your moment has come at last."

Lockhart blanched. . . .

"I certainly remember you saying you were sorry you hadn't had a crack at the monster before Hagrid was arrested," said Snape. "Didn't you say that the whole affair had been bungled, and that you should have been given a free rein from the first?" (HP/CoS, 293-4)

McGonagall finishes what Snape started, demonstrating once again that the two work beautifully together.

"We'll leave it to you, then, Gilderoy," said Professor McGonagall. "Tonight will be an excellent time to do it. We'll make sure everyone's out of your way. You'll be able to tackle the monster all by yourself. A free rein at last."

Lockhart gazed desperately around him, but nobody came to the rescue. He didn't look remotely handsome anymore. His lip was trembling, and in the absence of his usually toothy grin, he looked weak-chinned and feeble.

"V-very well," he said. "I'll—I'll be in my office, getting—getting ready." (HP/CoS, 294)

Notably, this man who is the opposite of Snape in every way "didn't look remotely handsome" when exposed, at last, for his true self. Rowling is training her young readers to understand that when they learn long-hidden truths about ugly characters, no matter how hook-nosed and greasy-haired, they may see these characters in a new light.

Snape's ugliness is reflected from a different angle by another character: Argus Filch, whose rage is as constant as Snape's but is played for laughs rather than bitterness. Alas for Filch, even Snape finds him a figure of fun. When Filch is distraught over the Petrified Mrs. Norris, Snape wears "a most peculiar expression," as though he was "trying hard not to smile." (HP/CoS, 141) It is rather unfair that Filch gets so little respect, considering that Filch has doctored Snape's dog bites, reported to him about wayward students, and backs him up on many issues, including Snape's conviction that Harry ought to be punished for withholding information about the attacks.

> "Innocent until proven guilty, Severus," [Dumbledore] said firmly.
>
> Snape looked furious. So did Filch.
>
> "My cat has been Petrified!" he shrieked, his eyes popping. "I want to see some *punishment!*" (*HP/CoS*, 144)

When Ron learns that Filch is a Squib, a non-magical person born into a wizarding family, he says, "It would explain a lot. Like why he hates students so much." (*HP/CoS*, 145) Filch deals with his worry over Mrs. Norris by "lunging out at unsuspecting students and trying to put them in detention for things like 'breathing loudly' and 'looking happy.'" (*HP/CoS*, 146) It's as though Filch is the burlesque version of Snape: Snape without the gravitas. In other words, Filch shows us what Snape would have been without magic.

Snape is offstage for much of *Chamber of Secrets*. He brews the Mandrake Restorative Draught that brings Hermione out of her fairy-tale stillness, but we don't see that. The effects of his teaching from this year on Harry's story are nearly invisible but profound.

Harry learns that some types of spells require specific emotions or thoughts from the caster. As he learned from Snape, and will never forget, the emotions of dueling an enemy create different magical conditions than dueling a friend. Spikes of loyalty and courage conjure Fawkes and the Sword of Gryffindor for Harry. And to open the Chamber of Secrets, you don't have to be the Heir of Slytherin. You just have to know how the Heir of Slytherin would *feel*—as Ginny does when she's possessed and as Ron will, years later, after the Horcrux. This is one of Rowling's most important themes: that empathy is the basis of powerful magic.

When he first learns he is a Parselmouth, Harry has to learn for himself how to work with this rare gift. He has no one to teach him: "Harry tried to say something in Parseltongue. The words wouldn't come. It seemed he had to be face-to-face with a snake to do it." (*HP/CoS*, 197)

But when the stakes are high—when Ginny's life is on the line—his elevated sense of urgency spurs him to work out a way to speak it at will.

The only times he'd ever managed to speak Parseltongue were when he'd been faced with a real snake. He stared hard at the tiny engraving, trying to imagine it was real.

"Open up," he said.

He looked at Ron, who shook his head.

"English," he said.

Harry looked back at the snake, willing himself to believe it was alive. If he moved his head, the candlelight made it look as though it were moving.

"Open up," he said.

Except that the words weren't what he heard; a strange hissing had escaped him, and at once the tap glowed with a brilliant white light and began to spin. (*HP/CoS*, 300)

Harry learns that his magic works the same whether he is actually facing a snake or just reproducing the feeling of facing one. It may be all in his mind, but that doesn't mean it isn't real.

. . . [H]e saw a solid wall ahead on which two entwined serpents were carved, their eyes set with great, glinting emeralds.

Harry approached, his throat very dry. There was no need to pretend these stone snakes were real; their eyes looked strangely alive.

He could guess what he had to do. He cleared his throat, and the emerald eyes seemed to flicker.

"*Open,*" said Harry, in a low, faint hiss. (*HP/CoS*, 304–5)

With this third attempt at Parseltongue, Harry has attained mastery of the conditions he needs to cast this magic. He's applied what he learned when Snape paired him with Draco rather than Ron to learn *Expelliarmus*: to learn to cast magic when truly threatened, it is not enough to practice the spell while calm. It works better to practice while experiencing, or imagining, the feeling of threat.

Expelliarmus, the Disarming Charm, is just a magical form of disarmament, the Muggle de-escalation of conflict or prevention of harm by the removal of weapons. The Cornish pixies from Lockhart's first

SEVERUS SNAPE
AND THE PRISONER OF AZKABAN

Harry Potter and the Prisoner of Azkaban is the happiest book of the seven-book series. Many readers cite it as their favorite. For one thing, there's no Voldemort. For another, almost everyone gets something they want. Harry gets a godfather. Sirius gets his freedom. Lupin gets a friend back. Hermione gets extra time. Wormtail escapes with his life. So does Buckbeak. The students get a good Defense teacher. Ron gets a wand and a sandwich from his mother that isn't corned beef.

Severus Snape and the Prisoner of Azkaban, on the other hand, is an unrelenting nightmare of a book. What Snape sees throughout Harry's third year is different from what almost anyone else sees, and this obstructed perspective compounds with ever more traumatic reminders of Snape's past until Snape has a full-blown meltdown in front of the Minister of Magic at the very moment that other characters are rejoicing. There is relief from trauma in this book, but not for Snape.

Plot: Spoilers Ahead

The plot of *Prisoner of Azkaban* features several intricately linked storylines with a common theme of returning to the past to gain perspective.

The Marauders

We learn about Harry's late father James and his friends Sirius Black, Remus Lupin, and Peter Pettigrew, who called themselves "The Marauders" when they were at Hogwarts.

The "Prisoner of Azkaban" of the title is Sirius Black, the first wizard ever to break out from Azkaban, the wizard prison. He is the most wanted man in magical Britain, wrongly believed to be a Death Eater who betrayed Harry's parents to Voldemort and then committed mass murder. We learn at the end of the book that Peter Pettigrew committed the crimes, framed Sirius, then faked his own death and went into hiding—as Ron Weasley's pet rat.

Sirius escapes Azkaban by somehow getting past the dementors, prison guards who destroy people by draining them of happiness. He heads to Hogwarts intending to kill Pettigrew, but is mistakenly believed to be targeting Harry.

Dumbledore hires Remus Lupin, the fourth member of the Marauders, to be the Defense Against the Dark Arts professor for the year. As James Potter is dead and Peter Pettigrew believed dead, Lupin knows Sirius better than any other living person and can provide the most insightful help to Dumbledore in defending Hogwarts students against his attacks. Dumbledore and the Hogwarts staff know Lupin is a werewolf, but they keep this information confidential to protect him from prejudice that excludes werewolves from schools and jobs.

Snape vs. the Marauders

The Marauders, all Gryffindors, bullied Snape when they were students together, culminating in near murder. As a prank, Sirius lured Snape into Lupin's path when Lupin was in werewolf form; he would have been killed if James hadn't risked his own life to pull Snape back. Dumbledore forbade teen Snape to speak of this event in any way that would reveal Lupin's lycanthropy. Judging from Snape's behavior at the end of this book, he seems to have been traumatized by the combination of these three elements: the sustained bullying, the near fatal prank, and the silencing.

Trauma

Azkaban is guarded by dementors, creatures who fill people's minds with their worst memories and suppress the good memories. The Ministry suspects that Sirius is headed to Hogwarts and sends dementors there to track him. As long as the dementors are on the grounds, everyone at Hogwarts is at greater risk of being overwhelmed by their worst memories. This is torment for everybody, but much more so for those who have trauma in their histories, as Harry finds out. Dementors put Harry into post-traumatic flashback.

We see an example when Harry is attacked by dementors at a Quidditch game. His flashbacks to his mother's murder when he was one year old, and his baby self's overwhelming need to defend her, supersede his awareness of the present moment. He forgets he's 13 years old, he forgets that he's flying, and he falls from the sky.

> At least a hundred dementors, their hidden faces pointing up at him, were standing beneath him. It was as though freezing water were rising in his chest, cutting at his insides. And then he heard it again. . . . Someone was screaming, screaming inside his head . . . a woman . . .
>
> *"Not Harry, not Harry, please not Harry!"*
>
> *"Stand aside, you silly girl . . . stand aside, now. . . ."*
>
> *"Not Harry, please no, take me, kill me instead—"*
>
> Numbing, swirling white mist was filling Harry's brain. . . . What was he doing? Why was he flying? He needed to help her. . . . She was going to die. . . . She was going to be murdered. . . .
>
> He was falling, falling through the icy mist. (*HP/PoA*, 178-9)

Prisoners of Azkaban live in two temporal realities: one in real time and another trapped in their minds. This is like what happens to survivors of trauma when they are in flashback: they lose awareness of the present moment because the terrible memory they're reliving feels more real. At times like Harry's third year, when dementors are prevalent, Rowling is indicating that her characters will be heavily affected by troubles from the past.

The Time-Turner

McGonagall has borrowed a Time-Turner this year so Hermione can turn back time to take more classes: "Professor McGonagall made me swear I wouldn't tell anyone. She had to write all sorts of letters to the Ministry of Magic so I could have one. She had to tell them that I was a model student, and that I'd never, ever use it for anything except my studies . . . ." (*HP/PoA*, 395-6)

Why might McGonagall have gone to such lengths to secure this opportunity for Hermione? As a Muggle-born, second-year Hermione had already been more invested in fighting the mysterious attacks than half-blood Harry or pureblood Ron, viewing learning as her best defense for survival. As a gifted student at a school with no accelerated track, she would have been meeting with her Head of House, anyway, for ways to meet her academic needs. And by the end of her second year, as someone who lost weeks of her education to being Petrified, she would have been even more anxious to make up the time.

She soon learns, in her third year, that a doubled school day is not sustainable. Harry notices that she looks "almost as tired as Lupin." (HP/PoA, 251) This serves as a comment on privilege. Those with disabilities, such as Lupin, or oppressed minorities, such as Hermione, must work much harder than their peers to stand any chance of holding their own. She discovers, though, that overwork and sleep deprivation lead to irritability and fits of temper. This will be a useful insight into Snape's temperament as his workloads increase through the series.

The Time-Turner and Snape

When Ron sees Snape glaring at Lupin and hisses to Harry to "Look at Snape," those words encapsulate Snape's function in the overall story. Anytime you want to know where the story is, look at Snape. Snape is always the story, whether he wants to be or not, and even if his work sometimes requires him to remain unseen. As Dumbledore explains to Harry about Hermione's Time-Turner, that's the cardinal rule for any magical person returning to scenes from their own past, especially if they're doing so with hopes for a different, better outcome: "If all goes well, you will be able to save more than one innocent life tonight. But remember this, both of you: *you must not be seen*. Miss Granger, you know the law—you know what is at stake. . . *You—must—not—be—seen."* (HP/PoA, 393)

We have seen the effect on Snape when he encounters bad memories from the past. *Sorcerer's Stone* was the first year that Snape had to teach Potter the Second, lookalike child of a hated old classmate, preselected for glory and favoritism above the people Snape is trying to nurture. All that year, he had to force himself to work undercover and without credit to protect this child, even when it put him into nightmare scenarios like a near-collision in mid-air at a Quidditch match.

In *Chamber of Secrets*, Snape covertly drilled students in de-escalation, including a protégé who was actively championing Death Eater ideas. We don't know it yet, but the sight of a young Slytherin spreading hate is certain to remind Snape of his past.

In *Prisoner of Azkaban*, though, Snape encounters full-on trauma. It builds throughout the year for him as the exact same people from his past return to Hogwarts to terrorize students and put them in actual mortal danger. Rowling carefully makes it tricky for readers to see this because Snape is operating on partial or incorrect information for much of this book, and as always, his good intentions are obscured by his personal ill will, but: through all of this school year, Snape is trying to save kids from suffering as he did. Eventually, his efforts are frustrated so thoroughly that he throws an uncontrollable screaming fit in front of the Minister of Magic. Fudge worries that Snape is mentally ill, but Dumbledore says he is not. He's experiencing post-traumatic flashback.

This is a fantastic volume for showing point of view. What one character sees is literally not what another sees. Harry and Lupin can read the map; Snape and Dumbledore cannot. Hermione can see the recent past from a different vantage point and so, later, can Harry. Snape's view of Lupin is informed by memories of bullying and near death, but Dumbledore has forbidden anyone to speak of those events, keeping the current students ignorant. At the beginning of this volume, Snape appears to hate the personable, gifted new teacher for no reason except that Snape covets the Defense Against the Dark Arts job that he's not virtuous enough to hold. At the end, Snape is literally knocked out for the part of the story that disproves his worst suspicions and sees only that once again, a Potter's involvement has helped Sirius get away with attempted murder. As far as Snape knows, nothing has changed.

Snape's Year in Overview

As mentioned in previous chapters, a few major issues remain constant from year to year, forming a sort of checklist of Snape's progress in the larger story.

Snape's personal dislike of Harry

On the first day of third-year Potions, Snape is as petty as ever, even teaming up with 13-year-old students to indulge his malice. He can be relied upon to act this way whenever he oversees Slytherins and Gryffindors together. When Draco fakes an injury and pretends he needs help with potions, Snape plays along with "an unpleasant smile," ordering Ron and Harry to do Draco's work.

> "And, sir, I'll need this shrivelfig skinned," said Malfoy, his voice full of malicious laughter.
>
> "Potter, you can skin Malfoy's shrivelfig," said Snape, giving Harry

the look of loathing he always reserved just for him. (*HP/PoA*, 124-5)

Snape's hostility to the new Defense teacher

This is a reliable predictor of the tenor of his upcoming school year. This year, there's a new twist: Snape appears to loathe this man the same way he loathes Harry. This hints that we will learn something about the origins of Snape's antipathy for a child who did nothing to incur it.

"Look at Snape!" Ron hissed in Harry's ear.

Professor Snape, the Potions master, was staring along the staff table at Professor Lupin. It was common knowledge that Snape wanted the Defense Against the Dark Arts job, but even Harry, who hated Snape, was startled at the expression twisting his thin, sallow face. It was beyond anger: It was loathing. Harry knew that expression only too well; it was the look Snape wore every time he set eyes on Harry. (*HP/PoA*, 93)

Look at Snape. Why does he loathe Lupin? We'll need a Time-Turner to find out.

Snape's reputation

In this book, Snape's reputation is connected to this rumor about Snape's desire for the Defense Against the Dark Arts job. It is bad enough that anyone is willing to believe this brilliant man's highest dream is to teach the same dunderheads a different subject. It is bad enough that, according to rumor, even Quirrell and Lockhart deserved the job more than he did. But the worst thing is when Snape must collude in perpetuating this image of himself while prohibited from saying anything in his own defense.

Through Harry's time with the Dursleys, we get a glimpse of how it feels to be silenced, forced to support defamatory lies about the self, and forbidden to speak in one's own defense. When the abusive Aunt Marge comes to visit, Vernon and Petunia lie that Harry attends "St. Brutus's Secure Center for Incurably Criminal Boys."

"What?" Harry yelled.

"And you'll be sticking to that story, boy, or there'll be trouble," spat Uncle Vernon. (*HP/PoA*, 19)

Harry restrains himself as long as Marge restricts her abuse to him, but when she insults his parents, he loses control. A sympathetic response to an attack on others can be harder to endure than an attack on the self, even if the threat is not real—after all, Harry's parents are dead. If it's compounded by love for the attacked, the distress can be beyond endurance—but as we shall see by the end of *Severus Snape and the Prisoner of Azkaban*, protectiveness of others can be stronger and harder to control than protectiveness for the self, even without personal liking for the victim.

The mystery of Snape's true motives

Above all, the mystery of Snape's true motives remains constant and in the foreground. Is his potion protecting Lupin or poisoning him? As usual, Hermione argues that whatever's going on in Snape's secretive mind, he's not trying to cause damage.

> "But if he—you know"—Hermione dropped her voice, glancing nervously around—"if he *was* trying to—to poison Lupin—he wouldn't have done it in front of Harry." (*HP/PoA*, 158)

But what *is* he trying to do? It's clearly something complex that the children, and the reader, are not yet allowed to know.

> "Some people reckon—" Harry hesitated, then plunged recklessly on, "some people reckon [Snape would] do anything to get the Defense Against the Dark Arts job."
>
> Lupin drained the goblet and pulled a face.
>
> "Disgusting," he said. "Well, Harry, I'd better get back to work. I'll see you at the feast later."
>
> "Right," said Harry, putting down his empty teacup.
>
> The empty goblet was still smoking. (*HP/PoA*, 157)

Still smoking. With this irresistible flourish, Rowling celebrates the joy of intrigue. There's a mystery afoot. The game is on.

Snape's attitude toward this Defense Against the Dark Arts teacher is very different from his attitudes toward Quirrell, whom he was ordered to tail (*HP/DH*, 679), and Lockhart, the decoy who took the brunt of the curse on the position while Snape surreptitiously taught Defense. Dumbledore hired Lupin in a different capacity: as an ally against an attacker believed to be using Dark Magic, not as a danger to be exposed. Unlike his predecessors, Lupin was hired to do actual teaching and does it well. Like his predecessors, Lupin has a secret: his lycanthropy, which Dumbledore has forbidden his staff to reveal to the students and their families. While Lupin holds the Defense position, Snape's overtime duties are downgraded from *de facto* Defense teacher and Auror to support staff: Lupin's on-call substitute and his private apothecary, since few other than Snape have the talent to brew Wolfsbane, the potion that allows werewolves to keep their human minds when transformed.

Hogwarts finally has a true Defense master, as even Snape acknowledges in his sneering way: "This is supposed to be your area of expertise, Lupin." (*HP/PoA*, 288) So why does Snape continue to rush to scenes of possible Dark Magic such as the slashing of the Gryffindor portrait, along with the Defense master, the Headmaster, and the Deputy Headmistress? (*HP/PoA*, 160) Snape is only a Head of House like Flitwick and Sprout, who are not hurrying forward. In previous years, Dumbledore has required his presence to hold the nominal Defense teacher in check and be the unofficial Hogwarts expert on the Dark Arts. This year, Lupin doesn't need to be checked, but as Lupin tells Harry, he is not particularly knowledgeable about some forms of fighting Dark Magic: "I don't pretend to be an expert at fighting dementors, Harry . . . quite the contrary. . . ." (*HP/PoA*, 189)

Snape, however, probably does have such knowledge, at least according to the description Percy Weasley gave Harry in his first year: "Knows an awful lot about the Dark Arts, Snape." (*HP/SS*, 126) It seems likely that Dumbledore requests and welcomes his presence as Dark Arts expert. But in this volume, it also seems likely that Snape's deep mistrust of Lupin is an additional factor propelling him to scenes of crisis.

> "You remember the conversation we had, Headmaster, just before—ah—the start of term?" said Snape, who was barely opening his lips, as though trying to block Percy out of the conversation.
>
> "I do, Severus," said Dumbledore, and there was something like

warning in his voice.

"It seems—almost impossible—that Black could have entered the school without inside help. I did express my concerns when you appointed—"

"I do not believe a single person inside this castle would have helped Black enter it," said Dumbledore, and his tone made it so clear that the subject was closed that Snape didn't reply. (*HP/PoA*, 165-6)

Dumbledore was right to shut down Snape in the Great Hall in front of students, but Snape's uncharacteristic lack of discretion shows that his panic is growing too urgent to suppress—and possibly that Dumbledore has not made it easy for him to bring up this topic in private.

Slytherin, Gryffindor, Grudges, and Dumbledore

With a subtlety that's extraordinary for a book aimed at younger readers, Rowling portrays Snape as a shamefully anti-Gryffindor teacher whose damaging behavior may be influenced by memories of long-ago mismanagement from Dumbledore. If readers look closely, we can see hints of that older history resurface gradually through Harry's third year along with pro-Gryffindor momentum that makes it all the more difficult for Snape to bring legitimate concerns to Dumbledore's attention.

Snape's worst bullying is directed at Neville, whose incompetence in Potions class is ninety percent fear of Snape. (*HP/PoA*, 125) When Neville's Shrinking Solution fails, Snape orders him to brew another batch to feed to his toad—threatening harm to a beloved pet, which crosses the line from bad teaching into abuse.

Neville was pink and trembling. He looked as though he was on the verge of tears.

"Please, sir," said Hermione, "please, I could help Neville put it right—"

"I don't remember asking you to show off, Miss Granger," said Snape coldly, and Hermione went as pink as Neville. (*HP/PoA*, 126)

Hermione helps Neville in secret. Snape tests the potion on the toad while the Slytherin students watch, looking "excited" (*HP/PoA*, 128) at the prospect of Neville's humiliation and distress for his pet. This is the divisive atmosphere Snape has encouraged in his classroom. The potion works correctly. "The Gryffindors burst into applause" (*HP/PoA*, 128), although the Slytherins, presumably, do not.

> "Five points from Gryffindor," said Snape, which wiped the smiles from every face. "I told you not to help him, Miss Granger. Class dismissed." (*HP/PoA*, 128)

Snape has just contradicted his capricious policy from the first book, when he punished Harry for *not* helping Neville. For these Gryffindors, there's no winning with Snape. But in the above paragraph, Rowling introduces a more subtle divisiveness as well. The omniscient narrator has just stated that Snape's punishment has wiped the smiles from "every" face, but it seems likely that at least some of the Slytherins who were "excited" at the prospect of Neville's failure had not been smiling. Presumably, the sentence means that the punishment wiped the smiles from every *smiling* face, but the wording could also suggest that *every* face was smiling—that is, every face that *mattered*, and the ones that were not smiling did not count. It's the way a Gryffindor teen who was pro-Neville and anti-Snape might have described the scene, discounting any Slytherin students who hadn't been smiling.

This instance of pro-Gryffindor bias in the narration is subtle and arguable, but later instances will be more pronounced and induce more opposition in readers who might not view the scene from a partisan Gryffindor perspective. This focus on ambiguous wording may seem like splitting hairs. But classroom tensions instigated by biased teachers are recognizable to many of Rowling's middle-grade readers as an authentically serious issue.

Snape's torment of Neville carries over into the first session of Lupin's Defense Against the Dark Arts class, which takes place in the staffroom. The sight of Lupin seems to put Snape in a fouler mood than usual. He vents by using Neville as a scapegoat in what is perhaps the most destructive act we see from him as a teacher: he cuts down Neville to another teacher in front of Neville and all his classmates.

> "Possibly no one's warned you, Lupin, but this class contains Neville Longbottom. I would advise you not to entrust him with anything difficult. Not unless Miss Granger is hissing instructions in his ear."

Neville went scarlet. Harry glared at Snape; it was bad enough that he bullied Neville in his own classes, let alone doing it in front of other teachers.

Professor Lupin had raised his eyebrows.

"I was hoping that Neville would assist me with the first stage of the operation," he said, "and I am sure he will perform it admirably." (*HP/PoA*, 132)

And with that single defensive move to block Snape's viciousness, Lupin becomes one of the most dearly loved characters of the series.

If only Lupin had left it at that.

In his practical lesson on overcoming boggarts through laughter, Lupin asks the students to reveal the thing they fear the most. Neville's reply is "Professor Snape." Lupin then instigates collective mockery of Snape using a sexist, ageist image that the students would never have come up with on their own. He prompts Neville to describe what his grandmother wears.

"When the boggart bursts out of this wardrobe, Neville, and sees you, it will assume the form of Professor Snape," said Lupin. "And you will raise your wand—thus—and cry '*Riddikulus*'—and concentrate hard on your grandmother's clothes. If all goes well, Professor Boggart Snape will be forced into that vulture-topped hat, and that green dress, with that big red handbag." (*HP/PoA*, 135)

To enormous hilarity, "all goes well" and the boggart gives the assembled class the opportunity to mock Snape in unattractive drag. Some good comes of this: Neville gains confidence from vanquishing the boggart and the students know they have a much-needed ally against Snape's bullying. But it comes at a painful price. Lupin has legitimized a form of hatred. Just as Snape created a classroom atmosphere in which his Slytherins were "excited" at the prospect of a classmate's failure, humiliation, and fear for his pet, Lupin has gotten a roomful of pubescent Gryffindors to engage in collective sexual ridicule behind a Slytherin teacher's back, including the alarming word "forced." They would not have done so openly, in class, without his instigation, not at a school where disrespectful student references to "Snape" are always corrected with a gentle "*Professor* Snape."

Unlike Lupin's assertion that he was sure Neville would do well in class, this is not an empowering response to Snape's bullying. This is retaliation, introducing an entirely unrelated image that implicates everybody who laughs at it, including the reader. The momentum of group laughter makes it even harder for anyone with an objection to speak out and be heard. It can, indeed, be funny to imagine the mean Snape in a vulture hat. And then, depending on your perspective and life experience . . . it can also be not so funny. Ask anyone who was singled out in adolescence by a crowd of 13-year-olds and mocked in a sexist, homophobic, or transphobic manner for being unattractive and sexually invalid. It can feel extraordinarily unpleasant to be subjected to the same experience in adulthood, long after one had hoped to leave such experiences in the past, especially when one of the original bullies is resuscitating the ordeal by introducing it into classroom instruction for an entire new generation of 13-year-olds. It is unlikely that these 13-year-olds, having once enjoyed a laugh at this novel transgression, will fail to relive the pleasure and spread it to their peers.

It is true that Snape has treated Neville unspeakably and harmed everyone who witnessed the scene. He deserves to be held accountable. But he should be confronted directly for what he has done, to bring a stop to his cruelty, not subjected to a fresh round of hostility using irrelevant and hurtful tactics. Both Lupin and Snape have perpetuated and escalated their ongoing conflicts by pulling in a new generation of enemies. Snape is not the only one who harmed his students by example. Lupin's actions have identifiable consequences, including retaliation against the student who is shouldering the credit or blame after obediently following Lupin's instruction.

> Snape was in a particularly vindictive mood these days, and no one was in any doubt why. The story of the boggart assuming Snape's shape, and the way that Neville had dressed it in his grandmother's clothes, had traveled through the school like wildfire. Snape didn't seem to find it funny. His eyes flashed menacingly at the very mention of Professor Lupin's name, and he was bullying Neville worse than ever. (*HP/PoA*, 142)

In an oddly metatextual moment, even the narrative itself seems to collude in mocking Snape at Christmas dinner. Are vulture hats more common than we realize in magical millinery? Or is this just how it feels when it seems like the whole world is laughing at you, from your boss to the Christmas crackers, and nobody seems to find anything wrong with this?

> "Crackers!" said Dumbledore enthusiastically, offering the end of a large silver noisemaker to Snape, who took it reluctantly and tugged. With a bang like a gunshot, the cracker flew apart to reveal a large, pointed witch's hat topped with a stuffed vulture.
>
> Harry, remembering the boggart, caught Ron's eye and they both grinned; Snape's mouth thinned and he pushed the hat toward Dumbledore, who swapped it for his wizard's hat at once. (*HP/PoA*, 227-8)

Lupin's boggart class is by far the best official Defense Against the Dark Arts class we see in the series. He teaches an essential skill well to the greatest number of students using an exercise that will make the lesson stick in their memories. Despite the harassment, he shows how good it feels to learn through practical action and how group efforts can make things easier. He leaves only two loose ends: everyone gets a turn to fight the boggart except Harry and Hermione. We learn that he thought Harry's boggart would be Voldemort, too frightening for the class to see. We never learn why he didn't give Hermione a turn, although he gave Neville two turns, so perhaps he was stinting on classroom instruction for the highest-scoring student in order to give extra time to one who needed reinforcement. Harry gets private lessons later, but under Lupin's tutelage, Hermione studies only the theory without the practice.

> "He seems like a very good teacher," said Hermione approvingly. "But I wish I could have had a turn with the boggart—"
>
> "What would it have been for you?" said Ron, sniggering. "A piece of homework that only got nine out of ten?" (*HP/PoA*, 140)

The Return of the Marauders

Harry's private lessons start to take shape when Lupin invites him to chat privately during the Hogsmeade trip that Harry cannot attend. As a teacher, Lupin is a wonderful match for Harry. He is intelligent, but not too advanced to understand the pace at which most students learn. More closely than perhaps anyone else Harry ever meets, Lupin knows how he feels living with extreme stigma and trauma, and he carries around a store of medicinal chocolate to treat those conditions—quite likely for his own depression as well as to revive students. But Harry's moment of receiving much-needed extra support is witnessed, and judged, by the last person Harry would want.

> The door opened, and in came Snape. He was carrying a goblet, which was smoking faintly, and stopped at the sight of Harry, his black eyes narrowing.
>
> "Ah, Severus," said Lupin, smiling. "Thanks very much. Could you leave it here on the desk for me?"
>
> Snape set down the smoking goblet, his eyes wandering between Harry and Lupin. (*HP/PoA*, 156)

Potter and Lupin in a cozy tête-à-tête behind closed doors is a sight certain to remind Snape unpleasantly of his own school years, especially when he's just exerted himself to brew what is, as we later learn, a complicated potion to keep Lupin from being a danger to others. Harry's physical resemblance to James already contributes to Snape's conflation of the two Potters, obscuring his recognition of Harry's very different background and temperament. But this erroneous conflation is intensified by Lupin's presence in Snape's workplace, which reminds Snape of how he used to feel the last time he was nervous about Lupin, a Potter, and Sirius Black near him.

> "I was just showing Harry my grindylow," said Lupin pleasantly, pointing at the tank.
>
> "Fascinating," said Snape, without looking at it. "You should drink that directly, Lupin."
>
> "Yes, yes, I will," said Lupin.
>
> "I made an entire cauldronful," Snape continued. "If you need more."
>
> "I should probably take some again tomorrow. Thanks very much, Severus."
>
> "Not at all," said Snape, but there was a look in his eye Harry didn't like. He backed out of the room, unsmiling and watchful. (*HP/PoA*, 156)

We know, from his encounter with Peeves chanting his singsong rhyme about "loony Lupin," that Lupin smiles pleasantly to cover his fear that his lycanthropy will be revealed. It's a tense moment between them. Snape is having none of these diversionary tactics. He leaves without revealing anything, but one can almost picture his fantasy of dipping Lupin into the "entire cauldronful" of Wolfsbane headfirst if Lupin does not take his dose. He "backed out," "unsmiling and watchful"—Professor Snape is afraid.

> "Why—?" Harry began. Lupin looked at him and answered the unfinished question.
>
> "I've been feeling a bit off-color," he said. "This potion is the only thing that helps. I am very lucky to be working alongside Professor Snape; there aren't many wizards who are up to making it."
>
> Professor Lupin took another sip and Harry had a crazy urge to knock the goblet out of his hands. (*HP/PoA*, 156-7)

At least Snape has the consolation of knowing the potion tastes foul, although he might well wish he could make it taste better—not to please Lupin but make him less likely to shirk drinking it. Once again, Harry mistakes Snape's protective efforts for murder attempts, quite understandably unable to see past Snape's overwhelming ill will. At 13, Harry does not yet understand the phenomenon of being genuinely helpful to a person for whom one feels enmity.

Meanwhile, Snape cannot help but be reminded of the Marauders. Potter the Second looks exactly like Potter the First; Sirius Black periodically breaks into the castle; Lupin is making himself at home on staff; and, by the tiniest of hints, Rowling shows that after Lupin led Neville to ridicule Snape in ways the Marauders might have done, Snape conflates Neville in his mind with Peter Pettigrew. Even Harry registers that Peter Pettigrew, in his parents' photos, "resembled Neville Longbottom." (*HP/PoA*, 213) And when Snape runs into Harry and Neville together, left behind at school on a Hogsmeade day, he thinks Harry and Neville are plotting together to escape through the statue of the one-eyed witch.

"And what are you two doing here?" said Snape, coming to a halt and looking from one to the other. "An odd place to meet—"

To Harry's immense disquiet, Snape's black eyes flicked to the doorways on either side of them, and then to the one-eyed witch.

"We're not—meeting here," said Harry. "We just—met here."

"Indeed?" said Snape. "You have a habit of turning up in unexpected places, Potter, and you are very rarely there for no reason. . . ." (*HP/PoA*, 277)

Snape's facts may be wrong, but his suspicions about Harry are unnervingly accurate; he has coexisted with the Invisibility Cloak and Marauders' Map for longer than Harry has. It is both sad and funny how wrong he is about guileless Neville, who may be a hanger-on but is otherwise nothing like Peter Pettigrew. Perhaps anyone who has treated a student as badly as Snape treated Neville harbors secret, guilty hopes of learning that this student is not blameless.

Snape's Assignment

The following month, Harry is horrified to find that Snape is covering for an indisposed Lupin in Defense Against the Dark Arts. Ignoring (and insulting) Lupin's lesson plans, Snape flips far ahead in the textbook and quizzes the class on werewolves. No one has answers except Hermione, whom he ignores.

> "Well, well, well, I never thought I'd meet a third-year class who wouldn't even recognize a werewolf when they saw one. I shall make a point of informing Professor Dumbledore how very behind you all are. . . ."
>
> "Please, sir," said Hermione, whose hand was still in the air, "the werewolf differs from the true wolf in several small ways. The snout of the werewolf—"
>
> "That is the second time you have spoken out of turn, Miss Granger," said Snape coolly. "Five more points from Gryffindor for being an insufferable know-it-all."
>
> Hermione went very red, put down her hand, and stared at the floor with her eyes full of tears. (*HP/PoA*, 171-2)

Snape assigns the class two rolls of parchment, "to be handed in to me, on the ways you recognize *and kill* werewolves" (*HP/PoA*, 173, emphasis mine). The following week, Lupin rescinds the assignment.

> "Don't worry. I'll speak to Professor Snape. You don't have to do the essay."

"Oh *no*," said Hermione, looking very disappointed. "I've already finished it!" (*HP/PoA*, 185-6)

One wonders how that conversation went. It seems likely that Snape and Lupin expressed differing opinions on the need for Lupin's students to learn how to defend themselves against a werewolf.

Snape alternately ignores Hermione and calls her names. Why does she not disregard his assignment as her classmates do? Why does she not turn bitter against him? Between Snape's contempt for Lupin's academic standards and his unimpressed response to the girl who commits textbooks to memory, we see that regardless of whether Snape and Hermione get along personally, they have the same kind of academic mind. A teacher like Lupin, who aims his teaching to the majority of his students, gives assignments that are generally irrelevant to Hermione's learning needs. Snape's assignment from the back of the textbook matches his idea of what third-years should be doing, and the only person who responds to it is Hermione. Hogwarts is full of pleasant-enough people who expect Hermione to function at a pace that frustrates her, more than 24 hours per day. Insulting or not, for Hermione, a teacher who expects others to function at Hermione's pace is a treasure. It is disappointing that, once again, Snape will not receive what she has to say.

When Snape backed out of Lupin's office looking wary, what was he afraid of? That night, Harry noticed that Snape's gaze was "flickering toward Lupin more often than was natural" (*HP/PoA*, 159), and after dinner, the school discovered that Sirius Black had slashed the Fat Lady's portrait after trying to break into Gryffindor tower. Not only does Snape think that Lupin may be colluding with Sirius, but he may wonder if Lupin is befriending Harry and cultivating his trust in order to deliver Harry to Sirius for murder. This chilling possibility is so far from Lupin's true feelings that it is startling for the reader to contemplate, but as we see in the next volume, *Harry Potter and the Goblet of Fire*, it is not unreasonable for Snape to worry about Harry being abducted.

If Lupin is indeed colluding with a murderer who wants to kill Harry, perhaps they plan to attack Harry while Lupin is in werewolf form. If Snape fears that may be possible, it makes sense that he would try to teach the students how to identify and kill werewolves. This stealth DADA approach worked the previous year with *Expelliarmus*, after all. And even if Potter resists the lesson, at least Granger will understand

and be able to help him. That approach worked two years ago with the potions puzzle. After all Snape's antagonism, Harry will not listen to him, but there are other ways to get messages through to Harry Potter's head.

For people who have read all of *Prisoner of Azkaban*, sometimes it seems startling to look back and remember that Snape wanted to teach the students how to *kill* werewolves. Surely, that is a bit extreme, is it not? But it is easy for readers to miss how the mid-year situation would have appeared to Snape because within this book, we only find out the full extent of the Marauders' "prank" against student Snape a few pages before learning that Sirius was innocent of betrayal and murder. In the ensuing rush of adventure, there is little leisure for the reader to reflect upon how teen Snape would have felt glimpsing a werewolf at the end of a narrow tunnel, set up by his enemies. From the time Sirius and Lupin both headed back to his adult workplace, Snape has been battling memories of that episode. As far as Snape knows, the boy who once tried to get him killed and saw nothing wrong with turning his own werewolf friend into a killer could easily have become a mass murderer. And the werewolf who remained fast friends with Sirius after that near-disaster could plausibly still be colluding with Sirius and lying to Dumbledore about it. Snape has no reason to believe the best of Sirius or Lupin and a great deal of evidence that they are dangerous.

When Sirius slashes his way into Gryffindor tower and stands over Ron with a knife (*HP/PoA*, 266), Snape must feel like his worst nightmares are unfolding. He may loathe Harry, but he doesn't think Harry deserves to be killed by Sirius Black. He believes Harry is worth saving, even if Harry shows no appreciation whatsoever for this sentiment and effort, going into Hogsmeade despite ample evidence that a violent mass murderer is hunting him. Snape must be bewildered by Harry's lack of appreciation: when Snape was a student, Sirius tried to get him killed and nobody cared. Now, when the wizarding world finally shares Snape's opinion of Sirius, Snape the teacher—fighting his personal distaste for Harry—is trying to extend the protection to Harry that he was denied. And then he learns that Harry, defying orders, has gone into Hogsmeade under his Invisibility Cloak and thrown mud at Draco Malfoy. Harry thought himself funny and undetectable until his cloak slipped. Oops.

Snape is genuinely aghast at Harry's heedlessness, but his own behavior has made it impossible for Harry to see this. After Snape's inflammatory role in the Slytherin-Gryffindor catfights, Harry thinks Snape is only trying to needle him for harassing Draco and shuts Snape out further. Snape has conditioned Harry to expend so much energy defending himself against Snape's pettiness that Harry can't perceive when Snape is worried about legitimate danger. His inimitable snarkiness in expressing this worry doesn't help:

> "Everyone from the Minister of Magic downward has been trying to keep famous Harry Potter safe from Sirius Black. But famous Harry Potter is a law unto himself. Let the ordinary people worry about his safety! Famous Harry Potter goes where he wants to, with no thought for the consequences." (*HP/PoA*, 284)

For once, there is no mystery to what is really exercising Snape at this moment. His major grievance is exactly what he says it is. He's frantic about the mortal danger posed by Sirius Black, and this trumps any other agenda he might have in this scene. He's wrong that Harry considers his own fame to place him above the law, but he is angry that Harry would ignore the danger he's in and flout the protective efforts put forth by the government and school. Keeping Harry Potter alive, it would seem, is a thankless endeavor.

> "How extraordinarily like your father you are, Potter," Snape said suddenly, his eyes glinting. "He too was exceedingly arrogant. A small amount of talent on the Quidditch field made him think he was a cut above the rest of us too. Strutting around the place with his friends and admirers . . . The resemblance between you is uncanny."
>
> "My dad didn't strut," said Harry, before he could stop himself. "And neither do I." (*HP/PoA*, 284)

Unfortunately for Harry, he is making this claim less than a week after he and his volunteer "honor guard" of Gryffindors made a spectacular entrance into the Great Hall with Harry's new Firebolt, leaving the Slytherins "thunderstruck" (*HP/PoA*, 257) by the conspicuous gift from Harry's mysterious benefactor.

> "I told you to shut up about my dad!" Harry yelled. "I know the truth, all right? He saved your life! Dumbledore told me! You wouldn't even be here if it wasn't for my dad!"
>
> Snape's sallow skin had gone the color of sour milk.

"And did the headmaster tell you the circumstances in which your father saved my life?" he whispered. "Or did he consider the details too unpleasant for precious Potter's delicate ears?" (*HP/PoA*, 285)

The whole of *Prisoner of Azkaban* is about Harry's yearning to know more about the popular, athletic father he reportedly resembles. Of the few things people have told Harry about James, none is stranger than Dumbledore's "dreamily" reported claim, from Harry's first year, that James once saved Snape's life: "Funny, the way people's minds work, isn't it? Professor Snape couldn't bear being in your father's debt. . . . I do believe he worked so hard to protect you this year because he felt that would make him and your father even. Then he could go back to hating your father's memory in peace. . . ." (*HP/SS*, 300) But nobody has ever explained to Harry about the different kinds of life debts in Rowling's universe and the ways they function. He's about to get a bit of an education.

The Nature of Life Debts

"I would hate for you to run away with a false idea of your father, Potter," he said, a terrible grin twisting his face. "Have you been imagining some act of glorious heroism? Then let me correct you—your saintly father and his friends played a highly amusing joke on me that would have resulted in my death if your father hadn't got cold feet at the last moment. There was nothing brave about what he did. He was saving his own skin as much as mine. Had their joke succeeded, he would have been expelled from Hogwarts." (*HP/PoA*, 285)

This account of the Marauders' "highly amusing joke" is necessarily limited, not only because Snape does not know the story from the Marauders' side but because he is also maintaining confidentiality about Lupin's lycanthropy. We shall see that Lupin's version, later in the book, contradicts Snape's account and adds significant detail. The life debt Snape describes here is of an ignoble sort. He thinks the Marauders planned the incident together and James changed his mind once it was underway. The underlying motive he's ascribing to James could be expressed as "I would kill you, but you're not worth the consequences." There is generally a feeling of relief when one is saved from the brink of death, but the emotion here is so contaminated with contempt that the very suggestion of gratitude feels unbearable to Snape.

Harry doesn't know it yet, but he is no longer in trouble with Snape; Lupin is. Snape's attention has gone back to the past. Like a Sneakoscope, he has detected that once again, there's something untrustworthy going on with Lupin—or he thinks he has—but he doesn't know what it is. Snape searches Harry for evidence to confirm his hunch that Lupin is luring Harry off school grounds. He finds the blank Marauder's Map.

> "So!" said Snape, his long nostrils quivering. "Is this another treasured gift from Mr. Weasley? Or is it—something else? A letter, perhaps, written in invisible ink? Or—instructions to get into Hogsmeade without passing the dementors?"
>
> Harry blinked. Snape's eyes gleamed. (*HP/PoA*, 286)

Harry and Snape draw conclusions about each other that are wrong and yet understandable based on the evidence. Snape commands the map to yield its information.

> As though an invisible hand were writing upon it, words appeared on the smooth surface of the map.
>
> *"Mr. Moony presents his compliments to Professor Snape, and begs him to keep his abnormally large nose out of other people's business."*
>
> Snape froze. Harry stared, dumbstruck, at the message. But the map didn't stop there. More writing was appearing beneath the first. (*HP/PoA*, 286-7)

The map offers further personal comments from Prongs, Padfoot, and Wormtail, insulting Snape's looks, intelligence, and greasy hair. In one thrillingly dreadful moment, Harry sees both the kind of words he'd love to say to Snape and the kind of insults that Snape used to endure from bullies who outnumbered him. Snape doesn't know the nicknames, but he knows the tenor of these taunts. He has probably heard them in his nightmares for the past 20 years. He summons Lupin.

> Snape pointed at the parchment, on which the words of Messrs. Moony, Wormtail, Padfoot, and Prongs were still shining. An odd, closed expression appeared on Lupin's face.
>
> "Well?" said Snape.

> Lupin continued to stare at the map. Harry had the impression that
> Lupin was doing some very quick thinking. (*HP/PoA*, 287-8)

At the sight of this artifact from his school days, Lupin, too, travels
back to the past. He reverts to bluffing and lying like a schoolboy. He
suggests Harry got the document from a joke shop, knowing he can trust
the map's enchantments to make it impossible to prove he is lying.

Snape knows Lupin is lying, of course: "You think a joke shop could
supply him with such a thing? You don't think it more likely that he got
it *directly from the manufacturers?*" (*HP/PoA*, 288)

Lupin knows Snape thinks he has been luring Harry out of the castle.
But Snape cannot prove anything, especially when Ron bursts in to lie
that he had bought the parchment for Harry at a joke shop. Lupin gets
Ron and Harry away from Snape, announces that he is not giving them
back the map, and then delivers a stinging reproach to Harry.

> "Don't expect me to cover up for you again, Harry. I cannot make
> you take Sirius Black seriously. But I would have thought that
> what you have heard when the dementors draw near you would
> have had more of an effect on you. Your parents gave their lives to
> keep you alive, Harry. A poor way to repay them—gambling their
> sacrifice for a bag of magic tricks."
>
> He walked away, leaving Harry feeling worse by far than he had at
> any point in Snape's office. (*HP/PoA*, 290)

This reproach, though understandable in its content, is startlingly
hurtful in its delivery. It is the kind of barbed comment people make
when they are shaken and guilty within themselves. The 13-year-old child
had not meant to dishonor his parents' sacrifice, and at any rate, they are
not even alive to be disappointed. Lupin could have reminded Harry of
this larger picture without using such unfairly loaded language.

But he has been shaken by the resurfacing of this artifact from his
own past, lost to him before he even graduated from Hogwarts and
suddenly back in circulation, exposing a new generation of children to
danger. This map is evidence. It documents the poor way Lupin repaid
the extraordinary efforts and trust Dumbledore extended to provide an
education for him: swearing the Hogwarts staff to secrecy about his
lycanthropy, creating the tunnel and the Shrieking Shack, purchasing the
"very valuable" Whomping Willow (*HP/CoS*, 79), and putting his own

good name on the line as guarantee that it would be perfectly safe to enroll a werewolf at Hogwarts. If Dumbledore saw this map, he would realize that Lupin, as a student, had left the secure Shrieking Shack in werewolf form and roamed the Hogwarts grounds and Hogsmeade along with other students out of bounds. Had anything gone wrong, Lupin might have attacked someone and Dumbledore's career would have been over.

Lupin tells Harry, Ron, and Hermione later, "All this year, I have been battling with myself, wondering whether I should tell Dumbledore that Sirius was an Animagus. But I didn't do it. Why? Because I was too cowardly. It would have meant admitting that I'd betrayed his trust while I was at school, admitting that I'd led others along with me . . . and Dumbledore's trust has meant everything to me. He let me into Hogwarts as a boy, and he gave me a job when I have been shunned all my adult life, unable to find paid work because of what I am." (*HP/PoA*, 356)

Dumbledore hired adult Lupin to protect Harry and the rest of the school against Sirius Black, but Lupin still did not tell Dumbledore that Sirius knew of two ways that might get him into Hogwarts past the dementors: his Animagus form and the secret passageway. He put his shame above the safety of the students and above Dumbledore's good name. This was the driving emotion behind his reproach to Harry for poor repayment of his parents' sacrifice. James and Lily are dead, but Lupin sees a trusting Dumbledore every day. He cannot let Dumbledore know this map exists.

The heavy burden of an elder's trust weighs on Hermione, as well. We see it when she fails the boggart portion of her Defense Against the Dark Arts final exam, the lesson that Lupin did not or would not teach this gifted child.

> Hermione did everything perfectly until she reached the trunk with the boggart in it. After about a minute inside it, she burst out again, screaming.
>
> "Hermione!" said Lupin, startled. "What's the matter?"
>
> "P-P-Professor McGonagall!" Hermione gasped, pointing into the trunk. "Sh-she said I'd failed everything!" (*HP/PoA*, 319)

McGonagall has gone to extraordinary measures to procure a Time-Turner for Hermione, putting her own good name on the line. As

Hermione tells Harry: "She had to write all sorts of letters to the Ministry of Magic so I could have one. She had to tell them that I was a model student, and that I'd never, ever use it for anything except my studies. . . ." (*HP/PoA*, 395-6) Hermione's greatest fear is that she will repay McGonagall poorly. If she uses her Time-Turner for any other purpose, she gambles with McGonagall's trust and reputation. What would be worth such a risk?

In her spare time, such as it is, Hermione has been singlehandedly preparing an exhaustive legal defense for Buckbeak the hippogriff, whom the Malfoys want killed as part of their campaign against Hagrid's appointment as a teacher. Her work is no use, of course, as Lucius Malfoy has bought off the committee. Buckbeak is found guilty.

Hermione comes to understand that the verdict has nothing to do with justice or evidence: "There'll be an appeal, though, there always is. Only I can't see any hope. . . . Nothing will have changed." (*HP/PoA*, 292)

Buckbeak's predetermined appeal marks the beginning of the children's loss of innocence about due process and believing in the system. In exchange, the children gain experience, informed skepticism, and wisdom. They decide to violate the ban on leaving the castle in order to visit Hagrid before Buckbeak's execution, but for this, they need Harry's missing Invisibility Cloak.

> Harry told her about leaving it in the passageway under the one-eyed witch.
>
> ". . . if Snape sees me anywhere near there again, I'm in serious trouble," he finished.
>
> "That's true," said Hermione, getting to her feet. "If he sees *you*. . . . How do you open the witch's hump again?" (*HP/PoA*, 326)

By this point, Hermione has adjusted so completely to Snape's refusal to notice her that she blithely exploits the loophole this creates. The kids stay with Hagrid until the executioner arrives and they slip out the back. They hear what they believe is Buckbeak's death: "without warning, the unmistakable swish and thud of an axe." (*HP/PoA*, 331)

With that sound, their trust in authority is severed. There was an appeal, but the committee didn't listen to it. If you hurt or destroy an innocent being—or even a guilty being with their own untold side of the story—because you refuse to hear their appeal, this damage cannot be reversed. You have to hear the appeal while you can. There's a chance that a different perspective could change something.

The stunned children head back to the school, but Sirius, in dog form, drags Ron and his rat (the disguised Peter Pettigrew) to the Shrieking Shack. When Harry and Hermione go to Ron's rescue, they find Sirius in human form. Harry attacks him with intent to kill, accusing Sirius of having killed James and Lily.

> "You've got to listen to me," Black said, and there was a note of urgency in his voice now. "You'll regret it if you don't. . . . You don't understand. . . ."
>
> Before either of them could say another word, something ginger streaked past Harry; Crookshanks leapt onto Black's chest and settled himself there, right over Black's heart. (*HP/PoA*, 342)

Crookshanks puts his own life at risk to support Sirius's plea for Harry to hear his appeal.

During the ensuing standoff, Lupin arrives on the scene, realizes that Peter Pettigrew was the traitor, and regains a friendship with Sirius. As the living person who knows Sirius Black the best, it makes sense that Lupin could not dismiss his doubts about Sirius committing the crimes for which he was jailed. It was at a dreadful cost: the entire school terrorized, poor Ron waking up to a vengeful convict standing over his bed with a knife. But perhaps Lupin knew that he had to hear Sirius's side of the story for himself before deciding to help apprehend him, because once Sirius was caught, the dementors were certain to Kiss him with no chance for him to appeal.

But Hermione, witnessing the friendship between Lupin and Sirius without knowing the story, comes to the same erroneous conclusions as Snape: "'NO!' Hermione screamed. 'Harry, don't trust him, he's been helping Black get into the castle, he wants you dead too—*he's a werewolf!*'" (*HP/PoA*, 345)

Like Snape, she's been keeping Lupin's secret for him. Everything she's seen of Lupin until now has affirmed that decision for her.

> Lupin stopped dead. Then, with an obvious effort, he turned to Hermione and said, "How long have you known?"
>
> "Ages," Hermione whispered. "Since I did Professor Snape's essay. . . ."

> "He'll be delighted," said Lupin coolly. "He assigned that essay hoping someone would realize what my symptoms meant. . . . Did you check the lunar chart and realize that I was always ill at the full moon? Or did you realize that the boggart changed into the moon when it saw me?"
>
> "Both," Hermione said quietly.
>
> Lupin forced a laugh.
>
> "You're the cleverest witch of your age I've ever met, Hermione." (HP/PoA, 345-6)

Lupin is straight-up afraid of Hermione. Perhaps he avoided giving her classroom instruction because he was afraid she would see his secrets. This girl is as sharp as Snape in putting clues together. Their minds work the same way. The only thing we see Hermione learning in Defense Against the Dark Arts this year is from Snape, not Lupin.

Lupin begins to tell his story when the door creaks open of its own accord, but nobody is there. None of them realize that Snape has just arrived under Harry's cloak and is listening to Lupin's history, including Dumbledore providing the Shrieking Shack for Lupin to inhabit during the full moon: "The villagers heard the noise and the screaming and thought they were hearing particularly violent spirits. Dumbledore encouraged the rumor. . . ." (HP/PoA, 353)

That detail about Dumbledore is Rowling's first clue about the origin of the persistent but unattributed rumor that Snape covets the Defense Against the Dark Arts position. The rumor about the Shrieking Shack is proof that at least once, Dumbledore has relied upon the human tendency to gossip in order to distract attention away from his secret agenda.

When Lupin tells of his friends becoming Animagi to keep him company and keep him in line, Hermione continues to think along the same lines as Snape:

> "That was still really dangerous! Running around in the dark with a werewolf! What if you'd given the others the slip, and bitten somebody?"
>
> "A thought that still haunts me," said Lupin heavily. "And there were near misses, many of them. We laughed about them

afterwards. We were young, thoughtless—carried away with our own cleverness." (*HP/PoA*, *355*)

Hermione's mind goes straight to this danger without her even knowing about the prank on Snape. Lupin admits she is right. Unbeknownst to them, Snape hears the admission and Lupin's subsequent confession that he lied to himself and Dumbledore all year. And then Snape hears Lupin's account of the prank that nearly killed him.

> "Professor Snape was at school with us. He fought very hard against my appointment to the Defense Against the Dark Arts job. He has been telling Dumbledore all year that I am not to be trusted. He has his reasons . . . you see, Sirius here played a trick on him which nearly killed him, a trick which involved me—"
>
> Black made a derisive noise.
>
> "It served him right," he sneered. "Sneaking around, trying to find out what we were up to . . . hoping he could get us expelled. . . ."
> (*HP/PoA*, *356*)

So Lupin finds Snape's response understandable. The prank, with all its implications for Lupin, was thought up by Sirius alone. And Sirius, whose development has been arrested by imprisonment, dementors, and rage for the past 12 years, expresses no remorse.

> "Severus was very interested in where I went every month," Lupin told Harry, Ron, and Hermione. "We were in the same year, you know, and we—er—didn't like each other very much. He especially disliked James. Jealous, I think, of James's talent on the Quidditch field . . . anyway Snape had seen me crossing the grounds with Madam Pomfrey one evening as she led me toward the Whomping Willow to transform. Sirius thought it would be—er—amusing, to tell Snape all he had to do was prod the knot on the tree trunk with a long stick, and he'd be able to get in after me. Well, of course, Snape tried it—if he'd got as far as this house, he'd have met a fully grown werewolf—but your father, who'd heard what Sirius had done, went after Snape and pulled him back, at great risk to his life . . . Snape glimpsed me, though, at the end of the tunnel. He was forbidden by Dumbledore to tell anybody, but from that time on he

knew what I was. . . ." (*HP/PoA*, 357)

Snape had thought he owed James a grudging, contemptuous kind of life debt, in which James felt that killing Snape would not be worth the consequences. We will see this kind of life debt later when Harry prevents Sirius and Lupin from killing Pettigrew.

> "Get off me," Harry spat, throwing Pettigrew's hands off him in disgust. "I'm not doing this for you. I'm doing it because I don't reckon my dad would've wanted his best friends to become killers—just for you." (*HP/PoA*, 375-6)

But Snape hears that the life debt he owes James was actually a different kind, an action that says: *I will risk my own life to save yours.* It may have meant: *Not even my enemy deserves to die this way.* But even if it didn't, even if James was still only trying to prevent his friends from becoming killers, still, he risked himself. It is the same risk that Snape has accepted in running to the Shrieking Shack to defend Harry, Ron, and Hermione from a werewolf. In intention, at least, Snape has just repaid his life debt to Harry's father.

> "So that's why Snape doesn't like you," said Harry slowly, "because he thought you were in on the joke?"
>
> "That's right," sneered a cold voice from the wall behind Lupin.
>
> Severus Snape was pulling off the Invisibility Cloak, his wand pointing directly at Lupin. (*HP/PoA*, 357)

He may be a git, but the moments Snape allows himself to be seen are always a thrill.

> Snape was slightly breathless, but his face was full of suppressed triumph. "You're wondering, perhaps, how I knew you were here?" he said, his eyes glittering. "I've just been to your office, Lupin. You forgot to take your potion tonight, so I took a gobletful along. And very lucky I did . . . lucky for me, I mean. Lying on your desk was a certain map. One glance at it told me all I needed to know. I saw you running along this passageway and out of sight." (*HP/PoA*, 358)

It was a full moon night and Lupin hadn't taken his potion. One can see how Snape might conclude that Lupin and Sirius planned to have Lupin attack Harry in werewolf form.

> "Severus, you're making a mistake," said Lupin urgently. "You haven't heard everything—I can explain—Sirius is not here to kill Harry—"
>
> "Two more for Azkaban tonight," said Snape, his eyes now gleaming fanatically. "I shall be interested to see how Dumbledore takes this. . . . He was quite convinced you were harmless, you know, Lupin . . . a *tame* werewolf—"
>
> "You fool," said Lupin softly. "Is a schoolboy grudge worth putting an innocent man back inside Azkaban?"
>
> BANG! Thin, snakelike cords burst from the end of Snape's wand and twisted themselves around Lupin's mouth, wrists, and ankles; he overbalanced and fell to the floor, unable to move. (*HP/PoA*, 359)

Several themes come to a head in this scene. Lupin begs for an appeal, but Snape denies him. He doesn't intend to kill, though; Snape is a master of defense, not a vigilante, and intends to turn his enemies over to the authorities. And Lupin raises the issue of *innocence*.

But Snape is not willing to hear what Lupin means by that. Hermione tries to reason with him.

> "But if—if there was a mistake—"
>
> "KEEP QUIET, YOU STUPID GIRL!" Snape shouted, looking suddenly quite deranged. "DON'T TALK ABOUT WHAT YOU DON'T UNDERSTAND!" (*HP/PoA*, 360)

Hermione is far from a stupid girl, and at the moment, she understands more about this situation than Snape can when he's in this "deranged" state. Standing in the place where Lupin regularly transformed, believing the same people intend to kill again—as they do, although not the person Snape thinks—Snape may be entering a state of post-traumatic flashback, reliving the emotions of the time he nearly died. This is a very different kind of time travel from the conscious, anchored return to the past afforded by a Time-Turner, which grants the traveler a second perspective overlaid on the first. Flashbacks return the sufferer to the old perspective without room for any new ones. At the moment,

Snape cannot hear other sides to the story. He is about to sentence Lupin and Sirius without an appeal.

> "YOU'RE PATHETIC!" Harry yelled. "JUST BECAUSE THEY MADE A FOOL OF YOU AT SCHOOL YOU WON'T EVEN LISTEN—"
>
> "SILENCE! I WILL NOT BE SPOKEN TO LIKE THAT!" Snape shrieked, looking madder than ever. "Like father, like son, Potter! I have just saved your neck; you should be thanking me on bended knee! You would have been well served if he'd killed you! You'd have died like your father, too arrogant to believe you might be mistaken in Black—now get out of the way, or I will *make you.* GET OUT OF THE WAY, POTTER!" (*HP/PoA*, 361)

Harry, Ron, and Hermione cast *Expelliarmus* on Snape simultaneously. The force of the combined spell knocks Snape unconscious, "a trickle of blood oozing from under his hair." (*HP/PoA*, 361)

Snape isn't ready to re-evaluate the past; he's still in it. He doesn't learn what the others are about to learn: that Pettigrew committed the crimes, that he's alive, and he's returning to Voldemort. Snape doesn't see Harry stop Sirius and Lupin from killing Pettigrew with the claim that James wouldn't have wanted them to become killers for someone so despicable. Pettigrew now owes Harry the kind of life debt that Snape thought he owed James: contemptuous, but still, absolutely, a debt. Harry suggests Azkaban for Pettigrew instead of the vigilante execution that Sirius and Lupin planned. Harry's form of justice aligns with James and Snape, not with Sirius and Lupin.

Most of all, Snape doesn't learn about Sirius Black's *innocence*, the magical power that kept him alive. Sirius says, "I think the only reason I never lost my mind is that I knew I was innocent. That wasn't a happy thought, so the dementors couldn't suck it out of me . . . but it kept me sane and knowing who I am. . . ." (*HP/PoA*, 371) His innocence was the source of strength *other than happiness* that was powerful enough to overcome the constant repetition of his worst memories.

Sirius is not blameless, certainly. His bullying was extreme, and years of torment from dementors destroyed his right and ability to mature into full adulthood during his unjust incarceration. But Sirius has never killed, saved from that guilt by the intervention of James Potter and then Harry. Sirius's actions have never led to anyone's death; he has never lost that innocence. This is something Snape is not yet ready to accept.

Snape's Flashback and Trauma

When Snape revives, he finds himself on the Hogwarts grounds with Harry, Ron, Hermione, and Sirius passed out near him, the dementors in retreat, Lupin gone. He binds and gags Sirius and levitates all four back to the castle, where the Minister of Magic promises him an Order of Merlin and predicts that Harry will thank Snape for returning Sirius Black to the dementors. Snape, with the unaccustomed luxury of a sympathetic listener, unburdens himself to Fudge about Dumbledore's leniency whenever Harry breaks rules to pursue danger.

> "Ah, well, Snape . . . Harry Potter, you know . . . we've all got a bit of a blind spot where he's concerned."
>
> "And yet—is it good for him to be given so much special treatment? Personally, I try and treat him like any other student. And any other student would be suspended—at the very least—for leading his friends into such danger. Consider, Minister—against all school rules—after all the precautions put in place for his protection—out-of-bounds, at night, consorting with a werewolf and a murderer—and I have reason to believe he has been visiting Hogsmeade illegally too—" (*HP/PoA*, 387)

Aside from the astonishing claim that Snape tries to treat Harry "like any other student," this paragraph is notable because it shows how Harry's behavior this year has reminded Snape of Lupin from his school days. After all the precautions put in place for Lupin's protection as a student, after all the special treatment, Lupin still led his friends into danger, out-of-bounds, at night, and visited Hogsmeade as a werewolf. Yet when Sirius nearly got him to kill another student, nobody was expelled; there is no evidence that anyone was even punished. The only consequence we know for sure is that Snape was "forbidden by Dumbledore to tell anybody" (*HP/PoA*, 357) that Lupin is a werewolf. He was forbidden to speak of his terrifying experience. His near murder, and his need to work through it by talking, were considered less important than Lupin's privacy and, perhaps, Dumbledore's chagrin.

If nothing else, this explains why Snape has always been so keen to propose expulsion anytime Harry breaks a rule.

Snape's trauma around the Marauders' "prank" has had two

components: the bullying that led to the near-attack and, just as damagingly, the subsequent silencing that accorded lower priority to his safety than the protection of his attackers. When it seems to him that Dumbledore is once again siding with the Marauders, Snape's memories of that long-ago betrayal push him toward insubordination.

> "You surely don't believe a word of Black's story?" Snape whispered, his eyes fixed on Dumbledore's face.
>
> "I wish to speak to Harry and Hermione alone," Dumbledore repeated.
>
> Snape took a step toward Dumbledore.
>
> "Sirius Black showed he was capable of murder at the age of sixteen," he breathed. "You haven't forgotten that, Headmaster? You haven't forgotten that he once tried to kill *me*?"
>
> "My memory is as good as it ever was, Severus," said Dumbledore quietly.
>
> Snape turned on his heel and marched through the door Fudge was still holding. (*HP/PoA*, 391)

After Snape's unhappy exit, Dumbledore tells Harry and Hermione that they can save Sirius from execution if they manage to do something magical and transgressive that they must figure out for themselves. He is remarkably stingy with specifics. No pressure, kids.

> "What we need," said Dumbledore slowly, and his light blue eyes moved from Harry to Hermione, "is more *time*."
>
> "But—" Hermione began. And then her eyes became very round. "OH!"
>
> "Now, pay attention," said Dumbledore, speaking very low, and very clearly. "Sirius is locked in Professor Flitwick's office on the seventh floor. Thirteenth window from the right of the West Tower. If all goes well, you will be able to save more than one innocent life tonight. But remember this, both of you: *You must not be seen*. Miss Granger, you know the law—you know what is at stake. . . . *You—must—not—be—seen*." (*HP/PoA*, 393)

This is the answer, then: this is the thing that is worth the risk of breaking the law, gambling with the good name of Professor McGonagall or other mentors, using magic in unauthorized ways. According to school rules, Dumbledore's authority transcends McGonagall's. According to the rules of magical power, his authority transcends the Ministry—something that the Ministry finds threatening, understandably. Hermione and Harry recognize and act upon Dumbledore's authority without hesitation. He does not often call upon it to override everyday order.

Hermione, Harry, and Ron have learned that sometimes there is no way to save the innocent through proper channels. Sirius was framed, imprisoned, and sentenced to the Kiss without trial. Sometimes, there is no lawful way for the innocent to live their lives. They must become fugitives, and those who love them must help.

When is it okay to take super-magical objects for one's own use? According to the rules of J.K. Rowling's universe, when you want them not for personal gain, but to protect others. But Dumbledore does not tell this to Harry and Hermione. He gives them only the first law of time travel: *You must not be seen.* The rest, as Hermione tells Harry in a terrified whisper, is apparently up to them to figure out as they go along: "Harry, *I don't understand what Dumbledore wants us to do.* Why did he tell us to go back three hours? How's that going to help Sirius?" (*HP/PoA*, 396)

Harry and Hermione go over their memories of the past three hours and figure out the one thing they could have changed without being seen: once Hagrid shooed them out of his hut, once the Ministry saw Buckbeak tethered, the kids could have lingered behind under the Invisibility Cloak and set Buckbeak free.

Dumbledore knew, of course, that there was no chance of Buckbeak winning his appeal. He knows about Hermione's Time-Turner. He must have recognized the moment for a possible rescue, after Hagrid had witnesses to prove he did not set free the condemned animal under his care but before the officials approached Buckbeak—although Dumbledore probably originally imagined setting Hermione and friends the much easier task of letting Buckbeak fly away immediately.

We see Dumbledore create a delay at the moment by insisting that the executioner sign the paperwork, which both marks this fissure in the proceedings and makes extra time for them to carry out the rescue. Once the rescue is effected, we see confirmation that the kids guessed correctly what Dumbledore wanted them to do.

"It was tied here!" said the executioner furiously. "I saw it! Just here!"

"How extraordinary," said Dumbledore. There was a note of amusement in his voice. (*HP/PoA*, 402)

The first innocent life has been saved without the time travelers being seen.

Saving the second innocent life proves harder because Harry has to learn the restraint required by the second law of time travel: *Do not change time.*

"Hermione," said Harry suddenly, "what if we—we just run in there and grab Pettigrew—"

"No!" said Hermione in a terrified whisper. "Don't you understand? We're breaking one of the most important Wizarding laws! Nobody's supposed to change time, nobody!" (*HP/PoA*, 398)

To observe, to know, but not to interfere: this is how it feels to relive an unbearable memory. The fantasy of going back in time to change something regrettable is universal but impossible. We can only understand what happened and learn to tolerate it; we can't change the past. But when we see history repeating itself and we must *choose* not to interfere, that's a different story. As Snape has found, the urge to interfere can overpower reason. The ability to overcome this urge is essential for experienced time travelers: that is, adults, parents, teachers, or anyone who has had to learn that each generation will make its own mistakes.

Harry is being tested on his ability to resist interfering for the first time. Hermione has to restrain him physically from keeping his Invisibility Cloak out of Snape's hands. Whether or not 13-year-old Harry can perceive this, Snape wants to use the Cloak to protect others, not for personal gain. Harry sees that his Cloak works for Snape without a hitch, even if Harry is snarling under his breath, "Get your filthy hands off it." (*HP/PoA*, 405)

Hermione's guidance is priceless to Harry. She has used extra time for studies so she can hold her own in a prejudiced society. This helps her understand how extra time can aid Harry's struggles with trauma and moments lost to flashback. When Harry returns to the moment that a powerful wizard drove away a hundred dementors, he watches from the bank opposite the spot where he first stood: a new perspective, with a friend and witness by his side.

And that friend calls his attention to a different element in the scene.

> "Harry, look at Snape!"
>
> Together they peered around the bush at the other bank. Snape had regained consciousness. He was conjuring stretchers and lifting the limp forms of Harry, Hermione, and Black onto them. A fourth stretcher, no doubt bearing Ron, was already floating at his side. Then, wand held out in front of him, he moved them away toward the castle. (HP/PoA, 412)

Hermione is regularly the only Gryffindor to be as concerned for Professor Snape as she is for others, despite Snape's usual refusal to listen to her or acknowledge her. Because of Hermione's vigilance, Harry gets a glimpse of how his nemesis behaves when he thinks nobody's looking. Snape is not acting here. He is careful even with the unconscious Sirius Black, in contrast to Sirius bumping Snape's head intentionally when Snape was unconscious. (HP/PoA, 378) It may be that the private Snape is a better man than the public persona Harry usually sees.

Snape brings the unconscious people back to the castle, certain that he has saved innocent students from the same murderer who once tried to kill him. But when he discovers that Sirius has somehow escaped again, Snape enters a state of full-blown post-traumatic flashback, the culmination of a year's worth of memories of being bullied, disbelieved, nearly killed, and silenced.

> "HE DIDN'T DISAPPARATE!" Snape roared, now very close at hand. "YOU CAN'T APPARATE OR DISAPPARATE INSIDE THIS CASTLE! THIS—HAS—SOMETHING—TO—DO—WITH—POTTER!"
>
> "Severus—be reasonable—Harry has been locked up—"
>
> BAM.
>
> The door of the hospital wing burst open.
>
> Fudge, Snape, and Dumbledore came striding into the ward. Dumbledore alone looked calm. Indeed, he looked as though he was quite enjoying himself. Fudge appeared angry. But Snape was beside himself.

"OUT WITH IT, POTTER!" he bellowed. "WHAT DID YOU DO?" (*HP/PoA*, 419)

This is a particularly effective instance of one of Rowling's favorite devices, calling characters by their surnames when she wants to emphasize the conflation of their identities with their parents or children who share the same name. Harry already resembles James, but when Snape is in flashback, dealing with a Potter who has conspired with Sirius Black, he cannot completely distinguish between Potter past and Potter present.

> "THEY HELPED HIM ESCAPE, I KNOW IT!" Snape howled, pointing at Harry and Hermione. His face was twisted; spit was flying from his mouth.
>
> "Calm down, man!" Fudge barked. "You're talking nonsense!"
>
> "YOU DON'T KNOW POTTER!" shrieked Snape. "HE DID IT, I KNOW HE DID IT—"
>
> "That will do, Severus," said Dumbledore quietly. "Think about what you are saying. This door has been locked since I left the ward ten minutes ago. Madam Pomfrey, have these students left their beds?" (*HP/PoA*, 419-20)

Dumbledore intervenes to halt Snape's flashback by recalling him to the present moment. With his calm demeanor and the words "Think about what you are saying," Dumbledore is signaling to Snape that whatever has happened, Dumbledore has authorized it. Dumbledore expects Snape to catch on, at least enough to play along while the Minister of Magic is there.

> "Of course not!" said Madam Pomfrey, bristling. "I would have heard them!"
>
> "Well, there you have it, Severus," said Dumbledore calmly. "Unless you are suggesting that Harry and Hermione are able to be in two places at once, I'm afraid I don't see any point in troubling them further." (*HP/PoA*, 420)

As one of Hermione's teachers, Snape knows about the Time-Turner. Dumbledore has just given him the explanation he demanded.

> Snape stood there, seething, staring from Fudge, who looked thoroughly shocked at his behavior, to Dumbledore, whose eyes were twinkling behind his glasses. Snape whirled about, robes swishing behind him, and stormed out of the ward.
>
> "Fellow seems quite unbalanced," said Fudge, staring after him. "I'd watch out for him if I were you, Dumbledore."
>
> "Oh, he's not unbalanced," said Dumbledore quietly. "He's just suffered a severe disappointment." (*HP/PoA*, 420)

Fudge is not the only one who has been shocked by this moment. Many readers have wondered at the insensitivity of Dumbledore's eyes twinkling at a time of extreme upset for Snape. Is Dumbledore enjoying Snape's powerlessness? Even, perhaps, mocking him? Is this another instance of Gryffindor versus Slytherin taunting?

There may certainly be an element of that on the surface. But the politics of the moment point to an even more complex dynamic between the two men. Dumbledore's twinkling eyes tell Snape that he has not only authorized Sirius Black's escape, but based on things Snape doesn't yet know, Dumbledore is glad of it and delighted to have pulled it off without Fudge being the wiser. As Snape's gaze moves between Fudge and Dumbledore, he reads the situation: he cannot say another word without inviting Fudge to investigate more closely, possibly jeopardizing Dumbledore's plans. Snape's screaming fit, in fact, has served the valuable purpose of distracting Fudge. The most helpful thing for Dumbledore's employee to do, in this case, is to consent to appear unbalanced before the Minister of Magic, taking another hit to his reputation and public image, his true self remaining—once again—unseen. Dumbledore's comment to Fudge about Snape's "severe disappointment" even suggests an employee who would be uncontrolled enough to throw a tantrum over the loss of the promised Order of Merlin.

After reading the situation, Snape consents. He plays the role. Bitterly, but with consent.

And when Dumbledore says "quietly" that Snape has suffered a severe disappointment, we know that he implies one thing to Fudge but means quite another. His eyes are not twinkling anymore. He does not, in fact, enjoy Snape's discomfort. Snape thought he would finally get reparations for a life-scarring event. Dumbledore's quietness and his understanding of Snape's reaction suggest that after Fudge leaves, Dumbledore will speak to Snape, and he will be more sensitive in private than he appears in front of the Prime Minister.

The next day, Harry learns from Hagrid that Lupin is leaving.

> "Er—Snape told all the Slytherins this mornin'. . . . Thought everyone'd know by now . . . Professor Lupin's a werewolf, see. An' he was loose on the grounds las' night. . . . He's packin' now, o' course."
>
> "He's *packing*?" said Harry, alarmed. "Why?"
>
> "Leavin', isn' he?" said Hagrid, looking surprised that Harry had to ask. "Resigned firs' thing this mornin'. Says he can't risk it happenin' again." (*HP/PoA*, 422)

Lupin confirms to Harry that Snape "*accidentally* let slip that I am a werewolf this morning at breakfast."

> "You're not leaving just because of that!" said Harry.
>
> Lupin smiled wryly.
>
> "This time tomorrow, the owls will start arriving from parents. . . . They will not want a werewolf teaching their children, Harry. And after last night, I see their point. I could have bitten any of you. . . . That must never happen again." (*HP/PoA*, 423)

Lupin stops short of blaming Snape for his resignation; if he resigned "first thing," it seems that Lupin resigned first and then Snape told his students the news. But was it Lupin's choice to resign?

> "Last night Sirius told me all about how they became Animagi," said Dumbledore, smiling. "An extraordinary achievement—not least, keeping it quiet from me." (*HP/PoA*, 428)

While Lupin was still in werewolf form, Sirius made the solo decision to tell Dumbledore the secrets Lupin has been keeping since his school days. By the time the moon set and Lupin reverted to human form, Dumbledore had time to realize that Lupin had roamed Hogwarts and Hogsmeade in werewolf form as a student, lied about this to Dumbledore, withheld information about Sirius when Lupin returned to teach, and finally, roamed the grounds again in werewolf form as a teacher. It would not have been fun to be Lupin during that morning's job performance review with his employer. We can see that perhaps Dumbledore showed Lupin mercy by permitting him to resign rather than firing him in disgrace.

Why did Snape choose to tell the Slytherins instead of letting Lupin leave quietly?

In the past, after Lupin's lycanthropy endangered Snape's life, nothing changed. Dumbledore enforced silence around the incident, compounding Snape's trauma. Dumbledore would not hear Snape's safety concerns when he appointed Lupin to a teaching position, but it turned out that Snape was right. It was not humanly possible to guarantee anyone's safety against lycanthropy, despite Dumbledore's precautions and Snape's inexorable production of Wolfsbane. The first time, another human who was in on the secret showed faulty judgment and exposed a student to the werewolf. The second time, Lupin's own human emotions prevented his self-care. Fortunately, nobody was hurt in either instance, but Snape was right: it would be impossible to guarantee that there wouldn't be a next time.

Did Dumbledore perhaps think it better to let Lupin's lycanthropy be known, rather than risk discovery and outrage if Lupin resigned without explanation? Did Dumbledore think it better to leak the news through his tactic of unofficial rumor, rather than through an official school announcement or Leaving Feast speech? Did he perhaps take advantage of Snape's well-known animosity against Lupin and ask the undoubtedly cooperative Snape to break the news in a spiteful manner, drawing attention away from Lupin's and Dumbledore's failures and inciting popular sympathy for Lupin because of Snape's disclosure?

These scenarios are possible, even likely, considering other tactics we have seen from Dumbledore, but neither confirmed nor contradicted by the book. What we do know is that Snape has had a chance to speak to Dumbledore after Fudge's departure and before breakfast. He would not have risked his position at Hogwarts by letting slip the information without checking with Dumbledore first. As far as we know, he was not reprimanded for what he said. It seems likely that Dumbledore knew Snape would speak and did not forbid it. It is certain that Dumbledore is no longer requiring confidentiality from his staff around Lupin's lycanthropy, as Hagrid has mentioned it to Harry. (HP/PoA, 422)

Snape once accepted Dumbledore's order of silence when his own life was endangered by the student Lupin in werewolf form. But when the adult Lupin reneges on his own contract with Dumbledore, forgetting to take Wolfsbane, he endangers the entire campus and grounds. Snape can no longer endure being silent. As Harry found when he blew up Aunt Marge, it can be easier to withstand attacks on the self than threatened attacks upon others. Snape is dedicated to protecting every student against attack, even the ones he can't stand.

As Dumbledore said, Snape suffered a severe disappointment when Sirius escaped: he had hoped for some closure. If Dumbledore was able to speak to Snape after his flashback, acknowledging what his gag order had cost Snape and admitting his errors, that conversation might have functioned like a Time-Turner for Snape. He and Dumbledore would have been able to think back to the moment of Snape's student trauma and acknowledge Snape's innocence and suffering in the matter. This would have enabled Dumbledore to see why Snape would go to any lengths to protect other students from undergoing the same ordeal and led to Dumbledore lifting the confidentiality ban.

Meanwhile, Harry is saying goodbye to the best Defense Against the Dark Arts teacher he will ever have. Lupin gives back the map, not only because he's no longer Harry's teacher but he no longer has to hide the map's secrets from Dumbledore. Dumbledore says goodbye to Lupin "soberly" (HP/PoA, 425), with no hint of apology for Snape's disclosure, and "Harry had the impression that Lupin wanted to leave as quickly as possible": it is Lupin and not Snape who has disappointed Dumbledore.

From Snape's point of view, *Harry Potter and the Prisoner of Azkaban* is not the story of a kind teacher with a stigmatized disability and a wrongly incarcerated man set free by his courageous godson. It is the story of bullies who once got away with nearly getting Snape killed, the headmaster who refused to expel Sirius but cracked down on *Snape* by forbidding him to talk about his ordeal, the werewolf who returned as a teacher and once *again* posed a fatal danger to Hogwarts students, and the same headmaster, older but apparently no wiser, refusing even to listen to Snape's concerns for student safety.

The reader feels the true magic of Lupin teaching Harry priceless lessons about fear and trauma, probably the best person in the world to connect with James Potter's son in that way; Snape sees him teaching children to retaliate using sexist mockery. The reader learns Sirius is innocent, 12 prime years of his life destroyed by wrongful imprisonment; Snape hears none of that but gets knocked unconscious shortly after he hears the adult Sirius say that when Snape was nearly killed, "it served him right." (HP/PoA, 356) The reader sees Snape destroying Lupin's ability to earn a living; Snape sees himself saying enough is enough, stepping in before Lupin's lycanthropy actually kills someone and destroys Dumbledore's career.

It's not an easy point of view to see. The emotion of the main story from Harry's perspective is overpowering, and rightly so. But it's all there, if buried, and it makes sense of Snape's bitterness in this volume.

The Time-Turner magic that we learn in this volume will also turn out to be the overarching story of Snape's second chance in life, going back to his own past to become somebody who is stronger and more protective than he knew he could be.

> "Dumbledore just said—just said we could save more than one innocent life. [. . .] We've got to fly Buckbeak up to the window and rescue Sirius! Sirius can escape on Buckbeak—they can escape together!"
>
> From what Harry could see of Hermione's face, she looked terrified.
>
> "If we manage that without being seen, it'll be a miracle!"
>
> "Well, we've got to try, haven't we?" said Harry. (*HP/PoA*, 396)

In a few years, the time will come when Snape must save more than one innocent life. He will rescue Harry and Draco from Voldemort's death sentences so they can escape together. He will manage it without being seen, and it will be a miracle.

SEVERUS SNAPE
AND THE GOBLET OF FIRE

When Harry is 14 years old, a goblet of fire shoots out his name, along with the names of three gifted adults, to be challenged to a series of mortally dangerous magical tests. The other three are tall, accomplished, poised; Harry is just now undergoing puberty. Meanwhile, a monstrously larval Voldemort gains strength throughout the year until, at the end, he arises from a cauldron, fully restored, to kill Harry. When Voldemort fails, to his shock and terror, only one person comes to him with comfort and answers: Severus Snape, former Death Eater and double agent for Dumbledore's side.

Snape, too, undergoes unstoppable bodily changes during this crucible of a year, nervous all the while about a more powerful opponent. We learn for the first time that he was once a Death Eater before recanting and becoming a spy for Dumbledore. Years after renouncing his Death Eater beliefs and living unchallenged by Voldemort, his ineradicable Dark Mark is growing ever clearer. Voldemort is coming back. Death Eater Barty Crouch, Jr., impersonating the intimidating Mad-Eye Moody, reminds Snape all year that there's no such thing as a *former* Death Eater. Snape must steel himself to be called back to Voldemort's side, prepared to convince Voldemort he has never defected while serving Dumbledore as a double agent.

The tasks of the Triwizard Tournament, along with the unexpected task of the Yule Ball, show the reader what Snape and Harry must learn this year.

In the first task, contestants must steal from the nest of a brooding mother dragon. This is what Lily Evans Potter felt when Voldemort came to kill her baby. This distress and protective aggression is the power that defeated Voldemort.

In the second task, contestants must rescue their dearest loved ones from drowning. Now they understand how the mother dragons felt.

They experience the adrenaline surge, the frantic emotions that can both help and hinder, the devastation if they fail. Harry rescues his own hostage, Ron; helps another contestant rescue his hostage, Hermione; and, with enormous effort, rescues a third hostage, a child he has never met. Harry learns that the power and relief from rescuing one's own loved ones make it easier to decide to risk oneself to rescue others. This will be a major lesson for Snape, as well.

In the third task, contestants have no choice but to battle oncoming dangers, and if they win, the prize is that they get whisked to face Voldemort. They have prepared as well as they can. Not all will survive the encounter.

In the midst of the three official tasks, the Triwizard Tournament throws an unexpected fourth task into the mix: the Yule Ball. This task is judged by the rules of romantic courtship, whether one enters the competition or not, and there is no limit to the number of ways a contestant can fail. Some contestants are hopelessly underqualified, competing much too early. Some disqualified themselves years ago by committing evil that they can never undo and are reduced to punishing those who are winning this game. Harry prefers fire-breathing dragons to this one. Snape might well feel the same.

Snape's Year in Overview

After the misadventures of the previous school year, things have gotten slightly worse from Snape's point of view.

Snape's personal dislike of Harry

When the Goblet of Fire spits out Harry's name, compelling a dumbstruck Harry to compete, Snape immediately thinks Harry did it on purpose.

> "It's no one's fault but Potter's, Karkaroff," said Snape softly. His black eyes were alight with malice. "Don't go blaming Dumbledore for Potter's determination to break rules. He has been crossing lines ever since he arrived here—"
>
> "Thank you, Severus," said Dumbledore firmly, and Snape went quiet, though his eyes still glinted malevolently through his curtain of greasy black hair. (HP/GoF, 276)

Why would Snape think such a thing? Based on Harry's pursuit of a troll, his defense of the Sorcerer's Stone, his flying car mishap, his battle in the Chamber of Secrets, his surreptitious Hogsmeade trips, and his unauthorized visits to Hagrid past the dementors, it is not an unreasonable guess.

Unfortunately, Harry's unsought status as a Triwizard competitor reinforces one of Snape's original misconceptions about Harry: that he pursues notoriety. More than once, Snape abuses his position as a teacher to needle Harry in class: "I don't care how many times your picture appears in the papers. To me, Potter, you are nothing but a nasty little boy who considers rules to be beneath him." (*HP/GoF*, 516)

Harry keeps his temper, more or less, but imagines different ways he would love to respond, including the Cruciatus curse, the Unforgivable Curse they have just learned about from the new Defense Against the Dark Arts teacher. (*HP/GoF*, 300)

Snape's usual hostility to the new Defense teacher

This year, there is a new note to it: intimidation. Mad-Eye Moody is a hardline law enforcement official, a veteran Auror, who has spent his career tracking down Dark wizards. A notoriously vigilant, possibly paranoid man, he is deeply skeptical of former Voldemort supporters who recanted after Voldemort lost power. His idiosyncrasies are so well known that it is not difficult for Death Eater Barty Crouch, Jr. to impersonate him all year, fooling everyone up to Dumbledore himself.

> It was common knowledge that Snape really wanted the Dark Arts job, and he had now failed to get it for the fourth year running. Snape had disliked all of their previous Dark Arts teachers, and shown it—but he seemed strangely wary of displaying overt animosity to Mad-Eye Moody. Indeed, whenever Harry saw the two of them together—at mealtimes, or when they passed in the corridors—he had the distinct impression that Snape was avoiding Moody's eye, whether magical or normal.
>
> "I reckon Snape's a bit scared of him, you know," Harry said thoughtfully. (*HP/GoF*, 209-10)

But Snape's fear turns venomous when Crouch, posing as Moody, gets away with a vicious attack on Draco Malfoy. He sees Draco hex Harry from the back during a fight, which angers him. He Transfigures Draco into a ferret, raises the ferret "ten feet into the air," and bounces him off the floor repeatedly. (*HP/GoF*, 204-5)

Crouch/Moody only stops when McGonagall shrieks and rescues Draco in disbelief. It's a striking instance of one of Rowling's themes for this volume: extremists at either end of the spectrum may have more in common with each other than they do with most of their ideological allies. McGonagall seems to find it credible that Mad-Eye Moody would get exercised over perceived violations of dueling honor, enough to beat a student; meanwhile, Death Eater Crouch hates Lucius Malfoy for renouncing Voldemort once he fell from power, so he takes out his hatred on Malfoy's child. The tenor of the ill will toward Draco feels equivalent whether coming from a Death Eater or an enemy of Death Eaters.

As Head of Slytherin, Snape must have felt sickened when he learned of this ignominious beating. A repeated ten-foot drop onto a stone floor is brutal. He wasn't there to defend his student.

> "I know your father of old, boy. . . . You tell him Moody's keeping a close eye on his son . . . you tell him that from me. . . . Now, your Head of House'll be Snape, will it?"
>
> "Yes," said Malfoy resentfully.
>
> "Another old friend," growled Moody. "I've been looking forward to a chat with old Snape. . . . Come on, you. . . ."
>
> And he seized Malfoy's upper arm and marched him off toward the dungeons. (*HP/GoF*, 206-7)

Whatever happened during the ensuing discussion, Snape and Draco must have felt humiliated and powerless. We are not told Moody's House as a student, but Gryffindor seems a decent bet. Judging by the Slytherins' amplified nastiness toward Harry and his friends this year, Crouch/Moody's threatening attitude toward former Death Eaters extended toward Slytherin house overall.

Snape's reputation

This is overshadowed by other topics at Hogwarts this year. He has no job other than Potions Master and Head of Slytherin, since the man appointed to the Defense Against the Dark Arts position is better qualified than he is and does not need to be tailed. He hates Harry; he favors Slytherin: to most observers, it looks like business as usual.

But Harry, Ron, and Hermione are re-evaluating what they know of him, trying to make sense of pieces that don't seem to fit. The author finds a fun way to tell the reader which of their theories are on target.

> "Moody said Dumbledore only lets Snape stay here because he's giving him a second chance or something. . . ."
>
> "What?" said Ron, his eyes widening, his next cushion spinning high into the air, ricocheting off the chandelier, and dropping heavily onto Flitwick's desk. "Harry . . . maybe Moody thinks Snape put your name in the Goblet of Fire!"
>
> "Oh Ron," said Hermione, shaking her head skeptically, "we thought Snape was trying to kill Harry before, and it turned out he was saving Harry's life, remember?"
>
> She Banished a cushion and it flew across the room and landed in the box they were all supposed to be aiming at. Harry looked at Hermione, thinking . . . it was true that Snape had saved his life once, but the odd thing was, Snape definitely loathed him, just as he'd loathed Harry's father when they had been at school together. (*HP/GoF*, 480)

Snape loathes Harry; Snape saves Harry. Perhaps their new clue about a second chance can make sense of that contradiction.

> "I just want to know what Snape did with his first chance, if he's on his second one," said Harry grimly, and his cushion, to his very great surprise, flew straight across the room and landed neatly on top of Hermione's. (*HP/GoF*, 481)

The mystery of Snape's true motives

Just when Crouch/Moody is about to kill Harry, someone crashes through the door to save him.

> Moody was thrown backward onto the office floor. Harry, still staring at the place where Moody's face had been, saw Albus Dumbledore, Professor Snape, and Professor McGonagall looking back at him out of the Foe-Glass. He looked around and saw the three of them standing in the doorway, Dumbledore in front, his wand outstretched. (*HP/GoF*, 679)

It's true that a foe of Barty Crouch, Jr. could either be a foe of Death Eaters or a former Death Eater afraid of Voldemort's return. But the unity of purpose from these three angry teachers suggests that Snape is allied completely with Dumbledore and McGonagall. After Dumbledore enters, Harry sees that "Snape followed him, looking into the Foe-Glass, where his own face was still visible, glaring into the room." (*HP/GoF*, 679) Perhaps Snape is checking for magical confirmation of what he knows to be true: his renunciation of Voldemort is genuine. He is so young and new to double agency, at this point, that he still looks for reassurance, for external mirroring of his internal reality, especially since he has so often been disbelieved. As he gets further into his mission, as more lives depend upon him, he will have to learn to avoid or fool magical mirrors so they don't give him away. There will come a point when he learns to hide his true self so deeply that he won't show up in mirrors at all.

At the end of this book, Harry, Ron, and Hermione watch as a resolute Snape openly declares himself convinced of Voldemort's return, baring his Dark Mark to the Minister of Magic, and goes alone to Voldemort to start the long mission that will likely end in his death. It is one of the few times they, and we, see him absolutely as he is. Prepared or not, it is time, and he is afraid.

Puberty, Time Travel, and Second Chances

Harry, Voldemort, and Snape all go through a form of puberty this year. All three are awkwardly changing out of their childish selves, struggling to mature their bodies and minds enough to meet adult challenges. Harry looks like a small child next to his Triwizard competitors. Voldemort requires round-the-clock care in an infant-sized body while he plans his full return. And Snape is undergoing his own version of Time-Turner travel. At 34, twice the minimum age for a Triwizard champion, he is living out his second chance to choose a side when Voldemort beckons. Adolescence would be a difficult time for many people to relive, but it is especially so for an ugly, unpleasant man who was even uglier and less pleasant as a teen.

Those who have been expecting Voldemort's return know what it means when people go missing or Dark Marks reappear. Shortly after Wormtail (Peter Pettigrew) escapes with intention to rejoin Voldemort, Harry tells Sirius about his curse scar hurting and receives an urgent reply: *If it hurts again, go straight to Dumbledore—they're saying he's got Mad-Eye out of retirement, which means he's reading the signs, even if no one else is.* (HP/GoF, 226)

Probably at the same time Harry's curse scar hurts him, the Dark Marks on former Death Eaters begin to come out of dormancy. Snape tells Dumbledore, "It's coming back . . . Karkaroff's too . . . stronger and clearer than ever . . ." (HP/GoF, 598)

Dumbledore is anchoring Snape's travel back to this pivotal moment in his past, serving as his mentor. As Hagrid says, Dumbledore "trusts people, he does. Gives 'em second chances. . . ." (HP/GoF, 455) Snape cannot change anything in the past; he cannot bring back anyone who died because of his choices. But if all goes well, more than one innocent life will be saved. His assignment is longer and less defined than the three hours that Dumbledore set Hermione and Harry the previous year. It stretches from the moment he notices his Dark Mark changing until the moment, whenever that will be, that Voldemort summons his followers again.

Karkaroff, who evaded a prison sentence after Voldemort's fall by giving names of fellow Death Eaters, including Snape, has no mentor to help him plan for Voldemort's return. Snape has been avoiding him, so he corners Snape while he's teaching, too panicked to worry about the expert eavesdroppers witnessing their interaction.

> Harry, peering around the edge of his cauldron, saw Karkaroff pull up the left-hand sleeve of his robe and show Snape something on his inner forearm.
>
> "Well?" said Karkaroff, still making every effort not to move his lips. "Do you see? It's never been this clear, never since—"
>
> "Put it away!" snarled Snape, his black eyes sweeping the classroom.
>
> "But you must have noticed—" Karkaroff began in an agitated voice.
>
> "We can talk later, Karkaroff!" spat Snape. "Potter! What are you doing?" (HP/GoF, 519)

With instincts like this, Karkaroff clearly will not last very long once Voldemort starts to track him. He is not defending himself properly; he is revealing his vulnerability, pulling up his sleeve of his own volition in front of witnesses, literally showing his weakness. Within the context of a roomful of teenagers with their merciless appraisals and mockery, he is also showing too much that he is a person like them, with a human body, rather than a well-defended and clothed authority figure. At age 11, Harry was horrorstruck to walk in on Filch tending Snape's bare, bitten leg; it can be just as horrifying for teens in mid-puberty to be confronted suddenly with the sight of their middle-aged, unattractive teachers, unclothed and vulnerable, going through their own bodily changes.

One of Rowling's most sophisticated points is that naïve teen political choices can have major, even lifelong repercussions on one's romantic and family future. Snape has no romance in his life and never will, for three reasons. On his first chance, he destroyed his own prospects and faith in himself when he repelled the love of his life with his hateful politics, which eventually brought about her death. On his second chance, he will atone for this with undercover work that makes romance too risky. Thirdly, he would have had a difficult time attracting romance in any case because life is painfully—agonizingly—unfair to the homely.

Snape doesn't get a date to the Yule Ball. His companion for a nighttime stroll is a panicking Karkaroff.

> "Severus, you cannot pretend this isn't happening!" Karkaroff's voice sounded anxious and hushed, as though keen not to be overheard. "It's been getting clearer and clearer for months. I am becoming seriously concerned, I can't deny it—"
>
> "Then flee," said Snape's voice curtly. "Flee—I will make your excuses. I, however, am remaining at Hogwarts." (*HP/GoF*, 426)

Snape patrols the grounds for teens enjoying the kind of romance that he has forfeited.

> Snape and Karkaroff came around the corner. Snape had his wand out and was blasting rosebushes apart, his expression most ill-natured. Squeals issued from many of the bushes, and dark shapes emerged from them.
>
> "Ten points from Ravenclaw, Fawcett!" Snape snarled as a girl ran past him. "And ten points from Hufflepuff too, Stebbins!" as a boy went rushing after her. (*HP/GoF*, 426)

The image of a spiteful Snape blasting rosebushes is an instant classic. In Snape, Rowling has given English literature the very archetype of the grumpy teacher who needs to get laid. She is careful to show that he's snarling at a Ravenclaw and a Hufflepuff, too; this has nothing to do with his usual Gryffindor-Slytherin issues.

This year, Snape expands his classroom bullying repertoire to include shots at his students' love lives. When he sees Rita Skeeter's tabloid article inventing a love triangle between Harry, Hermione, and Viktor Krum, Rowling gives us a character moment that is pricelessly mean and pricelessly funny.

> To Harry's fury, he began to read the article aloud.
>
> *"'Harry Potter's Secret Heartache'* . . . dear, dear, Potter, what's ailing you now? *'A boy like no other, perhaps . . .'"*
>
> Harry could feel his face burning. Snape was pausing at the end of every sentence to allow the Slytherins a hearty laugh. The article sounded ten times worse when read by Snape. Even Hermione was blushing scarlet now. (*HP/GoF*, 515)

You might not want him as your teacher, but this character is a literary treasure. When it comes to awfulness you can savor, Rowling's Snape always delivers.

When Draco calls Hermione a "Mudblood" again, Harry fights him and Hermione is accidentally hit by a hex that makes her teeth grow toward her chin. Goyle gets hexed as well. Snape's response shows that he has regressed to the immaturity level of his students, perhaps even further.

> "Hospital wing, Goyle," Snape said calmly.
>
> "Malfoy got Hermione!" Ron said. *"Look!"*
>
> He forced Hermione to show Snape her teeth—she was doing her best to hide them with her hands, though this was difficult as they had now grown down past her collar. Pansy Parkinson and the other Slytherin girls were doubled up with silent giggles, pointing at Hermione from behind Snape's back.
>
> Snape looked coldly at Hermione, then said, "I see no difference."
>
> Hermione let out a whimper; her eyes filled with tears, she turned on her heel and ran, ran all the way up the corridor and out of sight. (*HP/GoF*, 299-300)

What's going on? What kind of despicable adult gives in to such a mean impulse?

This exchange occurs the week after Harry is announced as a Triwizard champion, which might remind people of other times that Harry or Gryffindors have been exempted from rules. It's a couple of months after Crouch/Moody administered corporal punishment to Draco and then immediately took Draco along to have a "chat" with his "old friend" Snape. When Snape examines Goyle, a Slytherin from his own House, he reacts calmly. When his attention is drawn to Hermione, he is standing with a squadron of Slytherins behind him, facing the Gryffindors. He is not being a teacher of the school at large, as McGonagall was when she rescued Draco from being beaten after he attacked a Gryffindor in the back. He is standing at the head of Slytherins only, abusing his power as a teacher but otherwise acting like a child.

This is retaliation. It shows how powerless he feels. He feels his Slytherins are bullied and he has no hope of fairness toward them, so he indulges in petty revenge on a blameless teenage girl. It is excruciatingly embarrassing to watch, as well as cruel.

What's going on in the mind of Hermione, that preternaturally perceptive Gryffindor girl who reads Snape too correctly for his comfort? She is probably not surprised by his behavior. She's long accepted that he will not look at her or acknowledge her. She wasn't going to ask for his attention; she was probably already deciding to take herself to the Hospital Wing without asking permission, since Snape notices her so little that she can even steal from his office without getting caught. It is Ron, unattuned to the longstanding dynamic between Snape and Hermione, who forces the question. Not that Ron is expecting fair treatment from Snape, either. He is bent on showing that a Gryffindor has suffered as much damage as a Slytherin and deserves as much solicitude from Snape. It is a critique of Snape's handling of the situation, and it occasions the kind of response that Snape always gives to critiques.

Snape's cruelty about a teenage girl's looks could have caused true damage. Fortunately for the nerves of the reader, Hermione turns out to be remarkably resilient about it. She gets her teeth fixed and goes on to be the belle of the Yule Ball in Cinderella style, dating a surly, large-nosed, gifted wizard who has not forfeited his right to romance in life. And that's the final unspoken element of this scenario: the mixture of scorn and pity elicited by the sight of a loveless adult mocking a maturing teen. Hermione may have tears in her eyes, but she can walk away. There will be roses for her. She can leave this bitter man behind.

The Egg and the Eye

Harry gets a crash course in embittered manhood in one of Rowling's most masterfully crafted scenes: the end of Chapter 25, "The Egg and the Eye." (*HP/GoF*, 467-78) Out past curfew with his Invisibility Cloak, the Marauder's Map, and the golden egg holding the clue to his second task, Harry gets stuck in a trick stair and drops the egg and map. Immobilized, he watches helplessly as the three oddest-looking men at Hogwarts converge to squabble over the source of the din: Filch, Snape, and Crouch disguised as Mad-Eye Moody, with his scars and his magical eye.

Filch arrives first, "his horrible, pouchy face and bulging, pale eyes staring" to no avail (*HP/GoF*, 468); Harry is still under the Invisibility Cloak. Filch immediately blames the din on his nemesis, Peeves the poltergeist. Filch is obsessed with getting Dumbledore to throw Peeves out of the castle, in a burlesque version of Snape's deathless fantasy of getting Harry expelled.

Next to arrive: "At the foot of the stairs stood the only person who could make Harry's situation worse: Snape. He was wearing a long gray nightshirt and he looked livid." (*HP/GoF*, 469) Someone has broken into his office. There are no words to express Harry's horror at the sight of Snape in nothing but a nightshirt, gray and shell-less like a Blast-Ended Skrewt.

Filch tries pathetically to interest Snape in his pursuit of Peeves, but Snape is in the midst of snarling, "Filch, I don't give a damn about that wretched poltergeist," when Crouch/Moody arrives, "wearing his old traveling cloak over his nightshirt and leaning on his staff as usual." (*HP/GoF*, 470) He is better armored than Snape. With his magical eye, he can see Harry through the Invisibility Cloak. He is in control of the situation, and he takes advantage of it with insinuating threats to Snape.

> "Dumbledore happens to trust me," said Snape through clenched teeth. "I refuse to believe that he gave you orders to search my office!"
>
> "'Course Dumbledore trusts you," growled Moody. "He's a trusting man, isn't he? Believes in second chances. But me—I say there are spots that don't come off, Snape. Spots that never come off, d'you know what I mean?"

> Snape suddenly did something very strange. He seized his left forearm convulsively with his right hand, as though something on it had hurt him.
>
> Moody laughed. "Get back to bed, Snape."
>
> "You don't have the authority to send me anywhere!" Snape hissed, letting go of his arm as though angry with himself. (*HP/GoF*, 471-2)

Snape's response switches rapidly between anger, defensiveness, and intimidation like a pubescent boy's voice breaking. He knows he has nothing to hide, but the insinuation that Dumbledore might not trust him *hurts*. We see here how much Dumbledore's trust means to Snape's life.

It is hard enough for Snape to keep up the charade of being too untrustworthy for the Defense Against the Dark Arts position, but when he thinks he's faced with a DADA expert who genuinely believes this of him, who knows of Snape's past and doubts his change of heart, his composure breaks. The ominous return of his Dark Mark and the presence of the man he thinks is an Auror have reminded him of the ugliness he used to espouse. It's true that some spots don't come off. The mark hidden under his clothing no longer mirrors who he is on the inside, but for those who see it or know that it's there, it does reflect who he truly *used* to be. He is not yet seasoned enough to master his regret. It betrays him.

But just as Filch blames Peeves for everything, Snape's mind always turns to Harry Potter when he has a grievance with the world.

> But Snape's black eyes were darting from the egg in Filch's arms to the map in Moody's hand, and Harry could tell he was putting two and two together, as only Snape could. . . .
>
> "Potter!" Snape snarled, and he actually turned his head and stared right at the place where Harry was, as though he could suddenly see him. "That egg is Potter's egg. That piece of parchment belongs to Potter. I have seen it before, I recognize it! Potter is here! Potter, in his Invisibility Cloak!"
>
> Snape stretched out his hands like a blind man and began to move up the stairs; Harry could have sworn his over-large nostrils were

dilating, trying to sniff Harry out—trapped, Harry leaned backward, trying to avoid Snape's fingertips, but any moment now—(*HP/GoF*, 473)

Snape is a potent wizard to begin with, but when it comes to detecting Harry's wrongdoing, he manifests an almost monstrous genius, nearly equal to the most mystical magic we see from Ollivander or Dumbledore.

Crouch/Moody saves Harry from discovery by going on the offensive.

> "There's nothing there, Snape!" barked Moody, "but I'll be happy to tell the headmaster how quickly your mind jumped to Harry Potter!"
>
> "Meaning what?" Snape turned again to look at Moody, his hands still outstretched, inches from Harry's chest.
>
> "Meaning that Dumbledore's very interested to know who's got it in for that boy!" said Moody, limping nearer still to the foot of the stairs. "And so am I, Snape . . . very interested. . . ."
>
> . . . "I merely thought," said Snape, in a voice of forced calm, "that if Potter was wandering around after hours again . . . it's an unfortunate habit of his . . . he should be stopped. For—for his own safety." (*HP/GoF*, 473-4)

Bizarrely, in this upside-down conversation between a helpful man who wants to hurt Harry and a hateful man who wants to protect Harry, Snape's stammered explanation is the true one. He forgets himself, sometimes, because Harry enrages him so, but he really does want Harry to stay safe during this year when someone is clearly trying to kill him.

Once the defeated Snape and Filch leave the scene, Crouch/Moody borrows the Marauders' Map from Harry and drops a bombshell about Snape, the first hint Harry ever hears about this part of Snape's past.

> "Oh if there's one thing I hate," he muttered, more to himself than to Harry, and his magical eye was fixed on the left-hand corner of the map, "it's a Death Eater who walked free. . . ."
>
> Harry stared at him. Could Moody possibly mean what Harry thought he meant? (*HP/GoF*, 476-7)

Dumbledore's trust

Harry, Ron, and Hermione consult Sirius about the possibility that Snape was a Death Eater. For all of them, it comes down to one mystery: Why would Dumbledore trust Snape if he was?

> "Ever since I found out Snape was teaching here, I've wondered why Dumbledore hired him. Snape's always been fascinated by the Dark Arts, he was famous for it at school. Slimy, oily, greasy-haired kid, he was," Sirius added, and Harry and Ron grinned at each other. "Snape knew more curses when he arrived at school than half the kids in seventh year, and he was part of a gang of Slytherins who nearly all turned out to be Death Eaters."

> [. . .] But as far as I know, Snape was never even accused of being a Death Eater—not that that means much. Plenty of them were never caught. And Snape's certainly clever and cunning enough to keep himself out of trouble." (*HP/GoF*, 531)

Sirius's recollections introduce new information about Snape the student. He arrived knowing adult-level curses—defensive, angry, possibly power hungry, and smart, if not wise. He was notorious. He had friends, or at least a "gang"—he was not entirely unpopular, at least within his own House.

Sirius narrows it down to the central issue. There must be something important that we don't know: "There's still the fact that Dumbledore trusts Snape, and I know Dumbledore trusts where a lot of other people wouldn't, but I just can't see him letting Snape teach at Hogwarts if he'd ever worked for Voldemort." (*HP/GoF*, 532)

While left unattended in Dumbledore's office, Harry sneaks a look at his Pensieve, a magical device for viewing and sharing memories. He sees Karkaroff's Death Eater trial, presided over by Barty Crouch, Sr., the authoritarian father of the Death Eater posing as Mad-Eye Moody.

> Dumbledore had gotten to his feet.

> "I have given evidence already on this matter," he said calmly. "Severus Snape was indeed a Death Eater. However, he rejoined our side before Lord Voldemort's downfall and turned spy for us, at great personal risk. He is now no more a Death Eater than I am."

> Harry turned to look at Mad-Eye Moody. He was wearing a look of

deep skepticism behind Dumbledore's back. (*HP/GoF*, 590-1)

"Now no more a Death Eater than I am." Quite a statement. That addresses the issue that Sirius raised. Yes, Dumbledore believes there is a way for someone who had once worked for Voldemort to be as trustworthy as someone who has always worked against Voldemort. But when Harry asks Dumbledore how he can be sure, Dumbledore holds Harry's gaze for a few seconds, then says, "That, Harry, is a matter between Professor Snape and myself." (*HP/GoF*, 604)

Harry tells Ron and Hermione.

> "And he trusts Snape?" Ron said. "He really trusts Snape, even though he knows he was a Death Eater?"
>
> "Yes," said Harry.
>
> Hermione had not spoken for ten minutes. She was sitting with her forehead in her hands, staring at her knees. Harry thought she too looked as though she could have done with a Pensieve. (*HP/GoF*, 605-6)

We know the way Hermione's mind works. She is re-evaluating everything she knows about this man, this petty classroom tyrant who knew vicious curses as a child and now regularly saves the lives of people he doesn't even like. She is thinking about what it must have taken to join the Death Eaters and then secretly leave, turning spy. Ten minutes is a long time for a mind like hers. By the end of it, she surely understands more about Snape than she is telling Ron and Harry. She doesn't have to like people, but she cannot help but understand them; that's who she is. Her faith in Snape has just grown stronger.

Ugliness, mirroring, and double agency

With Voldemort's impending return to power, there is finally a concrete use for Snape's dislike of Harry. There is little point, at this moment, in trying to get Snape and Harry to hate each other less. They're both preoccupied with surviving past the end of this school year. But now that Snape is about to resume his career as a double agent, his visceral hatred for Harry can join all the other facets of his cover persona that he and Dumbledore have polished during Voldemort's dormancy. It hasn't been easy for Snape to maintain peace with being seen as incorrigibly evil at the core, less deserving of trust than such stellar worthies as Gilderoy Lockhart. But the sacrifice of his reputation is about to pay off. Everyone believes that he covets the Defense Against the Dark Arts position and resents being denied. His exterior image does not reflect his true self; it's uglier than he really is. But if people see past it, they can be persuaded—or at least distracted—by the waves of genuine loathing that Snape emanates in Harry's direction.

Ugliness is a significant element of Snape's persona. It is one of his foremost qualities when Snape bars Harry's access to Dumbledore, acting so much like a gargoyle that he even looks like one. (Rattlesnakeroot, 2011)

> "POTTER!"
>
> Harry skidded to a halt and looked around. Snape had just emerged from the hidden staircase behind the stone gargoyle. The wall was sliding shut behind him even as he beckoned Harry back toward him.
>
> "What are you doing here, Potter?"
>
> "I need to see Professor Dumbledore!" said Harry, running back up the corridor and skidding to a standstill in front of Snape instead. "It's Mr. Crouch . . . he's just turned up . . . he's in the forest . . . he's asking—"
>
> . . . "The headmaster is busy, Potter," said Snape, his thin mouth curling into an unpleasant smile. (*HP/GoF*, 557)

Dumbledore hears them and overrides Snape to follow Harry, "leaving Snape standing next to the gargoyle and looking twice as ugly." (*HP/GoF*, 558) Later, Harry notes bitterly that Snape's delay might have given the murderer of Barty Crouch, Sr. more time. (*HP/GoF*, 566)

Rowling gives the reader one last moment to consider the evidence she's given about Snape's true view of Voldemort. She's carefully included support for arguments that he could be any of the three absent followers that Voldemort mentions but does not name when he returns to power. She identifies each follower a few pages later, but it's a good moment for a roll call and an appreciation for the mystery.

> "One, too cowardly to return . . . he will pay. One, who I believe has left me forever . . . he will be killed, of course . . . and one, who

remains my most faithful servant, and who has already reentered my service."

... "He is at Hogwarts, that faithful servant, and it was through his efforts that our young friend arrived here tonight. . . ." (*HP/GoF*, 651-2)

Harry, and the reader, know that Snape and Karkaroff are among the three named by Voldemort. Whether or not Snape is the "faithful servant," he is also the person who taught Harry the Defense Against the Dark Arts spell that is about to save his life.

"You have been taught how to duel, Harry Potter?" said Voldemort softly, his red eyes glinting through the darkness.

At these words Harry remembered, as though from a former life, the dueling club at Hogwarts he had attended briefly two years ago. . . . All he had learned there was the Disarming Spell, "Expelliarmus" . . . and what use would it be to deprive Voldemort of his wand, even if he could, when he was surrounded by Death Eaters, outnumbered by at least thirty to one? He had never learned anything that could possibly fit him for this. (*HP/GoF*, 659-60)

Snape's surreptitious plan is working. He has drilled a simple spell into Harry that Harry has practiced and can perform under stress. It does not lead to escalation but an emotional connection between attacker and attacked. It *humanizes* the victim who would disarm the attacker rather than attack in return. The resulting emotion reminds Voldemort of Lily, James, and his other victims, so vividly that Harry can literally see and hear these memories. These sights reinforce Harry's faith in *Expelliarmus* and show him the spell's lingering power. The defense that Snape taught thus becomes Harry's signature magic.

Defense Against the Dark Arts: Antidotes

All year long, Snape has been trying to teach Harry about antidotes. He has been unsuccessful, possibly because students learn better from teachers who don't bully them.

"Professor Snape was forcing them to research antidotes. They took this one seriously, as he had hinted that he might be poisoning

one of them before Christmas to see if their antidote worked."
(*HP/GoF*, 234)

Would he actually do such a thing? Apparently so.

"Antidotes!" said Snape, looking around at them all, his cold black
eyes glittering unpleasantly. "You should all have prepared your
recipes now. I want you to brew them carefully, and then, we will
be selecting someone on whom to test one. . . ."

Snape's eyes met Harry's, and Harry knew what was coming. Snape
was going to poison *him*. Harry imagined picking up his cauldron,
and sprinting to the front of the class, and bringing it down on
Snape's greasy head—(*HP/GoF*, 300-1)

Harry's understandable hostility distracts him, and the reader, from
wondering why Snape is focusing on antidotes this year. Unlike other
years, there is a competent Defense Against the Dark Arts professor, so
his services are not needed in that department. Any Defense he teaches
should be within his own subject, Potions. And this year, Hogwarts is
hosting a Death Eater headmaster who teaches his students the Dark
Arts. (*HP/GoF*, 165)

Moody had told them all during their last Defense Against the
Dark Arts lesson that he preferred to prepare his own food and
drink at all times, as it was so easy for Dark wizards to poison an
unattended cup. (*HP/GoF*, 321-2)

In a year when someone is trying to get Harry killed, perhaps Snape
has reason to train Harry, in particular, on poisons and antidotes.
Unfortunately, Harry doesn't pay attention, distracted by the unexpected
task of asking Cho Chang to the Yule Ball: "He found it hard to
concentrate on Snape's Potions test, and consequently forgot to add the
key ingredient—a bezoar—meaning that he received bottom marks."
(*HP/GoF*, 396)

It seems that Harry learns from Snape better when there's an
intermediary, whether it's Gilderoy Lockhart and *Expelliarmus* or, a
couple of years from now, the owner of a decades-old textbook and
bezoars.

Snape never does poison Harry or any other student, despite his
threats.

> "Veritaserum—a Truth Potion so powerful that three drops would have you spilling your innermost secrets for this entire class to hear," said Snape viciously. "Now, the use of this potion is controlled by very strict Ministry guidelines. But unless you watch your step, you might just find that my hand *slips*"—he shook the crystal bottle slightly—"right over your evening pumpkin juice." (*HP/GoF*, 517)

Barty Crouch, Jr.'s confession is the only time we see Veritaserum being used in the series. We learn that everything he did as Mad-Eye Moody adhered to a consistent inner agenda that could not always be guessed from the evidence. For example, he helped Harry repeatedly because "I could not hurt Potter; my master needed him." (*HP/GoF*, 690) The same might be true, then, of Snape. He might be devoted to helping Harry against Voldemort despite every appearance of loathing Harry. By the same logic, of course, he might turn out to be working for Voldemort all along. What Barty Crouch, Jr.'s Veritaserum confession tells us, though, is that in this story, characters are likely to *have* agendas, hidden or not. There are fictional universes in which characters remain always unknown or ambiguous, or turn out to have no consistent agendas at all. That is not how Rowling's universe works.

Barty Crouch, Jr. describes the indirect way he furthered his agenda when he was posing as Mad-Eye Moody: "It hasn't been easy, Harry, guiding you through these tasks without arousing suspicion. I have had to use every ounce of cunning I possess, so that my hand would not be detectable in your success." (*HP/GoF*, 676) From this point in the story until the day he dies, Snape is going to have to apply the same standards of subtlety in guiding students against Voldemort and his followers.

His responsibilities will extend to students other than just Harry, as we see from his reaction to Harry's argument with the Minister of Magic.

> "Look, I saw Voldemort come back!" Harry shouted. He tried to get out of bed again, but Mrs. Weasley forced him back. "I saw the Death Eaters! I can give you their names! Lucius Malfoy—"
>
> Snape made a sudden movement, but as Harry looked at him, Snape's eyes flew back to Fudge. (*HP/GoF*, 706)

Snape knows some of his Slytherin students have parents who have just rejoined Voldemort. Their lives are about to become much more dangerous, and he will have to protect them without arousing the suspicions of their parents, Voldemort, or the rest of the school. Whatever anti-Slytherin bias they've suffered before is about to intensify. It's a heavy load on top of his own double agency. Perhaps thinking of them adds to his courage when confronting Fudge's denial.

> Finally, [Fudge] said, with a hint of a plea in his voice, "He can't be back, Dumbledore, he just can't. . ."
>
> Snape strode forward, past Dumbledore, pulling up the left sleeve of his robes as he went. He stuck out his forearm and showed it to Fudge, who recoiled.
>
> "There," said Snape harshly. "There. The Dark Mark. It is not as clear as it was an hour or so ago, when it burned black, but you can still see it. Every Death Eater had the sign burned into him by the Dark Lord."
>
> . . . He stared, apparently repelled by the ugly mark on Snape's arm, then looked up at Dumbledore and whispered, "I don't know what you and your staff are playing at, Dumbledore, but I have heard enough." (*HP/GoF*, 709-10)

After a year of hiding his body's secret, shameful changes, Snape bares his vivid Dark Mark to the Minister of Magic. His puberty is over; he is a young man with nothing to hide. The lack of shame changes him. Unlike every other glimpse we have had of the skin under his robes, this time, the sight does not seem shell-less or ugly. Fudge is repelled by the "ugly mark" on his arm, not by Snape. The ugliness is not *in* Snape anymore; it is on his surface, evident in the Mark that shows the growing terror he's been enduring all year in private and the terror that is coming to all of them soon, whether they deny it or not. The self that has grappled with this truth and prepared to accept the consequences is not ugly; it is brave.

He will soon have to begin years of keeping his emotions tightly hidden, but at this moment, when it counts, Snape reveals his true self and nothing else. The witnesses in the room, aside from the Prime Minister, are Dumbledore, Harry, Ron, Hermione, McGonagall, Mrs. Weasley, Bill Weasley, Madam Pomfrey, the unconscious Mad-Eye Moody, and, unbeknownst to Snape, Sirius Black. The secretive Snape would not normally be so unguarded in front of such a crowd, but this is a turning point in his life, when he diverges forever from easier paths.

The Time-Turner-like journey he has taken with Dumbledore this year into his own past, preparing to make different choices so he can save innocent lives without being seen, has arrived at the critical moment. His preparations are finished. The grand operation of his second chance starts now.

> Dumbledore made sure that the door was closed, and that Madam Pomfrey's footsteps had died away, before he spoke again.
>
> "And now," he said, "it is time for two of our number to recognize each other for what they are. Sirius . . . if you could resume your usual form."
>
> The great black dog looked up at Dumbledore, then, in an instant, turned back into a man.
>
> Mrs. Weasley screamed and leapt back from the bed. (*HP/GoF*, 712)

Dumbledore equates Sirius being in Animagus form with Snape's cover as an untrustworthy teacher with a weakness for the Dark Arts.

That is a rather weighty equation. In Dumbledore's eyes, Snape has had a true self all along that is no more like that public image than Sirius Black is actually a dog.

This is the answer to Sirius's question about why Dumbledore would hire someone who once worked for Voldemort. People can change, even if their spots cannot. Appearances and inner reality are not always the same. There are sometimes good reasons to present the self untruthfully, even if that can be a grueling ordeal, as Sirius well knows. And people who have undergone such transformations know things, can do things, that those innocent of such ordeals cannot. Snape knows everything about how it feels to be a Death Eater; his Mark still burns. But he also knows how it feels to fight Voldemort's cause at mortal risk. Most people are neither Death Eaters nor active fighters; some few are one or the other; very few know how it feels to be both. There are some things that only Snape can do.

Overcoming his loathing of Sirius may or may not be one of them.

> "Him!" he snarled, staring at Sirius, whose face showed equal dislike. "What is he doing here?"
>
> "He is here at my invitation," said Dumbledore, looking between

them, "as are you, Severus. I trust you both. It is time for you to lay aside your old differences and trust each other."

Harry thought Dumbledore was asking for a near miracle. Sirius and Snape were eyeing each other with the utmost loathing. (*HP/GoF*, 712)

Sirius's second chance starts now, too. He can begin to work against the man who killed his best friend and destroyed his young adulthood. He and Snape both have good reason for their arrested development, though that can be hard to remember when they're behaving like children.

The enormity of the task before Snape makes him seem young in this scene in a way that normally is not part of his image. He is 35.

"Severus," said Dumbledore, turning to Snape, "you know what I must ask you to do. If you are ready . . . if you are prepared. . ."

"I am," said Snape.

He looked slightly paler than usual, and his cold, black eyes glittered strangely.

"Then good luck," said Dumbledore, and he watched, with a trace of apprehension on his face, as Snape swept wordlessly after Sirius.

It was several minutes before Dumbledore spoke again. (*HP/GoF*, 713)

Snape is afraid.

The several minutes of silence from Dumbledore echo the ten minutes of silence from Hermione when she first learned that Snape had been a Death Eater. Snape may be alone, but there are others who are thinking about what he's doing, and by including these silences from two of the series' most insightful characters, the author signals that the reader should, too. Rowling slows down time in her own story to mark a few pivotal moments of importance, but they are usually Harry's moments. This is one time the story belongs to Snape.

Snape goes to Voldemort and returns to his duties at Hogwarts, seemingly unchanged. Harry watches him at the Leaving Feast. The aperture has closed, but now Harry knows what's underneath Snape's façade.

His eyes lingered on Harry for a moment as Harry looked at him. His expression was difficult to read. He looked as sour and unpleasant as ever. Harry continued to watch him, long after Snape had looked away.

What was it that Snape had done on Dumbledore's orders, the night that Voldemort had returned? And why . . . why . . . was Dumbledore so convinced that Snape was truly on their side? He had been their spy, Dumbledore had said so in the Pensieve. Snape had turned spy against Voldemort, "at great personal risk." Was that the job he had taken up again? Had he made contact with the Death Eaters, perhaps? Pretended that he had never really gone over to Dumbledore, that he had been, like Voldemort himself, biding his time? (*HP/GoF*, 720-1)

What Harry knows is that Voldemort was shocked and fearful when his rebirth went awry. He had expected to kill Harry and ascend triumphantly back to power, not to be overpowered, for the first time, by the memories of his own crimes. Something went terribly wrong, humiliating him in front of his followers, and Voldemort didn't understand it—Voldemort, who thought he understood everything. He had ordered the Death Eaters to do nothing and they had obeyed, directionless and just as confused.

Snape's arrival must have been the most comforting thing to happen to Voldemort in years, this dictator who would sooner kill a person than admit that he needs comfort. After Voldemort lived a year dependent on Wormtail, after years of living bodiless and alone, after a night of failure and terrifying emotion and rage at the followers who never searched for him, Snape came to him to say: *My Lord, I have been working for you all along. I have never forgotten you.*

Snape would have told Voldemort stories of spying, of Dumbledore, of the profound mediocrity of Harry Potter, of Dumbledore's folly in seeing anything in the vexing child. The stories would have rung true for Wormtail, for Lucius Malfoy, for anyone who had known Snape during the years of Voldemort's absence. The stories would have accorded with what Voldemort witnessed of Harry's first year. If Voldemort looked into Snape's mind, as he surely must have, he would have seen nothing but Snape's genuine loathing of Harry. He would have sent Snape back to Hogwarts to spy again, glad of the one servant who was able to bring him answers. Like Dumbledore, Voldemort would have found that there are some things only Snape can do.

SEVERUS SNAPE
AND THE ORDER OF THE PHOENIX

Voldemort's return to a full body adds three jobs to Snape's workload and an unexpected fourth burden, as well. In addition to being Potions master and Head of Slytherin, Snape is now an active Death Eater, answering Voldemort's calls to strategy meetings about his campaign to seize power. He is the primary source of spy intelligence at Order of the Phoenix meetings. He tutors Harry privately in Occlumency, a magical way to seal the mind against intrusion. And he is part of the resistance to Dolores Umbridge, a bureaucrat posted to Hogwarts by the Minister of Magic to implement a totalitarian regime denying that Voldemort has returned and cracking down on anyone preparing to defend themselves against him.

Snape and Dumbledore spend the year in a desperate race to stay a step ahead of Voldemort's plans to kill Harry, defeat Dumbledore, gather troops, and infiltrate the Ministry. Their undercover work is so demanding that they seem virtually absent from Hogwarts for much of the year. Dumbledore quietly invests McGonagall with responsibility for heading Hogwarts while he is preoccupied. Hermione assumes some of Snape's role: covertly, she ensures that students get training in Defense Against the Dark Arts without running afoul of Voldemort's curse. This year, they must also evade government decrees against students being trained to defend themselves. Harry combines what he's learned from Lupin and Snape to pass on his defense expertise to his fellow students.

The mood of this book is magnificently grim. Dumbledore predicts, correctly, that at moments when he's speaking one-on-one to Harry, Voldemort will attempt to possess Harry in order to confront Dumbledore. Voldemort usually destroys the animals and people he possesses, so a terrified Dumbledore essentially abandons Harry during this volume. Partway through the year, Dumbledore is forced on the run, abandoning Hogwarts as well. Dumbledore usually seems near-omnipotent, but fighting Voldemort with one hand and the Ministry with the other, he is stretched past his limits. Harry must hide his true agenda to survive; he doesn't know it yet, but this brings him closer to understanding Snape.

Plot: Learning from Snape

Our first glimpse of Snape in this book shows him as a spy, not a teacher. Harry spots "the dark, greasy-haired head and prominent nose of his least favorite teacher" at Grimmauld Place, Sirius Black's house, now headquarters for the Order of the Phoenix. Snape leaves before Harry can find out anything about what he is doing, though; Ron tells Harry, "Snape never eats here." (HP/OotP, 76-7) Snape wants to get away from Sirius Black's house, no doubt. But as a double agent, he might not have time to linger, anyway.

In this volume, Snape is gone from the school narrative for chapters at a time, busy with his spy work. In his absence, the reader sees Harry experience many of the emotions that we have seen in Snape.

In the opening chapter, grieving and angry, Harry goads his cousin Dudley in much the same way that Snape has baited Harry: "It gave Harry enormous satisfaction to know how furious he was making Dudley; he felt as though he was siphoning off his own frustration into his cousin, the only outlet he had." (HP/OotP, 13) But when Harry and Dudley are attacked by dementors, Harry goes into protective mode, gets Dudley home, then gets threatened with expulsion by the Ministry of Magic for performing underage magic. Dumbledore testifies for Harry at his trial, but Dumbledore, like Harry, has been targeted by a government smear campaign all summer. Harry has suffered smear campaigns before, but never to such a serious degree.

Harry hopes that he'll be vindicated in the end and the public understanding of him will mirror his true self, but under Dolores Umbridge's regime, he has to learn to suppress his urge to contradict lies about himself, a skill that Snape has been struggling with for years. McGonagall tells him as much when Umbridge punishes him for insisting that he witnessed Voldemort's return.

> "For heaven's sake, Potter!" said Professor McGonagall, straightening her glasses angrily (she had winced horribly when he had used Voldemort's name). "Do you really think this is about truth or lies? It's about keeping your head down and your temper

under control!" (*HP/OotP*, 249)

The sadistic Umbridge punishes Harry by forcing him to cut the words "I must not tell lies" into his own skin every night for a week. He learns that in order to endure the ongoing punishment, he cannot permit others to offer sympathy, which will lower his defenses. Harry takes comfort in identifying with Sirius.

> "And with a surge of sympathy for his godfather, Harry thought that Sirius was probably the only person he knew who could really understand how he felt at the moment, because Sirius was in the same situation; nearly everyone in the Wizarding world thought Sirius a dangerous murderer and a great Voldemort supporter and he had had to live with that knowledge for fourteen years. . . ." (*HP/OotP*, 300)

Harry does not realize that much of his ordeal might mirror Snape's, as well, but the reader can note that Harry's and Snape's tensions are probably rising in parallel.

Prime Minister Fudge has placed Professor Umbridge in the Defense Against the Dark Arts position at Hogwarts to prevent students from gaining any practical experience in defensive magic; they are to memorize written theory only. Three years ago, when Professor Lockhart held the position, Snape circumvented him by staging an extracurricular practical lesson in dueling. Snape reinforced the effectiveness of this defensive lesson by ensuring that the most volatile students practiced against their worst enemies. This year, Snape is too busy to plot subversive supplemental lessons, but Hermione rises to the challenge magnificently.

While treating Harry's wounds from another detention with Umbridge, Hermione shocks Ron and Harry by declaring that nothing, not even homework, is as important as learning Defense Against the Dark Arts, and that learning from books is not enough: "We need a teacher, a proper one, who can show us how to use the spells and correct us if we're going wrong." (*HP/OotP*, 325) She proposes that Harry teach the lessons, provoking an outburst from Harry that makes the argument for her.

> "*You don't know what it's like!* You—neither of you—you've never had to face him, have you? You think it's just memorizing a bunch of spells and throwing them at him, like you're in class or

something? The whole time you know there's nothing between you and dying except your own—your own brain or guts or whatever—like you can think straight when you know you're about a second from being murdered, or tortured, or watching your friends die—they've never taught us that in their classes, what it's like to deal with things like that—" (*HP/OotP*, 327-8)

After Lupin's boggart lesson, the students know that some lessons are best learned through moving and doing, not through theory. After Snape's Disarming lesson, they know that practicing in safety feels very different from fighting true attack. Hermione organizes a secret resistance group, which they name the D.A., "Dumbledore's Army," as a cheeky joke about the Ministry's fears. Harry signs on to be the true Defense Against the Dark Arts teacher for the year and he begins with what he learned from Snape.

"I was thinking, the first thing we should do is *Expelliarmus*, you know, the Disarming Charm. I know it's pretty basic but I've found it really useful—"

"Oh *please*," said Zacharias Smith, rolling his eyes and folding his arms. "I don't think *Expelliarmus* is exactly going to help us against You-Know-Who, do you?"

"I've used it against him," said Harry quietly. "It saved my life last June." (*HP/OotP*, 392)

The successful D.A. meetings give Harry two different kinds of internal strength that provide some insight into how Snape might experience his undercover work. After the initial gathering, he gets validation from his peers that lifts one of his worst stressors: the way people view him mirrors his true inner self. We have seen the toll it takes on Snape to be seen wrongly. It may be necessary for a greater goal, but it is costly. Being believed, especially by the people one most esteems, brings immediate relief.

The knowledge that they were doing something to resist Umbridge and the Ministry, and that he was a key part of the rebellion, gave Harry a feeling of immense satisfaction. . . The knowledge that all those people did not think him a lying weirdo, but someone to be admired, buoyed him up so much that he was still cheerful on Monday morning, despite the imminent prospect of all his least favorite classes. (*HP/OotP*, 350-1)

The following practice session of the D.A. builds on that strength to bring Harry a more durable, deeply rooted defense, one that does not depend on being mirrored back by others.

> Harry felt as though he were carrying some kind of talisman inside his chest over the following two weeks, a glowing secret that supported him through Umbridge's classes and even made it possible for him to smile blandly as he looked into her horrible bulging eyes. He and the D.A. were resisting her under her very nose, doing the very thing that she and the Ministry most feared, and whenever he was supposed to be reading Wilbert Slinkhard's book during her lessons he dwelled instead on satisfying memories of their most recent meetings, remembering how Neville had successfully disarmed Hermione, how Colin Creevey had mastered the Impediment Jinx after three meetings' hard effort, how Parvati Patil had produced such a good Reductor Curse that she had reduced the table carrying all the Sneakoscopes to dust. (*HP/OotP*, 397)

In addition to feeling buoyed by others' confidence in him, Harry is nourished by his pride in *them*. He has helped to teach others to defend themselves. The glow of power he has had from mastering these skills is now glowing in others as well because of him, and he has watched it happening. No matter what, the mere *memory* of this shared learning can fortify him, whether or not he is being accurately mirrored by those around him. It is a more self-sufficient joy. It gives us a glimpse into one of the ways a reviled teacher might be able to sustain himself, even when he has committed himself to the guarantee of being misunderstood by all around him.

Snape's Year in Overview

What's going on with Snape himself, in the brief glimpses we get of him between top-secret missions for one omnipotent overlord or another?

Snape's personal dislike of Harry

He finds Harry as irritating as ever. He sinks to the same depths of perversity and pettiness as ever when griping at this student for daring to exist. It's true that his dislike of Harry now serves the utilitarian purpose of obscuring Voldemort's view of his true agenda, but that probably has little bearing on the heartfelt nature of Snape's loathing.

Harry, though, has a loss of innocence this year about how loathsome a teacher can be.

> He had never before considered the possibility that there might be another teacher in the world he hated more than Snape, but as he walked back toward Gryffindor Tower he had to admit he had found a contender. (*HP/OotP*, 271)

Some readers have posited that Snape's twisted punishments, such as Vanishing Harry's imperfect potions instead of giving partial marks, point to sadism. Rowling, however, distinguishes clearly in degree between Snape's twistedness and true sadism, as seen in Umbridge when she prepares herself to cast *Crucio* on Harry, "panting slightly as she pointed her wand at different parts of Harry's body in turn, apparently trying to decide what would hurt the most." (*HP/OotP*, 746-7) When it comes to actual harm, just as Harry instantly saves Dudley from dementors, Snape goes immediately into protective mode, unlike Umbridge, who pushes Harry "in front of her like a shield" when endangered. (*HP/OotP*, 753)

Snape's usual hostility to the new Defense teacher

With Voldemort's return, and the government's reactionary crackdown on practical defense studies, Snape has no time for concern about the Defense Against the Dark Arts teacher's curriculum. There are more urgent worries. Snape must put as much effort as possible into his double agency and the maintenance of his cover.

As a person, we see that Snape views Umbridge as contemptible and lets the students know as much when she demands he produce Veritaserum.

> "You took my last bottle to interrogate Potter," he said, observing her coolly through his greasy curtains of black hair. "Surely you did not use it all? I told you that three drops would be sufficient."
>
> Umbridge flushed.
>
> "You can make some more, can't you?" she said, her voice becoming

more sweetly girlish as it always did when she was furious.

> "Certainly," said Snape, his lip curling. "It takes a full moon cycle to mature, so I should have it ready for you in around a month."
> (*HP/OotP*, 744)

A dozen students were present for this exchange. Snape didn't need to let them know that Umbridge found it reasonable to use an entire bottle of a highly regulated concentrate to interrogate one child. Umbridge shrieks at him, "You are being deliberately unhelpful!" (*HP/OotP*, 745) Yes. Yes, he is. Even Harry must have noted and enjoyed Snape's resistance to Umbridge.

Snape's reputation

As a teacher, Snape finds Umbridge irrelevant. As an outsider bearing down on the strategy that he and Dumbledore have developed to fight Voldemort, however, he finds her presence nearly intolerable.

> "Well, the class seems fairly advanced for their level," she said briskly to Snape's back. "Though I would question whether it is advisable to teach them a potion like the Strengthening Solution. I think the Ministry would prefer it if that was removed from the syllabus."
>
> Snape straightened up slowly and turned to look at her. (*HP/OotP*, 363)

Surely even Snape-hating Gryffindors enjoyed the moment Snape turned to face Umbridge. Rowling carefully unites the sentiments of Slytherins, Gryffindors, and the reader behind Snape for this scene: even Umbridge can find no fault with Snape's academic standards. His classroom manner has indisputably caused damage, but his students have put in the labor. One way or another, together, he and the students have created something unassailable by this intruder.

But then, in front of Harry and the other students, she asks Snape about his employment history. He has been teaching at Hogwarts for fourteen years—our first indication that Snape joined the staff the year Harry's parents died.

> "You applied first for the Defense Against the Dark Arts post, I believe?" Professor Umbridge asked Snape.

"Yes," said Snape quietly.

"But you were unsuccessful?"

Snape's lip curled.

"Obviously."

"And you have applied regularly for the Defense Against the Dark Arts post since you first joined the school, I believe?"

"Yes," said Snape quietly, barely moving his lips. He looked very angry. (*HP/OotP*, 363-4)

Harry listens closely as Umbridge asks what Harry has been dying to know for years.

"Do you have any idea why Dumbledore has consistently refused to appoint you?" asked Umbridge.

"I suggest you ask him," said Snape jerkily.

"Oh I shall," said Professor Umbridge with a sweet smile. (*HP/OotP*, 364)

This is the first confirmation that Snape has reapplied for the Defense position every year. His application has been rejected each time in favor of other candidates, even when there have been no other applicants, as Hagrid tells us in *Chamber of Secrets* when he says Gilderoy Lockhart was "the *on'y* man for the job." (*HP/CoS*, 115) Either Snape is indeed vulnerable to the lures of the Dark Arts, so unstable that Dumbledore refuses to count his application, or this is a paper trail that he and Dumbledore have laid as part of a strategy. Snape's supposed vulnerability to the lure of the Dark Arts is part of their cover story, but Snape has never found that lie easy to swallow, and he certainly cannot bear to choke it out in front of Umbridge and his avidly listening students. It was Dumbledore's idea for Snape to include this ignoble rumor in his cover persona. Let him be the one to perform it for Umbridge.

At long last, Umbridge moves on to question the students and Snape sees Harry, who has not, of course, been paying attention to his cauldron.

"No marks again, then, Potter," said Snape maliciously, emptying

Harry's cauldron with a wave of his wand. "You will write me an essay on the correct composition of this potion, indicating how and why you went wrong, to be handed in next lesson, do you understand?" (*HP/OotP*, 364)

Snape is certainly taking out his stress on Harry. But he is also defying Umbridge's order to remove the Strengthening Solution from the syllabus. Anything this Ministry might deem a threat is something the Boy Who Lived needs to know. This is a textbook example of Rowling loading Snape's actions with exactly equal motives of protectiveness, sound strategy, and hostility toward Harry.

No matter what other work he has, Snape remains grimly conscientious about his teaching duties. He warns his class about the upcoming O.W.L. examinations with the usual threats and insults, with the promise of disqualifying most students from Potions study in sixth and seventh years.

"After this year, of course, many of you will cease studying with me," Snape went on. "I take only the very best into my N.E.W.T. Potions class, which means that some of us will certainly be saying good-bye."

His eyes rested on Harry and his lip curled. Harry glared back, feeling a grim pleasure at the idea that he would be able to give up Potions after fifth year.

"But we have another year to go before that happy moment of farewell," said Snape softly, "so whether you are intending to attempt N.E.W.T. or not, I advise all of you to concentrate your efforts upon maintaining the high-pass level I have come to expect from my O.W.L. students." (*HP/OotP*, 232)

It's a shame this teacher has to be inflicted on introductory-level students. We see that where possible, he has adjusted his workload to focus on advanced or gifted classes, where his temperament makes him a better match.

The mystery of Snape's true motives

All of the *Harry Potter* series is designed to require rereading for full understanding, but from this volume onward, Rowling seeds the story with many more details that hint at her endgame and the crucial role that

Snape plays in it. Harry learns that Aunt Petunia knows things about the Wizarding World because she overheard "that awful boy—telling her about them—years ago" (*HP/OotP*, 32), but when Harry assumes she means James and Lily, Petunia doesn't correct him. Rowling has hinted at a Snape-Lily connection before this point through selective omissions, showing James's social circle but not Lily's, but this is the first active hint she introduces.

In *Order of the Phoenix*, Rowling continues to maintain a careful equilibrium between positive and negative readings of Snape's motives behind everything he says and does. Harry, Ron, and Hermione have a great deal of new evidence, but between Snape's treatment of Harry, his work for the Order, and the lack of explanation for Dumbledore's trust, their conclusions about him remain stalemated.

> "I did think he might be a bit better this year," said Hermione in a disappointed voice. "I mean . . . you know. . ." She looked carefully around; there were half a dozen empty seats on either side of them and nobody was passing the table. ". . . Now he's in the Order and everything."
>
> "Poisonous toadstools don't change their spots," said Ron sagely. "Anyway, I've always thought Dumbledore was cracked trusting Snape, where's the evidence he ever really stopped working for You-Know-Who?"
>
> "I think Dumbledore's probably got plenty of evidence, even if he doesn't share it with you, Ron," snapped Hermione. (*HP/OotP*, 235)

We will find, though, that Snape's true motives can be discerned in this volume through a close reading of the private lessons in Occlumency that Dumbledore orders him to provide for Harry.

Occlumency

Just before Christmas, 15-year-old Harry gets his first kiss from his longtime crush, Cho Chang. He would have enjoyed it more if she hadn't also been crying and talking about the death of Cedric Diggory, who had been her boyfriend at the time that Harry saw him be killed. That night, Harry dreams of the same image he's dreamed for months: a plain door at the end of a corridor. But this time, he dreams he is a venomous snake who bites a man guarding that door. Harry wakes up screaming and tells

Dumbledore, who discovers that Arthur Weasley has been bitten while on duty for the Order. Harry has not told anybody, but Dumbledore seems to know that Harry saw the vision from the snake's point of view. Dumbledore has been ignoring Harry and avoiding eye contact with him since summer, but for one instant, they look at each other and Harry is overwhelmed by Voldemort's emotions.

> Harry looked up at him—they were very close together—and Dumbledore's clear blue gaze moved from the Portkey to Harry's face.
>
> At once, Harry's scar burned white-hot, as though the old wound had burst open again—and unbidden, unwanted, but terrifyingly strong, there rose within Harry a hatred so powerful he felt, for that instant, that he would like nothing better than to strike—to bite—to sink his fangs into the man before him—(HP/OotP, 474-5)

On the last day of holidays at Grimmauld Place, Harry receives the ominous news that Professor Snape is in the kitchen and wants a word with him. He enters to find Snape and Sirius incandescent with mutual hostility, goading each other like schoolboys.

Snape explains that Dumbledore has ordered him to give Harry secret weekly lessons in Occlumency, "the magical defense of the mind against external penetration. An obscure branch of magic, but a highly useful one." (HP/OotP, 519)

> "Why can't Dumbledore teach Harry?" asked Sirius aggressively. "Why you?"
>
> "I suppose because it is a headmaster's privilege to delegate less enjoyable tasks," said Snape silkily. "I assure you I did not beg for the job." He got to his feet. "I will expect you at six o'clock on Monday evening, Potter. My office. If anybody asks, you are taking Remedial Potions. Nobody who has seen you in my classes could deny you need them." (HP/OotP, 519)

Remedial Potions. At last, Snape gets to watch someone *else* writhe as they collude in spreading an intolerable lie about themselves for the greater good. Snape has had long, bitter years to reflect on the efficacy of this tactic.

Why *does* it have to be Snape who teaches Harry? Dumbledore's reasoning is not difficult to follow. Occlumency is obscure, so few people have mastered the skill, possibly none as expertly as Snape. They must keep the lessons secret from Umbridge, so the teacher has to be at Hogwarts and part of the Order, which limits candidates to Snape, Dumbledore, McGonagall, or Hagrid. Hagrid can't keep secrets and, as we see from her fights with Umbridge, self-control is not McGonagall's strong suit, either. Dumbledore is terrified that if he is near Harry, Voldemort will sense this and feel such a surge of rage that his emotions will overpower Harry and possess or destroy him. We know from *Goblet of Fire* that possession is Voldemort's signature magic, a power he retains even when he has no body or wand, and that his possession of animals and humans shortens their lives. (*HP/GoF*, 653-4) Voldemort has only been in his full body for a few months; nobody knows yet the limits of his connection with Harry or how badly he could hurt Harry.

So that leaves Snape to teach Harry. Considering Snape's history of antagonizing Harry, Sirius is so worried that he starts a confrontation. In an almost unbearable show of immaturity, these two men in their mid-thirties name-call each other like children, leaving the actual child in the room to hold them apart.

> "I've warned you, *Snivellus*," said Sirius, his face barely a foot from Snape's, "I don't care if Dumbledore thinks you've reformed, I know better—"
>
> "Oh, but why don't you tell him so?" whispered Snape. "Or are you afraid he might not take the advice of a man who has been hiding inside his mother's house for six months very seriously?"
>
> "Tell me, how is Lucius Malfoy these days? I expect he's delighted his lapdog's working at Hogwarts, isn't he?"
>
> "Speaking of dogs," said Snape softly, "did you know that Lucius Malfoy recognized you last time you risked a little jaunt outside? Clever idea, Black, getting yourself seen on a safe station platform . . . gave you a cast-iron excuse not to leave your hidey-hole in future, didn't it?"
>
> Sirius raised his wand.
>
> "NO!" Harry yelled, vaulting over the table and trying to get in between them, "Sirius, don't—" (*HP/OotP*, 520)

This scene is cringe-worthy and heartbreaking. Twelve years of wrongful imprisonment, followed by two and a half years as a fugitive, have kept Sirius in a state of arrested development. Snape has had the freedom denied Sirius, but when threatened by his least favorite bully from his past, he regresses to taunting Sirius about something that Gryffindors find intolerable: forced inactivity during crisis. Yet there is beauty in both men in this scene, too. Harry sees someone who cares about nothing in the world more than Harry's happiness and is willing to fight for it. Snape gives Sirius a genuine warning. It is delivered amidst barbs, old arguments about cowardice and Snape's Death Eater past, but as with everything Snape says, there is a kernel, too, of: *keep yourself safe.* It is Snape's idiosyncratic brand of warning, hostile on the personal level and yet useful.

Fortunately, Arthur Weasley and his family come into the kitchen at that moment and Snape leaves without further conflict. Molly Weasley reports that the St. Mungo's healer "found an antidote to whatever that snake's got in its fangs." (*HP/OotP*, 522) This antidote is never mentioned again, but it seems likely that members of the Order, having once encountered Voldemort's snake, probably carried some with them. It would make sense for the Order to respond to the near-death of a member by having the resident potioneer add to their store of antidotes.

Back at Hogwarts, Harry reports to Snape's dungeon for Occlumency lessons. He recognizes Dumbledore's Pensieve on Snape's desk: Dumbledore has lent his support to Snape. Snape explains the lesson, "dislike etched in every line of his face." (*HP/OotP*, 529) The scene is a tour de force from Rowling. Almost every line is worth a close reading.

Snape explains that Voldemort is skilled at Legilimency, "the ability to extract feelings and memories from another person's mind—" (*HP/OotP*, 530) Legilimency, he says, is not quite the same as the Muggle concept of mind-reading:

> "Thoughts are not etched on the inside of skulls, to be perused by any invader. . . It is true, however, that those who have mastered Legilimency are able, under certain conditions, to delve into the minds of their victims and to interpret their findings correctly. The Dark Lord, for instance, almost always knows when somebody is lying to him. Only those skilled at Occlumency are able to shut down those feelings and memories that contradict the lie, and so utter falsehoods in his presence without detection." (*HP/OotP*, 530-1)

Why this emphasis on the distinction between Legilimency and mind-reading? It tells us how Snape is able to lie to Voldemort. The Legilimens detects feelings, sees memories, and forms a conclusion, but not necessarily the correct one. An Occlumens can obscure truths by presenting strong feelings that overwhelm other details or by leading the Legilimens into emotional territory they can't understand. Snape can show Voldemort with utter faith that he loathes Harry Potter and credits Harry with no gifts at all.

> "So he could know what we're thinking right now? Sir?"
>
> "The Dark Lord is at a considerable distance and the walls and grounds of Hogwarts are guarded by many ancient spells and charms to ensure the bodily and mental safety of those who dwell within them," said Snape. "Time and space matter in magic, Potter. Eye contact is often essential to Legilimency." (*HP/OotP*, 531)

We know that Voldemort can connect with Harry through the scar, from a distance, so why does Rowling give us this information about proximity, protective spells, and eye contact? Voldemort might be able to see into Harry's mind, but not Snape's—not at this distance, not with Snape's Occlumency defenses—*unless* he manages to look at Snape through Harry's eyes, as Harry looked through Voldemort's eyes when Voldemort was possessing the snake. With Voldemort's strength of mind, it is conceivable that he could use the scar link with Harry to spy on Harry's surroundings and even perform Legilimency on others.

> "The usual rules do not seem to apply with you, Potter. The curse that failed to kill you seems to have forged some kind of connection between you and the Dark Lord. The evidence suggests that at times, when your mind is most relaxed and vulnerable—when you are asleep, for instance—you are sharing the Dark Lord's thoughts and emotions. The headmaster thinks it inadvisable for this to continue. He wishes me to teach you how to close your mind to the Dark Lord." (*HP/OotP*, 531)

We know Harry is highly resistant to mind control because he can fight the Imperius curse. (*HP/GoF*, 232) When he is asleep, however, or when his defenses are lower, he will be less so, unless he has training.

> "But why does Professor Dumbledore want to stop it?" he asked

> abruptly. "I don't like it much, but it's been useful, hasn't it? I mean . . . I saw that snake attack Mr. Weasley and if I hadn't, Professor Dumbledore wouldn't have been able to save him, would he? Sir?"
>
> Snape stared at Harry for a few moments, still tracing his mouth with his finger. When he spoke again, it was slowly and deliberately, as though he weighed every word. (*HP/OotP*, 531-2)

Harry has a good point. Snape weighs every word in his reply because he has many considerations to juggle. He serves two masters, and he's a teacher. He must obey Dumbledore's global order not to tell Harry any more than Harry "needs to know." (*HP/OotP*, 88) Yet he must tell Harry enough to convince him and help him learn. And he must strike the exact right note of authenticity so if Voldemort should see this interaction through Legilimency, it will be believable as the performance of a double agent who pretends to obey Dumbledore but remains loyal to Voldemort. With all these requirements, Snape has no room for gratuitous insults. For once, he's got too much on his mind to hate Harry.

> "It appears that the Dark Lord has been unaware of the connection between you and himself until very recently. Up till now it seems that you have been experiencing his emotions and sharing his thoughts without his being any the wiser. However, the vision you had shortly before Christmas—"
>
> "The one with the snake and Mr. Weasley?"
>
> "Do not interrupt me, Potter," said Snape in a dangerous voice. "As I was saying . . . the vision you had shortly before Christmas represented such a powerful incursion upon the Dark Lord's thoughts—"
>
> "I saw inside the snake's head, not his!"
>
> "I thought I just told you not to interrupt me, Potter?" (*HP/OotP*, 532)

That didn't take long. Snape dislikes Harry again. Or does he? Does he just want to limit what they discuss? Why?

> But Harry did not care if Snape was angry; at last he seemed to be

getting to the bottom of this business. He had moved forward in his chair so that, without realizing it, he was perched on the very edge, tense as though poised for flight.

"How come I saw through the snake's eyes if it's Voldemort's thoughts I'm sharing?"

"Do not say the Dark Lord's name!" spat Snape.

There was a nasty silence. They glared at each other across the Pensieve. (*HP/OotP*, 532)

Harry is on the edge of his seat. He's never connected this hard before with anything Snape had to teach him. Ever since summer, he's been starved for information about himself, information that should belong to him by rights, that Dumbledore has kept from him. This is the first time anyone seems able to give answers. Snape must remain measured so he adheres, word by word, to the guidelines set by both masters. If he engages with Harry, if he forgets himself, he could accidentally reveal something that gets them in trouble. Harry must not interrupt. Snape must remain in control of the interaction and for once, it's not because he wants to wield power over Harry. The danger is what makes Snape angry here, not his dislike of Harry.

"Professor Dumbledore says his name," said Harry quietly.

"Dumbledore is an extremely powerful wizard," Snape muttered. "While *he* may feel secure enough to use the name . . . the rest of us. . ." He rubbed his left forearm, apparently unconsciously, on the spot where Harry knew the Dark Mark was burned into his skin. (*HP/OotP*, 532)

It's an honest interaction between these old adversaries. His vulnerability reaches Harry, who makes more of an effort.

"I just wanted to know," Harry began again, forcing his voice back to politeness, "why—"

"You seem to have visited the snake's mind because that was where the Dark Lord was at that particular moment," snarled Snape. "He was possessing the snake at the time and so you dreamed you were inside it too. . ."

"And Vol—he—realized I was there?" (*HP/OotP*, 532-3)

Snape loses control and snarls, which is dangerous, but he gives Harry the priceless gift of a definite answer. Harry continues to cooperate. This time, he catches himself before saying Voldemort's full name. That seems to help Snape recollect himself and calm down. He will need to be more careful about maintaining boundaries. He can't get caught up in emotion.

> "It seems so," said Snape coolly.
>
> "How do you know?" said Harry urgently. "Is this just Professor Dumbledore guessing, or—?"
>
> "I told you," said Snape, rigid in his chair, his eyes slits, "to call me 'sir.'"
>
> "Yes, sir," said Harry impatiently, "but how do you know—?"
>
> "It is enough that we know," said Snape repressively. (*HP/OotP*, 533)

Snape must shut down this line of inquiry. Anything about the Order's spying and Dumbledore's thinking is definitely more than Harry "needs to know."

> "The important point is that the Dark Lord is now aware that you are gaining access to his thoughts and feelings. He has also deduced that the process is likely to work in reverse; that is to say, he has realized that he might be able to access your thoughts and feelings in return—"
>
> "And he might try and make me do things?" asked Harry. *"Sir?"* he added hurriedly.
>
> "He might," said Snape, sounding cold and unconcerned. "Which brings us back to Occlumency." (*HP/OotP*, 533)

Snape has regained control of the interaction. He has gotten information to Harry without major blunder. He must confirm that Dumbledore is worried about Voldemort possessing Harry without revealing, in case Voldemort is listening, that Dumbledore and Snape find this prospect terrifying.

Snape pulled out his wand from an inside pocket of his robes and Harry tensed in his chair, but Snape merely raised the wand to his temple and placed its tip into the greasy roots of his hair. When he withdrew it, some silvery substance came away, stretching from temple to wand like a thick gossamer strand, which broke as he pulled the wand away from it and fell gracefully into the Pensieve, where it swirled silvery white, neither gas nor liquid. Twice more Snape raised the wand to his temple and deposited the silvery substance into the stone basin, then, without offering any explanation of his behavior, he picked up the Pensieve carefully, removed it to a shelf out of their way and returned to face Harry with his wand held at the ready.

"Stand up and take out your wand, Potter." (*HP/OotP*, 533)

So there are three memories Snape doesn't want Harry to see, and Dumbledore has lent his support to this. Why?

"You may use your wand to attempt to disarm me, or defend yourself in any other way you can think of," said Snape.

"And what are you going to do?" Harry asked, eyeing Snape's wand apprehensively.

"I am about to attempt to break into your mind," said Snape softly. "We are going to see how well you resist. I have been told that you have already shown aptitude at resisting the Imperius Curse. . . . You will find that similar powers are needed for this. . . . Brace yourself, now. . . . *Legilimens!*" (*HP/OotP*, 534)

Blanket permission for Harry to use his wand against Snape. Acknowledgment of one of Harry's strengths, in a manner that is useful for the lesson. This is what it looks like when Snape actually teaches Harry magic. It's a private lesson tailored to him because he needs the protection, delivered as sincerely as Lupin's Patronus tutoring.

Snape had struck before Harry was ready, before Harry had even begun to summon any force of resistance: the office swam in front of his eyes and vanished, image after image was racing through his mind like a flickering film so vivid it blinded him to his surroundings. . . .

He was five, watching Dudley riding a new red bicycle, and his heart was bursting with jealousy. . . . He was nine, and Ripper the bulldog was chasing him up a tree and the Dursleys were laughing below on the lawn. . . . He was sitting under the Sorting Hat, and it was telling him he would do well in Slytherin. . . . Hermione was lying in the hospital wing, her face covered with thick black hair. . . . A hundred dementors were closing in on him beside the dark lake. . . . Cho Chang was drawing nearer to him under the mistletoe. . . .

No, said a voice in Harry's head, as the memory of Cho drew nearer, *you're not watching that, you're not watching it, it's private—* (HP/OotP, 534)

Like a trauma flashback or an Imperius curse, an outside influence is overpowering Harry's awareness of his reality in the present moment. Harry has been feeling isolated and frightened all year, ignored by Dumbledore as the Dursleys used to ignore him; many of these memories contain those emotions, and Harry cannot stop them. The clue comes when the thought of Cho enables Harry to resist. Unlike the other memories, it's a positive one: it involves warmth and connection with someone who likes him. This kind of emotion can give Harry the strength to Occlude. Without knowing it, when Harry felt a surge of resistance, he produced a burst of defensive magic.

He felt a sharp pain in his knee. Snape's office had come back into view and he realized that he had fallen to the floor; one of his knees had collided painfully with the leg of Snape's desk. He looked up at Snape, who had lowered his wand and was rubbing his wrist. There was an angry weal there, like a scorch mark.

"Did you mean to produce a Stinging Hex?" asked Snape coolly.

"No," said Harry bitterly, getting up from the floor.

"I thought not," said Snape contemptuously. "You let me get in too far. You lost control."

"Did you see everything I saw?" Harry asked, unsure whether he wanted to hear the answer.

"Flashes of it," said Snape, his lip curling. "To whom did the dog belong?"

"My Aunt Marge," Harry muttered, hating Snape.

"Well, for a first attempt that was not as poor as it might have been," said Snape, raising his wand once more. "You managed to stop me eventually, though you wasted time and energy shouting. You must remain focused. Repel me with your brain and you will not need to resort to your wand." (*HP/OotP*, 534–5)

A compliment. Snape has paid Harry a compliment. In his own negative way, of course, but still. "For a first attempt that was not as poor as it might have been" is high praise when it's from Severus Snape to Harry Potter. The Occlumency lessons are the only times in the entire series that Snape praises Harry. He must be really impressed.

Harry has physically hurt Snape, and Snape is not angry. He meant it when he said Harry could defend himself in any way. He has seen flashes of Harry's memories; he has seen the pathos, and he is curious. Jealousy: Snape understands that feeling. Child abuse from people whom, as Rowling hints in this volume, Snape has actually met. So Harry didn't exactly have the "famous Harry Potter" arrogant childhood Snape has long assumed. So the Sorting Hat considered Slytherin for Harry; Snape didn't know that before. *That* would have been interesting, perhaps not in a good way. Hermione: never mind that; Snape never finds Hermione interesting. A hundred dementors: ah, so that's how that scene looked from Harry's point of view before Snape revived. That's actually . . . terrifying. More than any 13-year-old or adult wizard should have to confront. And Harry repelled them, alone. And then romance: a place where Snape cannot follow without feeling actual pain.

That's more thought than Snape has ever given to the real Harry Potter. He asks about the dog, perhaps because he identifies with that feeling of being tortured, perhaps because he's thinking about Harry's relatives. Harry is real to him here. He can acknowledge that Harry's first attempt was not bad, even if Harry did let him in too far.

"Let's go again . . . on the count of three . . . one—two—three—*Legilimens!*"

A great black dragon was rearing in front of him. . . . His father and mother were waving at him out of an enchanted mirror. . . . Cedric Diggory was lying on the ground with blank eyes staring at him . . .

"NOOOOOOO!"

He was on his knees again, his face buried in his hands, his brain aching as though someone had been trying to pull it from his skull.

"Get up!" said Snape sharply. "Get up! You are not trying, you are making no effort, you are allowing me access to memories you fear, handing me weapons!"

Harry stood up again, his heart thumping wildly as though he had really just seen Cedric dead in the graveyard. Snape looked paler than usual, and angrier, though not nearly as angry as Harry was. (*HP/OotP*, 535-6)

Snape gets deeper into Harry's memories. The dragon: fear and adrenalin. This kid has been through a lot. James and Lily: what a shock it must have been for Snape to see them through Harry's eyes and know that their presence in his life is "the deepest, most desperate desire" of Harry's heart. (*HP/SS*, 213) And then Cedric's death. That's how it looked when an innocent young man died on that terrible night. These memories are more draining for Snape to see than he probably expected. They are the things Harry shouted about to Hermione and Ron the previous summer when he first came to Grimmauld Place, things he needed to talk about but couldn't when he was isolated on Privet Drive, traumas that make his heart thump as though he were living them again.

No wonder Snape is looking pale. He, too, has been going through traumas he needs to talk about, but there is too much work to do and not enough time. He is responding sharply and with anger, the way he always responds when he is anxious because someone is not adequately defended. There is no manipulation when he scolds Harry, "You are not trying, you are making no effort, you are allowing me access to memories you fear, handing me weapons!" This is not a man who is secretly sabotaging Harry. His agitation is real.

"We shall try again! Get ready, now! *Legilimens!*"

He was watching Uncle Vernon hammering the letter box shut. . . . A hundred dementors were drifting across the lake in the grounds toward him. . . . He was running along a windowless passage with Mr. Weasley. . . . They were drawing nearer to the plain black door at the end of the corridor. . . . Harry expected to go through it . . . but Mr. Weasley led him off to the left, down a flight of stone steps. . . .

"I KNOW! I KNOW!"

He was on all fours again on Snape's office floor, his scar was
prickling unpleasantly, but the voice that had just issued from his
mouth was triumphant. He pushed himself up again to find Snape
staring at him, his wand raised. It looked as though, this time,
Snape had lifted the spell before Harry had even tried to fight back.
(*HP/OotP*, 536-7)

Harry recognized the door on his own, but the surge of magical
power when he made the connection was jolting enough to alert
Voldemort, causing the prickling in his scar. Voldemort is now sharing
Harry's thoughts. Snape has recognized the door, too. He has been
listening to the Dark Lord obsess over it for months.

"I saw—I remembered," Harry panted. "I've just realized . . ."

"Realized what?" asked Snape sharply.

Harry did not answer at once; he was still savoring the moment of
blinding realization as he rubbed his forehead. . . .

He had been dreaming about a windowless corridor ending in a
locked door for months, without once realizing that it was a real
place. Now, seeing the memory again, he knew that all along he
had been dreaming about the corridor down which he had run with
Mr. Weasley on the twelfth of August as they hurried to the
courtrooms in the Ministry. It was the corridor leading to the
Department of Mysteries, and Mr. Weasley had been there the
night that he had been attacked by Voldemort's snake. . . .

He looked up at Snape.

"What's in the Department of Mysteries?"

"What did you say?" Snape asked quietly and Harry saw, with deep
satisfaction, that Snape was unnerved. (*HP/OotP*, 537)

Snape is afraid that Harry has realized what the Order has been
guarding, which falls squarely under Dumbledore's heading of things
Harry doesn't need to know. But much more than that, he fears that
Voldemort is now aware of Harry's keen attention to visions of this door

and will attempt to manipulate Harry through their mental connection. This is one of the dangers Dumbledore was hoping to block with Occlumency lessons. Snape will have to tread carefully, or both of his masters will be angry with him, and Harry will be in greater danger.

> "I said, what's in the Department of Mysteries, *sir*?" Harry said.
>
> "And why," said Snape slowly, "would you ask such a thing?"
>
> "Because," said Harry, watching Snape closely for a reaction, "that corridor I've just seen—I've been dreaming about it for months— I've just recognized it—it leads to the Department of Mysteries . . . and I think Voldemort wants something from—"
>
> *"I have told you not to say the Dark Lord's name!"*
>
> They glared at each other. Harry's scar seared again, but he did not care. Snape looked agitated. When he spoke again he sounded as though he was trying to appear cool and unconcerned. (*HP/OotP*, 537)

Snape's fears are confirmed. Harry's scar is visibly hurting him; Voldemort is definitely aware of Harry in the present moment. Harry saying Voldemort's name makes Voldemort's Legilimency stronger: Harry's mental image of Voldemort grows more focused when he says the name rather than a euphemism, opening his mind more to Voldemort's intrusions. Through Harry's eyes, it's possible that Voldemort can see and hear everything Snape does. Snape must shut down the emotional urgency he was feeling earlier and say the cold things that Voldemort would expect to hear him say to Harry Potter, whom he has claimed to despise.

> "There are many things in the Department of Mysteries, Potter, few of which you would understand and none of which concern you, do I make myself plain?"
>
> "Yes," Harry said, still rubbing his prickling scar, which was becoming more painful.
>
> "I want you back here same time on Wednesday, and we will continue work then."
>
> "Fine," said Harry. He was desperate to get out of Snape's office and find Ron and Hermione.

> "You are to rid your mind of all emotion every night before sleep—
> empty it, make it blank and calm, you understand?" (*HP/OotP*,
> 538)

Harry doesn't understand the sudden change in Snape's tone. This
repressive condescension is how Snape usually speaks to him. He doesn't
detect that this time, it's an act. He doesn't know why Snape has just
shut down their session or why Snape cannot give more supportive
instructions about how Harry is supposed to rid his mind of all emotion
during this turbulent time.

After his lesson, Harry's scar aches and he feels almost feverish. He
falls asleep and shares Voldemort's thoughts in his dreams.

> Maniacal laughter was ringing in his ears. . . . He was happier than
> he had been in a very long time. . . . Jubilant, ecstatic,
> triumphant . . . A wonderful, wonderful thing had happened. . . .
>
> "Harry? HARRY!"
>
> Someone had hit him around the face. The insane laughter was
> punctuated with a cry of pain. The happiness was draining out of
> him, but the laughter continued. . . .
>
> He opened his eyes and as he did so, he became aware that the wild
> laughter was coming out of his own mouth. (*HP/OotP*, 541)

When Harry awakens fully and opens his eyes, he regains power
over himself, but while he was asleep, Voldemort's laughter was coming
out of Harry's mouth. Their connection is growing stronger and more
frightening. Harry feels that "his first foray into Occlumency had
weakened his mind's resistance rather than strengthening it" (*HP/OotP*,
542), which is standard for a beginner but very unfortunate, especially
coming at a time when Voldemort's powers are growing. Rowling
carefully weights the evidence so that it is not entirely certain, to Harry
and perhaps to the reader, whether Snape is on Voldemort's side.

> Harry's sessions with Snape, which had started badly enough, were
> not improving; on the contrary, Harry felt he was getting worse
> with every lesson.
>
> Before he had started studying Occlumency, his scar had prickled
> occasionally, usually during the night, or else following one of

those strange flashes of Voldemort's thoughts or moods that he experienced every now and then. Nowadays, however, his scar hardly ever stopped prickling, and he often felt lurches of annoyance or cheerfulness that were unrelated to what was happening to him at the time, which were always accompanied by a particularly painful twinge from his scar. He had the horrible impression that he was slowly turning into a kind of aerial that was tuned in to tiny fluctuations in Voldemort's mood, and he was sure he could date this increased sensitivity firmly from his first Occlumency lesson with Snape. (*HP/OotP*, 553-4)

Certainly, something happened in the first lesson: Voldemort shared Harry's thoughts and realized that Dumbledore has ordered Snape to teach Harry Occlumency. Snape has had to meet with Voldemort since then and spin a plausible account of how he is sabotaging these lessons, or how Harry is not working hard enough for them to be effective—that is an argument that Snape can certainly make with conviction. Voldemort is using the scar connection to monitor Snape as well as spy on Harry and Dumbledore. Snape is performing under tight constrictions that must satisfy Voldemort while trying to teach Harry to defend himself. Meanwhile, a jubilant Voldemort is rapidly growing proficient in manipulating the scar connection. He surely inhabits Harry's mind during the lessons. No wonder Harry's sessions feel like they are getting worse.

In a stroke of brilliance, Hermione gets Harry's account of Voldemort's return published in the *Quibbler*, the tabloid run by the father of Ravenclaw fourth-year Luna Lovegood. This single act turns the tide of public opinion against the Ministry's propaganda, invigorates the resistance against Umbridge's regime, and restores Harry's credibility. It also exposes the fathers of several students as Death Eaters. (*HP/OotP*, 583)

Snape's job has just gotten harder.

He remembers how it feels to be reviled at school for connections to Dark Magic. He sees his Slytherin students' fathers at Death Eater gatherings. He knows things are only going to get worse. He's their Head of House, possibly the only adult at Hogwarts that these boys trust, and unlike his work with Harry, protective feelings toward his Slytherins have always come naturally to him. Vengeful, ugly, angry boys with family crises and a tendency to Dark Magic: this hits home for him.

Speaking of unprotected, Harry's dreams of Voldemort and the unmarked door are preoccupying him, though he can't tell Ron and Hermione, or Hermione will scold him for not blocking the dreams.

> He wished very much that he could have talked to Sirius about it, but that was out of the question, so he tried to push the matter to the back of his mind.
>
> Unfortunately, the back of his mind was no longer the secure place it had once been.
>
> "Get up, Potter." (*HP/OotP*, 589)

In a rare conjunction, Harry's thoughts, the narrator's voice, and Snape's dialogue join together in wry humor about Harry's travails. No, there is no hiding in Harry's mind now that Voldemort has access to it. Snape guesses, accurately, that Harry is too interested in Voldemort's thoughts to block them. That leads him back to his favorite misconception about Harry: that he enjoys notoriety.

> "Perhaps," said Snape, his dark, cold eyes narrowing slightly, "perhaps you actually enjoy having these visions and dreams, Potter. Maybe they make you feel special—important?"
>
> "No, they don't," said Harry, his jaw set and his fingers clenched tightly around the handle of his wand.
>
> "That is just as well, Potter," said Snape coldly, "because you are neither special nor important, and it is not up to you to find out what the Dark Lord is saying to his Death Eaters."
>
> "No—that's your job, isn't it?" Harry shot at him. (*HP/OotP*, 591)

Oh. Harry shouldn't have said that. Snape hates insolence. Surely he will punish Harry for this in some unspeakably inventive way . . .
But he doesn't.

> He had not meant to say it; it had burst out of him in temper. For a long moment they stared at each other, Harry convinced he had gone too far. But there was a curious, almost satisfied expression on Snape's face when he answered.
>
> "Yes, Potter," he said, his eyes glinting. "That is my job."
> (*HP/OotP*, 591)

Dumbledore cannot possibly have authorized this kind of answer. Surely it is more than Harry "needs to know." But Dumbledore is not there to support either of them. Snape is—all of them are—stretched thin past the breaking point this year and if Harry is starved to talk to someone about what he's enduring, it makes sense that Snape must be, too. He risks his life every time he goes near the foul Voldemort to learn his evil plans. He is special, he is important, but he is a double agent and can tell no one. But when Harry names his job, he takes "a long moment" to think. Does Voldemort know it's Snape's job to find out what he thinks? Yes. Does Dumbledore know? Yes. Will it hurt Harry to know? No; in Snape's classic manner of delivering protection and ill will to Harry in equal measure, it will put Harry in his place and relieve him of responsibility.

For once, Snape can tell the truth. It gives Snape that "curious, almost satisfied expression."

He has been seen.

And Harry has been trusted with an adult reply that has everything to do with his life.

They practice again.

> A hundred dementors were swooping toward Harry across the lake in the grounds. . . . He screwed up his face in concentration. . . . They were coming closer. . . . He could see the dark holes beneath their hoods . . . yet he could also see Snape standing in front of him, his eyes fixed upon Harry's face, muttering under his breath. . . . And somehow, Snape was growing clearer, and the dementors were growing fainter . . . (*HP/OotP*, 591)

Harry is able to hold on to the present this time, even while Snape is delving into his mind. He's never been able to do that before. His defenses are stronger because Snape has trusted him with the truth. They've connected.

> Harry raised his own wand.
>
> *"Protego!"*
>
> Snape staggered; his wand flew upward, away from Harry—and suddenly Harry's mind was teeming with memories that were not his—a hook-nosed man was shouting at a cowering woman, while a small dark-haired boy cried in a corner. . . . A greasy-haired

teenager sat alone in a dark bedroom, pointing his wand at the ceiling, shooting down flies. . . . A girl was laughing as a scrawny boy tried to mount a bucking broomstick—

"ENOUGH!"

Harry felt as though he had been pushed hard in the chest; he took several staggering steps backward, hit some of the shelves covering Snape's walls and heard something crack. Snape was shaking slightly, very white in the face. (*HP/OotP*, 591-2)

Snape's defenses are down. It felt too good to be seen. Like Harry being too curious to shut out Voldemort's thoughts, Snape is not trying hard enough to hide his true self from someone with whom he feels kinship. Snape's memories feel different from Harry's. The first scene suggests spousal abuse or domestic violence; the third has a distinctly sexual quality to the humiliation. But the second could have come straight from Harry's most recent summer in Privet Drive.

Surely Snape is going to punish Harry for seeing his vulnerability. But he doesn't.

"Well, Potter . . . that was certainly an improvement . . . ." Panting slightly, Snape straightened the Pensieve in which he had again stored some of his thoughts before starting the lesson, almost as though checking that they were still there. "I don't remember telling you to use a Shield Charm . . . but there is no doubt that it was effective . . ." (*HP/OotP*, 592)

Snape isn't defensive about what Harry has seen. Apparently, anything but the three memories in the Pensieve is fair game; he has nothing else to hide. Once again, he is praising Harry and noting Harry's initiative in finding defenses. Snape is teaching Harry in good faith. Meanwhile, Harry is adjusting to his newly mature power to see the humanity of an authority figure he dislikes.

Harry did not speak; he felt that to say anything might be dangerous. He was sure he had just broken into Snape's memories, that he had just seen scenes from Snape's childhood, and it was unnerving to think that the crying little boy who had watched his parents shouting was actually standing in front of him with such loathing in his eyes. . . . (*HP/OotP*, 592)

They practice again.

> He was hurtling along the corridor toward the Department of Mysteries, past the blank stone walls, past the torches—the plain black door was growing ever larger; he was moving so fast he was going to collide with it, he was feet from it and he could see that chink of faint blue light again—

> The door had flown open! He was through it at last, inside a black-walled, black-floored circular room lit with blue-flamed candles, and there were more doors all around him—he needed to go on—but which door ought he to take—?

> "POTTER!"

> Harry opened his eyes. He was flat on his back again with no memory of having gotten there; he was also panting as though he really had run the length of the Department of Mysteries corridor, really had sprinted through the black door and found the circular room. . . . (*HP/OotP*, 592-3)

Voldemort has succeeded in planting a vision in Harry's mind and Snape has seen this. Voldemort wants to show Harry where to go. Harry's scar has been prickling nonstop for weeks; Voldemort knows that Harry has been unable to resist thoughts of the door, and he probably knows that Harry is in an Occlumency lesson with Snape at the moment. He may even have chosen this moment to plant the vision so that Snape can encourage Harry's curiosity.

> "Explain yourself!" said Snape, who was standing over him, looking furious.

> "I . . . dunno what happened," said Harry truthfully, standing up. There was a lump on the back of his head from where he had hit the ground and he felt feverish. "I've never seen that before. I mean, I told you, I've dreamed about the door . . . but it's never opened before . . ."

> "You are not working hard enough!"

> For some reason, Snape seemed even angrier than he had done two minutes before, when Harry had seen into his own memories.

> "You are lazy and sloppy, Potter, it is small wonder that the Dark

Lord—"

"Can you tell me something, *sir*?" said Harry, firing up again. "Why do you call Voldemort the Dark Lord, I've only ever heard Death Eaters call him that—" (*HP/OotP*, 593)

As ever, when Snape feels fear for a student, it manifests as anger. Between the scolding and the name-calling, Harry can scarcely be blamed for being unable to see that Snape is so worried for Harry's safety that he doesn't care about his own old memories—or that he's supposed to appear inscrutable about teaching Harry Occlumency, rather than frantic to shield him from Voldemort. Fortunately, Harry's question interrupts him before he can betray himself further, and the session comes to an end when they hear Professor Trelawney scream as Umbridge evicts her.

Life at Hogwarts is steadily worsening under Umbridge. Cho Chang's friend, Marietta Edgecombe, betrays Dumbledore's Army to Umbridge. To save the students from repercussions, Dumbledore assumes the blame for this group and goes on the run from the Ministry. Umbridge and Fudge have successfully chased him out of Hogwarts, and other than the Order, no one knows how to get in touch with him. Umbridge replaces Dumbledore as headmistress, although the Head's office seals itself against her and will not recognize her authority. She forms the Inquisitorial Squad, a group of students authorized to discipline their peers at will, and hand-appoints Slytherins to staff it.

The Inquisitorial Squad is one of Snape's worst nightmares come true. His students are being ordered to emphasize the most destructive elements of their natures and suppress their more humane traits. This harms them and also singles them out for their peers to target. Under Umbridge's rule, Snape is powerless to stop this.

"Malfoy just docked us all about fifty points," said Harry furiously, as they watched several more stones fly upward from the Gryffindor hourglass.

"Yeah, Montague tried to do us during break," said George.

"What do you mean, 'tried'?" said Ron quickly.

"He never managed to get all the words out," said Fred, "due to the fact that we forced him headfirst into that Vanishing Cabinet on the first floor."

Hermione looked very shocked.

"But you'll get into terrible trouble!"

"Not until Montague reappears, and that could take weeks, I dunno where we sent him," said Fred coolly. (*HP/OotP*, 626-7)

Hermione is wrong about one thing: in this climate, Fred and George do not get in trouble, even though they have put Montague in mortal danger. The Inquisitorial Squad may be hand-picked by Umbridge, but as individuals, they are just as expendable to her as the other students. *Harry Potter and the Order of the Phoenix* provides young readers with extraordinarily precise insight into the thinking of tyrants.

Fortunately for Fred and George, Montague turns up alive. Draco runs for Snape, bursting into the beginning of an Occlumency lesson. Snape tells him Harry is there for Remedial Potions.

"They've found Montague, sir. He's turned up jammed inside a toilet on the fourth floor."

"How did he get in there?" demanded Snape.

"I don't know, sir, he's a bit confused . . . ."

"Very well, very well—Potter," said Snape, "we shall resume this lesson tomorrow evening instead."

He turned and swept from his office. Malfoy mouthed "*Remedial Potions?*' at Harry behind Snape's back before following him. (*HP/OotP*, 638-9)

If Snape's "Remedial Potions" lie convinces even Draco, it will stand up to anyone. Snape's well-known contempt for Harry's potion-making gives it credence. The lie delivers a hit of pleasure to anyone who enjoys Harry's misfortunes, a brilliant tactic for distracting attention away from a true interpretation of the scene. It may also, by coincidence or design, set up Harry to understand the impotent rage Snape has often experienced while maintaining the cover he needs to protect Harry's ungrateful self. We do not know whether Dumbledore ever learned of the "Remedial Potions" cover story, but it takes little effort to imagine that Snape would have been ready to repeat back every argument Dumbledore ever made about the benefits of presenting Snape as a man so corrupt that he would be a worse Defense Against the Dark Arts teacher than Lockhart or Umbridge.

Snape drops everything to care for Montague. He is responsible for Montague as Head of House. But in addition, in Dumbledore's absence, Snape has assumed unofficial duties as deputy headmaster, supporting McGonagall in doing what they can to protect everyone covertly from Umbridge's rule. Running toward Trelawney's screams, tending to Montague, training Harry to shut out Voldemort: these all come from the same urge within Snape to defend against the Dark Arts. He goes where he is needed. In his urgency, he leaves Harry unattended with Dumbledore's Pensieve, containing the memories he removes during Occlumency lessons: "Harry gazed at the Pensieve, curiosity welling inside him . . . . What was it that Snape was so keen to hide from Harry?" (*HP/OotP*, 639)

Harry enters the memory and discovers Snape, James, Sirius, Lupin, Wormtail, and his mother Lily, all the same age that he is now, taking their exams.

> Snape-the-teenager had a stringy, pallid look about him, like a plant kept in the dark. His hair was lank and greasy and was flopping onto the table, his hooked nose barely half an inch from the surface of the parchment as he scribbled. Harry moved around behind Snape and read the heading of the examination paper:
>
> ### DEFENSE AGAINST THE DARK ARTS—ORDINARY WIZARDING LEVEL
>
> So Snape had to be fifteen or sixteen, around Harry's own age. His hand was flying across the parchment; he had written at least a foot more than his closest neighbors, and yet his writing was minuscule and cramped. (*HP/OotP*, 640-1)

Rowling shows Snape as even more unattractive in his teens than he is as a teacher. Her writing dwells minutely on the details of his ugliness in an insistent way that fixes the reader's attention unpleasantly close to his greasiness and tension, long past the point of comfort. His ugliness is repellent, but we cannot look away; the author will not let us. True to everyone's recollection, teen Snape is fascinated with the Dark Arts, unsurprisingly prolific on the topic. The minuscule, cramped writing suggests both intensity and defensiveness, as though the thoroughness of his scholarship has been the target of ridicule.

Harry notices that teen Snape "walked in a twitchy manner that recalled a spider, his oily hair swinging about his face." (*HP/OotP*, 643) Rowling often compares Snape to a spider, referring both to his movement quality and, indirectly, his career as a spy. The sphinx's riddle in the Triwizard Tournament associates spies with spiders (a "creature you would be unwilling to kiss," *HP/GoF*, 629), characterizing them as people too creepy to be eligibile for romance.

Teen Snape is shown as poorly groomed in ways often associated with growing up neglected or uncomfortable in one's own skin. We have seen memories that hint strongly at a childhood of neglect and tension. But appearances alone do not disqualify one from romance. Something other than attractiveness or grooming sets Snape apart as a creature that one would not want to kiss.

Harry follows James and his friends in Snape's memory and finds, to his horror, that James and Sirius ambush Snape for fun.

> As [Snape] emerged from the shadows of the bushes and set off across the grass, Sirius and James stood up. Lupin and Wormtail remained sitting: Lupin was still staring down at his book, though his eyes were not moving and a faint frown line had appeared between his eyebrows. Wormtail was looking from Sirius and James to Snape with a look of avid anticipation on his face. (*HP/OotP*, 645)

It's no surprise that Wormtail enjoys the ambush. Lupin's inner discomfort with his bystander role is more interesting to note. He's unable to make peace with his reluctance to object to behavior he knows is wrong.

James and Sirius advance on Snape. James hexes Snape while several students watch. Two on one, and no one moves to intervene; the hexes only escalate. Handsome Sirius taunts Snape about his unattractiveness, and others laugh at the unpopular Slytherin. Eighteen years later, Snape will remember this humiliation when Professor Lupin teaches Gryffindor children to mock an image of him dressed as an old lady.

> "Leave him ALONE!"
>
> James and Sirius looked around. James's free hand jumped to his hair again.
>
> It was one of the girls from the lake edge. She had thick, dark red hair that fell to her shoulders and startlingly green almond-shaped

eyes—Harry's eyes. Harry's mother . . .

"Leave him alone," Lily repeated. She was looking at James with every sign of great dislike. "What's he done to you?"

"Well," said James, appearing to deliberate the point, "it's more the fact that he *exists*, if you know what I mean . . ." (*HP/OotP*, 647)

Harry's eyes. Harry started viewing this scene with pleasure in the sight of his father and repelled fascination with teen Snape, but now, he's seeing it from his mother's viewpoint. Snape has done nothing to deserve this torment.

While Lily confronts James, though, the jinx on Snape wears off and he can move again.

Snape had directed his wand straight at James; there was a flash of light and a gash appeared on the side of James's face, spattering his robes with blood. James whirled about; a second flash of light later, Snape was hanging upside down in the air, his robes falling over his head to reveal skinny, pallid legs and a pair of graying underpants.

Many people in the small crowd watching cheered. Sirius, James, and Wormtail roared with laughter.

Lily, whose furious expression had twitched for an instant as though she was going to smile, said, "Let him down!" (*HP/OotP*, 647-8)

Snape retaliates with violence. James responds with sexual humiliation. This is an argument Snape cannot win. Lily almost smiles: whatever she thinks, she is not invested enough in Snape to feel sickened at the sight of his humiliation, as Ron was when Death Eaters revealed a Muggle woman's underwear at the Quidditch World Cup. (*HP/GoF*, 120) Perhaps she was taken aback by the violence of Snape's retaliation.

James lets Snape down, ungently, and Sirius hexes him again immediately. That final bit of insincerity and double-teaming pushes Lily to draw her wand. She puts her own safety at risk to fight the bullying of Snape. James backs down.

". . . [Y]ou're lucky Evans was here, Snivellus—"

"I don't need help from filthy little Mudbloods like her!"

Lily blinked. "Fine," she said coolly. "I won't bother in future. And I'd wash your pants if I were you, *Snivellus.*"

"Apologize to Evans!" James roared at Snape, his wand pointed threateningly at him.

"I don't want *you* to make him apologize," Lily shouted, rounding on James. "You're as bad as he is . . ."

"What?" yelped James. "I'd NEVER call you a—you-know-what!" (*HP/OotP*, 648)

Lily blinked: she was surprised to hear Snape call her a "filthy little Mudblood." She hadn't been expecting it. Snape could not endure being told that he owed his relief to Lily's willingness to put herself on the line for him. We don't see in this memory how well they know each other, but her surprise shows that it's something that hasn't happened before. The betrayal causes enough of a change in her attitude that she calls him by the same name that the bullies do and makes her own sexually humiliating observation. James's outrage shows that he thinks his own behavior was morally superior to Snape's hate speech, a view that Lily does not share. She tells James he makes her sick, then leaves.

James covers for this loss of face by resuming his bullying and playing to the crowd.

"Who wants to see me take off Snively's pants?"

But whether James really did take off Snape's pants, Harry never found out. A hand had closed tight over his upper arm, closed with a pincerlike grip. Wincing, Harry looked around to see who had hold of him, and saw, with a thrill of horror, a fully grown, adult-sized Snape standing right beside him. (*HP/OotP*, 649)

Snape is standing alongside Harry in the Pensieve memory: he knows which memory it is and how much Harry has seen. Snape pulls Harry back into the present.

It was scary: Snape's lips were shaking, his face was white, his teeth were bared.

"Amusing man, your father, wasn't he?" said Snape, shaking Harry so hard that his glasses slipped down his nose.

"I—didn't—"

Snape threw Harry from him with all his might. Harry fell hard onto the dungeon floor.

"You will not tell anybody what you saw!" Snape bellowed.

"No," said Harry, getting to his feet as far from Snape as he could. "No, of course I w—"

"Get out, get out, I don't want to see you in this office ever again!"

And as Harry hurtled toward the door, a jar of dead cockroaches exploded over his head. (*HP/OotP*, 649-50)

What, exactly, has shaken Snape so badly?

Rowling gives us a clue in the chapter title: "Snape's Worst Memory." We don't see the whole memory, but for her to give it that title, we can assume that we have seen most or all of what we need to know. Snape is not the one who labels the memory this way; the chapter title is a message from author to reader.

The bullying is bad, but Snape has been through worse: these same people almost killed him. The sexual humiliation is bad, but that's not it, either, or the scene would not have cut off before the attempt to remove Snape's pants. Rowling is showing that it was Snape's own response to Lily that makes this his worst memory. His shame is one reason why he orders Harry not to tell anyone what he saw. We know from other characters, such as Lupin, that shame can drive people to secrecy that is nearly impossible to break. Surely, nothing else in the memory would be newsworthy enough for Snape to forbid Harry to speak of it; nobody would be surprised that teens bullied another teen or that the bullied teen struck back.

Snape certainly hates the memory of James Potter and dislikes seeing Harry's face, but for him to be able to say right away, "Amusing man, your father, wasn't he?" shows that he expects Harry to see his point about James. He knows he is right in this assumption; Harry and Snape have seen repeatedly that they can empathize with each other's experiences of being bullied. It is not Snape's hatred of James or Harry's similarity to James that drives him to banish Harry from his office. Whatever it is, he wouldn't have been able to voice anything about it at all, so soon after discovering Harry in the Pensieve.

As with so many other interactions between Snape and Harry, there are at least two separate and equally weighty things going on, one hostile to Harry and one protective of Harry, and the hostility masks the rest of the story.

Snape doesn't want to see Harry in his office ever again. He has broken trust. He knew explicitly that Snape did not want him to see those memories.

Teen Snape betrayed Harry's mother, someone who confronted bullies for him at her own risk.

Harry has his mother's eyes.

Snape knows Harry saw the scene through his mother's eyes, feeling empathy for the bullied Snape and then shock at the racial slur. If Snape faces Harry, it is like looking into Lily's eyes while feeling the full force of his shame and regret—yet not having Lily there to receive his abject apology, only the face of his enemy, James Potter. Shame can be unbearable. Snape did what he could to bear it and teach Harry anyway, and Harry's intrusion destroyed that protection.

But the other thing that has so shaken Snape is also connected to Harry having his mother's eyes, though readers will not have enough information to understand Snape's reaction until the end of the series. We don't know yet that Lily knew and loved Snape before his eyes turned dark and cold and Occluded. Lily saw his true self; she knew how to read the person who became this inscrutable man.

Harry, too, can see Snape's mind. He is a Legilimens where Voldemort is concerned, sharing his thoughts through the scar, but he has also been a Legilimens where Snape is concerned. In part, this is because Snape did not put up any defenses against him except for placing a few memories in a Pensieve. But Harry is also able to understand what he has seen of Snape because Harry has his mother's eyes, his mother's empathy.

Snape can Occlude Voldemort as perhaps no other person can. This enables him to spy on Voldemort for the Order. When Voldemort scans Snape's thoughts, he cannot see that Snape is working against him because Snape is able to defend certain thoughts from Voldemort's view. But if Voldemort looks at Snape through *Harry's* eyes, he will be able to see those things. Snape let Harry see past his defenses.

By viewing one of Snape's off-limits memories, Harry has just endangered them all and exposed Snape to mortal risk. There is nothing in the memory he has just seen that would be risky for Voldemort to know: so Snape was bullied and he used a racist term against a Muggle-born. In that sense, it is not too late. But we don't know the other two memories and how they inform the one Harry has seen. We don't know what other images Harry might see in Snape's mind and how he might put them together with this memory. Harry would be able to conclude things that are beyond Voldemort's comprehension. Snape and Harry cannot continue the Occlumency lessons. Snape cannot interact with him at all, except to show hostility. This will not pose a hardship.

At another time, Snape might have stormed into Dumbledore's office and hammered out a way to ensure that Harry would learn Occlumency, preferably with much suffering. But there is no Dumbledore. Snape is already stretched beyond his limits with spying and the Order and helping McGonagall keep Hogwarts afloat. The children of Death Eaters need his attention. With her Inquisitorial Squad, Umbridge is training his most vulnerable Slytherins to become monsters, and Fred and George have already nearly killed one of them for it. There is no one who can help Snape. Under the circumstances, halting the lessons and keeping an eye on Harry from afar is probably the least dangerous course of action.

Snape's Worst Memory: fallout and recovery

Snape and Harry didn't complete the Occlumency lessons, but their empathic connection gave such support to Harry's moral development that Harry is able to continue to work things out on his own.

What is an orphan to do with feelings of empathy for the nasty man bullied by the father he loves but barely remembers? Harry tries to square what he's seen with what others have said about the Marauders.

> Yes, he had once overheard Professor McGonagall saying that his father and Sirius had been troublemakers at school, but she had described them as forerunners of the Weasley twins, and Harry could not imagine Fred and George dangling someone upside down for the fun of it . . . not unless they really loathed them . . . Perhaps Malfoy, or somebody who really deserved it . . . (HP/OotP, 653)

This is a funny thought. Draco would certainly have it coming to him if someone hung him upside down for using racial slurs. But the amusement dies down quickly when we remember: Montague "deserved it" for abusing power and ended up lost, nearly dead. What Fred and George did wasn't so harmless after all. They could have become murderers. This is the sort of realization that led to James risking his own life to warn Snape about the werewolf or Snape bringing unconscious Sirius to the castle in a stretcher rather than leaving him for the dementors: *Not even my enemy deserves to die this way.*

> Harry tried to make a case for Snape having deserved what he had suffered at James's hands—but hadn't Lily asked, "What's he done to you?" And hadn't James replied, "It's more the fact that he exists, if you know what I mean?" Hadn't James started it all simply because Sirius said he was bored? Harry remembered Lupin saying back in Grimmauld Place that Dumbledore had made him prefect in the hope that he would be able to exercise some control over James and Sirius. . . . But in the Pensieve, he had sat there and let it all happen. . . . (*HP/OotP*, 653)

Harry knows too much now about how Snape feels, and how ashamed Lupin has felt for being inactive in the face of harm, to ignore the implications of these thoughts. He's learning that he cannot justify keeping quiet about harm, even when the victims themselves have hurt others.

> To cap matters, Montague had still not recovered from his sojourn in the toilet. He remained confused and disorientated and his parents were to be observed one Tuesday morning striding up the front drive, looking extremely angry. (*HP/OotP*, 678)

As Head of Slytherin, it was Snape's job to meet with Montague's parents, temper anything unwise Umbridge said to them, and do what he could to defuse plans for vengeance against the Order-related blood traitors responsible. Even during a notably stressful year, that Tuesday must have stood out for Snape.

Snape is reinforcing his mental protections against Voldemort after showing too much concern for Harry's protection during the Occlumency lessons: "Snape, meanwhile, seemed to have decided to act as though Harry were invisible." (*HP/OotP*, 660) He avoids eye contact with Harry, in case Voldemort is watching Snape through the scar connection, and behaves spitefully so Voldemort will feel the mutual antipathy between Snape and Harry. This is the easiest thing in the world for Snape to pull off and affords him some nasty enjoyment, but Snape is behaving this way to protect them all. He may enjoy aggravating Harry, but it cannot be argued that these moments of "gloating pleasure" (*HP/OotP*, 661) interfere with the strategy in any way.

Despite this hostility, Harry continues to be haunted by what he saw in the Pensieve and talks to Sirius and Lupin about it. James never stopped hexing Snape, but 20 years later, after cooperating with Snape for the Order, Sirius and Lupin are gaining perspective, too.

> "Snape was just this little oddball who was up to his eyes in the Dark Arts and James—whatever else he may have appeared to you, Harry—always hated the Dark Arts."
>
> "Yeah," said Harry, "but he just attacked Snape for no good reason, just because—well, just because you said you were bored," he finished with a slightly apologetic note in his voice.
>
> "I'm not proud of it," said Sirius quickly.
>
> Lupin looked sideways at Sirius . . .
>
> "We were all idiots! Well—not Moony so much," he said fairly, looking at Lupin, but Lupin shook his head.
>
> "Did I ever tell you to lay off Snape?" he said. "Did I ever have the guts to tell you I thought you were out of order?"
>
> "Yeah, well," said Sirius, "you made us feel ashamed of ourselves sometimes. . . . That was something . . ." (*HP/OotP*, 670-1)

This is a change from the argument about Occlumency lessons when Sirius refused to believe that Snape had reformed. We don't know whether Sirius has understood Snape better or whether being a parent figure for Harry has matured his thinking, but we see that Lupin notices the change. Lupin, too, has gained in perspective since his secretive year teaching DADA.

Harry gets a painful reminder of his mother's defense of Snape's innocence when he witnesses Ministry officials coming stealthily at nighttime, on Umbridge's order, to remove Hagrid from Hogwarts. Professor McGonagall runs out to intervene, using the same argument and nearly the same words that Lily used.

> "Leave him alone! *Alone*, I say!" said Professor McGonagall's voice through the darkness. "On what grounds are you attacking him? He has done nothing, nothing to warrant such—" (*HP/OotP*, 721)

The Ministry workers attack McGonagall so severely that she is removed to St. Mungo's, leaving a frantic Harry with no support when he sees a vision of Voldemort torturing Sirius in the Department of Mysteries. Voldemort has planted this image deliberately to lure Harry into a trap.

> There was nobody left to tell. Dumbledore had gone, Hagrid had gone, but he had always expected Professor McGonagall to be there, irascible and inflexible, perhaps, but always dependably, solidly present. . . . (*HP/OotP*, 730)

Umbridge catches Harry using her Floo to check for Sirius at Grimmauld Place. It is not until she calls for Professor Snape to help her that Harry remembers there is one member of the Order of the Phoenix still at Hogwarts, one whom Umbridge has not thought to remove because, after investigating his background, she believes him to be a Death Eater.

Umbridge demands that Snape provide Veritaserum and Snape lies that she has used up his entire store.

> "But I need it this evening, Snape! I have just found Potter using my fire to communicate with a person or persons unknown!"
>
> "Really?" said Snape, showing his first, faint sign of interest as he looked around at Harry. "Well, it doesn't surprise me. Potter has never shown much inclination to follow school rules."
>
> His cold, dark eyes were boring into Harry's, who met his gaze unflinchingly, concentrating hard on what he had seen in his dream, willing Snape to read it in his mind, to understand . . . (*HP/OotP*, 744-5)

Now that it's an emergency, Snape and Harry snap immediately into Legilimency. They know how to do this. For good measure, Snape protects their communication against detection by either Umbridge or Voldemort by presenting an outward show of dislike for Harry while, incidentally, warning everyone else that Umbridge is capable of poisoning students.

> "Unless you wish to poison Potter—and I assure you I would have the greatest sympathy with you if you did—I cannot help you. The only trouble is that most venoms act too fast to give the victim

much time for truth-telling . . ."

Snape looked back at Harry, who stared at him, frantic to communicate without words.

Voldemort's got Sirius in the Department of Mysteries, he thought desperately. Voldemort's got Sirius—

"You are on probation!" shrieked Professor Umbridge, and Snape looked back at her, his eyebrows slightly raised. "You are being deliberately unhelpful! I expected better, Lucius Malfoy always speaks most highly of you!" (*HP/OotP*, 745)

So that's what it takes to get Snape on probation. Not bullying Neville, not favoritism, but refusing to fight Harry Potter. Umbridge expected him to comply; unsurprisingly, Lucius Malfoy seems to have been bribing Umbridge, encouraging her to purge Harry's allies from the staff, expecting fellow Death Eater Snape to cooperate from the inside.

Harry cannot be sure Snape has understood his nonverbal message. After all, Legilimency is not mind-reading, only the reading of feelings and memories. He has to risk speaking aloud in code: "He's got Padfoot at the place where it's hidden!" (*HP/OotP*, 745)

"Padfoot?" cried Professor Umbridge, looking eagerly from Harry to Snape. "What is Padfoot? Where what is hidden? What does he mean, Snape?"

Snape looked around at Harry. His face was inscrutable. Harry could not tell whether he had understood or not, but he did not dare speak more plainly in front of Umbridge.

"I have no idea," said Snape coldly. "Potter, when I want nonsense shouted at me I shall give you a Babbling Beverage. And Crabbe, loosen your hold a little, if Longbottom suffocates it will mean a lot of tedious paperwork, and I am afraid I shall have to mention it on your reference if ever you apply for a job." (*HP/OotP*, 745-6)

Snape does what he can. His face has to be inscrutable: Voldemort is surely watching every moment through Harry's eyes since planting the image of Sirius. All Snape can do for Harry is show that he heard.

His comment to Crabbe is another instance of hiding his true motives. His argument sounds as though he feels that Neville is not worth the trouble of killing. Crabbe and Voldemort can believe that

Snape is thinking: *Not even my enemy deserves to die like this.*

But Neville is not Snape's enemy. If Snape has never wished Harry dead, he certainly has not wished Neville dead. Snape words his warning impersonally, seemingly concerned only about inconvenience, but he's privately motivated by a more powerful sentiment: *This is somebody under my protection.* Regardless of personal feelings, a protector like Snape will go into immediate intervention mode when a vulnerable person is endangered. Whether it's Dumbledore stopping Umbridge from shaking Marietta Edgecombe (*HP/OotP*, 616), Snape giving Neville some air, or Dumbledore carrying Umbridge out of the forest (*HP/OotP*, 848), the protectiveness supersedes any personal conflict.

The Locked Room in the Department of Mysteries

Snape walks out of Umbridge's office, and the reader doesn't find out if he understood Harry's message until 55 pages later, when other members of the Order of the Phoenix arrive at the Department of Mysteries to help Harry and his friends battle Death Eaters. It must have been a long night for Snape. He had to investigate Harry's coded message. He had to patch up members of the Inquisitorial Squad without letting them know their family members were in a battle that would determine his future and theirs. He had to hold Hogwarts together as the senior administrator with Dumbledore, McGonagall, and even Umbridge out of commission. He had to know what was happening from both sides, hide what he knew for the sake of the students, remain immobile, and wait.

After the battle, Dumbledore confirms to Harry that Snape understood:

> "You see, when you gave Professor Snape that cryptic warning, he realized that you had had a vision of Sirius trapped in the bowels of the Department of Mysteries. He, like you, attempted to contact Sirius at once. I should explain that members of the Order of the Phoenix have more reliable methods of communicating than the fire in Dolores Umbridge's office. Professor Snape found that Sirius was alive and safe in Grimmauld Place." (*HP/OotP*, 830)

The method used by the Order, as we learn later, is via Patronus.

Snape communicated with his bitterest childhood enemy by showing him the form of his Patronus. A Patronus is a pure projection of the self; it cannot lie. Before he died, Sirius Black saw Snape for his true self and understood that Dumbledore was right to trust Snape.

> "When, however, you did not return from your trip into the forest
> with Dolores Umbridge, Professor Snape grew worried that you
> still believed Sirius to be a captive of Lord Voldemort's. He alerted
> certain Order members at once."

> Dumbledore heaved a great sigh and then said, "Alastor Moody,
> Nymphadora Tonks, Kingsley Shacklebolt, and Remus Lupin were
> at headquarters when he made contact. All agreed to go to your aid
> at once. Professor Snape requested that Sirius remain behind, as he
> needed somebody to remain at headquarters to tell me what had
> happened, for I was due there at any moment. In the meantime he,
> Professor Snape, intended to search the forest for you." (*HP/OotP*,
> 830)

Sirius, however, rushed to the Ministry to fight for Harry and got
killed. A grieving Harry lashes out, telling Dumbledore why he blames
Snape for Sirius's death:

> "Snape stopped giving me Occlumency lessons!" Harry snarled. "He
> threw me out of his office!"

> "I am aware of it," said Dumbledore heavily. "I have already said
> that it was a mistake for me not to teach you myself, though I was
> sure, at the time, that nothing could have been more dangerous
> than to open your mind even further to Voldemort while in my
> presence—"

> "Snape made it worse, my scar always hurt worse after lessons with
> him—" Harry remembered Ron's thoughts on the subject and
> plunged on. "How do you know he wasn't trying to soften me up
> for Voldemort, make it easier for him to get inside my—"

> "I trust Severus Snape," said Dumbledore simply. "But I forgot—
> another old man's mistake—that some wounds run too deep for the
> healing. I thought Professor Snape could overcome his feelings
> about your father—I was wrong." (*HP/OotP*, 833)

Dumbledore knows that he is not telling Harry the whole truth.
Snape's wounds that run too deep for the healing are not about Harry's
father. We will find out later that in telling this lie, Dumbledore is
upholding a promise. He can only ask Harry to trust in Dumbledore's

assessment of Snape.

Dumbledore can tell Harry what he has realized now, in hindsight, about the way that the Occlumency lessons *should* have gone. He and Snape were trying to appeal to Harry's sense of self-preservation, expecting him to volunteer to remain ignorant, empty his mind, shut out knowledge for his own safety. They should have appealed instead to his chivalry and protectiveness—what Hermione calls Harry's "saving-people-thing." (*HP/OotP*, 733) The teen boy with the irrepressible sense of curiosity might have been able to keep out Voldemort if he'd thought about the people he could protect by doing so, filling his mind with protectiveness rather than emptying it of desire.

Dumbledore spells out the strategy he should have used, the strategy that he and Snape will commit to from this moment.

> "There is a room in the Department of Mysteries," interrupted Dumbledore, "that is kept locked at all times. It contains a force that is at once more wonderful and more terrible than death, than human intelligence, than forces of nature. It is also, perhaps, the most mysterious of the many subjects for study that reside there. It is the power held within that room that you possess in such quantities and which Voldemort has not at all. That power took you to save Sirius tonight. That power also saved you from possession by Voldemort, because he could not bear to reside in a body so full of the force he detests." (*HP/OotP*, 843-4)

The unnamed force in this oft-quoted passage is "love," true, but it is a specific sort of love: protectiveness. It need not contain affection, although affection, empathy, intimacy, romance, and gratitude are among the things that strengthen it. Snape uses this force to hide his protection of Harry from Voldemort, who would not be able to understand why anyone would protect a person they truly dislike. This is what powers Snape's Occlumency. We saw hints of it in the Occlumency lessons: the first time Harry was able to repel Snape, he wanted to protect the privacy of his time with Cho. When he sees into Snape's memories, it is because Snape has just strengthened him with the truth. Dumbledore's decision to avoid contact with Harry and keep Harry isolated, motivated though it was by genuine protective fear, weakened Harry's ability to Occlude. Dumbledore knows now that the support he could have provided in Occlumency lessons would have helped Harry overpower even Voldemort's invasive abilities, although there was no way for him to know that would work until he saw Harry's emotions drive Voldemort out of his mind.

Snape devotes the remainder of his school year to behind-the-scenes care for affected students. Hermione most likely racks up another life debt to him: "The curse Dolohov had used on her, though less effective than it would have been had he been able to say the incantation aloud, had nevertheless caused, in Madam Pomfrey's words, 'quite enough damage to be going on with.'" (HP/OotP, 847) Hermione is cured by "ten different types of potion every day," and it seems probable that the resident potioneer and Dark Magic expert had a hand in brewing some of them.

Draco, Crabbe, and Goyle need his support more than ever. Not only is Snape their Head of House, but he must also monitor hostilities between them and the student fighters who put their fathers in prison. When Draco threatens to Harry, "*I'm* going to make you pay for what you've done to my father . . ." and Harry draws his wand, Snape is on the scene immediately.

> "What are you doing, Potter?" said Snape coldly as ever, as he strode over to the four of them.
>
> "I'm trying to decide what curse to use on Malfoy, sir," said Harry fiercely.
>
> Snape stared at him.
>
> "Put that wand away at once," he said curtly. "Ten points from Gryff—"
>
> Snape looked toward the giant hourglasses on the walls and gave a sneering smile.
>
> "Ah. I see there are no longer any points left in the Gryffindor hourglass to take away. In that case, Potter, we will simply have to—" (HP/OotP, 852)

In Snape's version of a happily-ever-after, we know that Hogwarts returns to some form of equilibrium at the close of this volume because Snape regains his friend and work partner, the good cop to his bad cop, and they can outwit students together again.

> "Add some more?"
>
> Professor McGonagall had just stumped up the stone steps into the

castle. She was carrying a tartan carpetbag in one hand and leaning heavily on a walking stick with her other, but otherwise looked quite well.

"Professor McGonagall!" said Snape, striding forward. "Out of St. Mungo's, I see!"

"Yes, Professor Snape," said Professor McGonagall, shrugging off her traveling cloak, "I'm quite as good as new. You two—Crabbe—Goyle—" (*HP/OotP*, 852)

McGonagall has no compunction about ordering Snape's Slytherins to carry her luggage. She dispatches Harry and Draco just as briskly while Snape indulges himself in grumbling about the points she's just awarded Gryffindor and Ravenclaw. It's been a long year.

Harry doesn't know it yet, but in his grief over Sirius, he is learning another of Snape's strategies for remaining steadfast while unable to show his true self to the world. As painful as it is to be seen falsely, such concerns recede compared to the emotion of wishing to protect someone—or grieving the failure to protect them.

"Ev'ryone knows you've bin tellin' the truth now, Harry," said Hagrid softly and unexpectedly. "Tha's gotta be better, hasn' it?"

Harry shrugged. . . .

A few days ago, before his exams had finished and he had seen the vision Voldemort had planted in his mind, he would have given almost anything for the Wizarding world to know that he had been telling the truth, for them to believe that Voldemort was back and know that he was neither a liar nor mad. Now, however . . . (*HP/OotP*, 854-5)

That's how Snape stands being thought evil when he is actually risking more than almost anyone as a double agent against Voldemort. The longer he can remain hidden, the more he can protect not only Harry but his own Slytherins, boys as needy as he was at their age. The Inquisitorial Squad showed him how easy it would be for others to turn them toward evil. He will do what he must to stay close and protect them.

SEVERUS SNAPE

AND THE HALF-BLOOD PRINCE

This is the year that Snape's past and present collapse spectacularly into one another. His second chance in life is counting down to the moment when he must remain unseen, yet perform the one action that will change time and save innocent lives. He must be a passive, often horrified witness to his old mistakes but be unable to change anything about who he once was and where he came from, whether he has repressed these things in shame or simply forgotten.

It's as if he's gone back in time. Slughorn is back. Voldemort is back. A young man takes the Dark Mark and will never be able to remove it. Potter wins at Quidditch and dates a redheaded girl. Snape's old Potions book resurfaces, and along with it, the Dark Magic spells he invented in his teens. And just below the surface of the story, never mentioned but nearly tangible, is the haunting memory of his ruined friendship with Lily Evans.

Rowling interweaves three major plots for the story of this eventful year. With Lucius Malfoy in Azkaban, Voldemort punishes the Malfoy family by ordering Draco to kill Dumbledore. Draco's mother, Narcissa, begs Snape to help Draco or to kill Dumbledore in his stead. Snape takes an Unbreakable Vow to do so; he will help Draco or die.

Dumbledore appoints Snape to the Defense Against the Dark Arts position at last. He brings Professor Slughorn out of retirement to teach Potions. Harry becomes the top student in Potions class by following the tips written in his 50-year-old textbook by someone who called himself the Half-Blood Prince.

An injured Dumbledore teaches Harry privately how to hunt down Horcruxes, relics of Voldemort's murders that contain fragments of his soul. Draco lets Death Eaters into Hogwarts and disarms Dumbledore but cannot bring himself to attack. Snape kills Dumbledore in Draco's stead and leads Draco and the other Death Eaters out of Hogwarts.

157

Above all, *Harry Potter and the Half-Blood Prince* is about the missing story of the mother. Tom Marvolo Riddle was named after his father and maternal grandfather, but we learn his mother Merope's story to understand why Voldemort chose Harry to mark as his equal. Severus Snape bears the surname of his Muggle father, but in his magical textbook, he names himself after his witch mother, Eileen Prince. Harry hears about his father's friends and about his mother herself, but on the topic of Harry's mother's friends, everyone is conspicuously silent.

Themes of jealousy, covetousness, and romantic desire run riot through this book. If Harry is overwhelmed by hostility toward Dean Thomas merely for dating Ginny, it is no wonder that Voldemort nearly died of jealousy at the sight of a baby with a loving mother. Hermione is wild with frustration at coming in second at Potions, by proxy, to a rival she doesn't trust and can't engage—someone who doesn't even really exist. Harry is so distracted by desire that he would rather throw away his lucky potion on wooing Ginny than defeating Voldemort, not knowing yet that natural euphoria works better for romance, forgetting that romance is a luxury he can ill afford. Felix Felicis, Amortentia, *Sectumsempra*, and other ambiguous magic is on everyone's minds. The same spells can be appropriated for good purposes or evil and sometimes the only thing that separates mischief from murder is sheer chance. Or a bezoar. Or Snape with healing magic that Harry cannot understand.

In selecting Draco for the Dark Mark, Voldemort gives himself a second chance to solve a mystery. When he marked Harry as his equal, he was defeated by the blood magic of Lily Potter, whose Muggle-born blood he considered dirty. This time he marks a different child, a pureblood, and repeats his observation of a mother's response to a threat to her child. We know Harry and Draco are underage for the entire school year, since they didn't make the cut-off for the Apparition test. (*HP/HBP*, 473-4) Voldemort can still use them to test the protective magic of a mother's love.

Snape and Dumbledore know Draco's new standing with the Death Eaters. Dumbledore remembers that he failed to connect with student Tom Riddle and prioritized others over connecting with Snape. Slughorn failed to see the danger in Tom and didn't find Snape worth cultivating. Snape, Dumbledore, and McGonagall work together to do better for Draco. They have to isolate him: Voldemort finds it too painful to share Harry's thoughts anymore, but he performs Legilimency regularly on Draco, so they cannot jeopardize Draco by letting him know the Order wants to protect him. Dumbledore keeps his distance and focuses on training Harry. Snape tries to keep communication open with Draco and prevent him and Harry from killing each other. McGonagall keeps an eye on inter-house conflict. Both assign detentions liberally to Gryffindors and Slytherins alike. Never have Snape and McGonagall worked together so closely.

Snape plans his endgame for the limited time remaining before he has to kill Dumbledore. Like Nicolas and Perenelle Flamel, they have the gift of time to set affairs in order. (HP/SS, 297) Through emphasizing Dumbledore's trust in him, they ensure that when Snape kills Dumbledore and openly joins the Death Eaters, his former allies will believe in their shock that Dumbledore was wrong. There will be nobody left alive who knows Snape's true self.

Snape's Year in Overview

Snape's personal dislike of Harry

Now that Dumbledore is tutoring Harry, Snape's protective focus is on Draco. He's not worried about protecting Draco from being hurt; he's trying to protect Draco from the lifelong regret of hurting others irreversibly, as Snape did at his age. Every time Harry antagonizes Draco, it makes Snape's job harder. Restricting Harry's movement makes things safer for Draco. The irritating sight of Slughorn fawning over Harry further provokes Snape to relapse into his resentment of "famous Harry Potter." When Slughorn asks Snape to release Harry from a detention so he can be the star at a Slug Club soirée, Snape sends a message that sums up his attitude toward Harry for the year:

> "He says you're to come to his office at half past eight tonight to do your detention—er—no matter how many party invitations you've received. And he wanted you to know you'll be sorting out rotten flobberworms from good ones, to use in Potions and—and he says there's no need to bring protective gloves." (HP/HBP, 236)

Snape's usual hostility to the new teacher

For a change, the unfamiliar face at the Head Table isn't here to teach Defense Against the Dark Arts. Horace Slughorn, the Potions Master before Snape, has accepted Dumbledore's invitation to resume the post. Slughorn reinstates his Slug Club, an invitation-only group of elite students he selects for their future promise, their charm, or their connections. This creates the atmosphere of resentment that typically results from such favoritism. It is clear that Slughorn never thought unpopular, working-class Snape good enough for his inner circles, despite being aware of teen Snape's genius for Potions. (*HP/HBP*, 319)

As a teacher, Slughorn's genial classroom manner is an improvement over Snape's, but his standards are lower. He has lower requirements for students to qualify for N.E.W.T.-level classes and he teaches from the textbook rather than providing custom-written lessons on the board, as Snape used to do. In his classroom, Harry, who is working from teen Snape's modifications to the textbook, has better results than Hermione, who follows the book's instructions.

Dumbledore confirms at last that the jinx on the Defense Against the Dark Arts job is real, dating from Voldemort's second application for that position.

> "Oh, he definitely wanted the Defense Against the Dark Arts job," said Dumbledore. "The aftermath of our little meeting proved that. You see, we have never been able to keep a Defense Against the Dark Arts teacher for longer than a year since I refused the post to Lord Voldemort." (*HP/HBP*, 446)

At least Dumbledore has been able to use the jinx to his advantage. Some years, as with Quirrell, Lockhart, and Umbridge, he has depended on the jinx to help neutralize enemies. With Lupin and Mad-Eye Moody, he worked within the confines of the jinx to bring in specialists for a guaranteed maximum stint of one year, to counter a specific danger. Readers and observers are free to speculate about which tactic applies to his appointment of Snape.

Snape's reputation

After an unbroken buildup over five novels, Rowling springs a glorious break in the pattern on her readers: Dumbledore announces Snape as the Defense Against the Dark Arts professor, causing a commotion at the Welcoming Feast.

> "No!" said Harry, so loudly that many heads turned in his direction. He did not care; he was staring up at the staff table, incensed. How could Snape be given the Defense Against the Dark Arts job after

all this time? Hadn't it been widely known for years that
Dumbledore did not trust him to do it? (*HP/HBP*, 166-7)

Despite ample evidence that Snape is trustworthy, despite years of
Dumbledore's avowals that he trusts Snape, Snape has been so
unpleasant that Harry has bought into the rumor. If Harry is convinced,
the rumor will have worked on the many others who have not seen
Snape and Dumbledore working together.

> Snape, who was sitting on Dumbledore's right, did not stand up at
> the mention of his name; he merely raised a hand in lazy
> acknowledgment of the applause from the Slytherin table, yet
> Harry was sure he could detect a look of triumph on the features he
> loathed so much. (*HP/HBP*, 167)

Even though Snape knows his exoneration will last less than a year,
he cannot help but show defiant pleasure at finally being acknowledged
Dumbledore's right-hand man. Moving him into this position is a clever
move on the characters' parts and also on the author's. It telegraphs that
Dumbledore and Snape expect something major to change for Snape by
the end of the year, putting the reader in increasing suspense. It
reimburses Snape for years of accepting an unflattering reputation that is
the opposite of his true self. It removes the need for Snape to be covert
about teaching Defense during this frightening year. It broadcasts to
Death Eaters that Dumbledore foolishly trusts the man they believe to
be on their side. It suggests that Snape is less than impressive, just a petty
man of limited vision whose "heart's desire" is nothing grander than a
lateral move at his place of employment. (*HP/HBP*, 167)

Within Harry's circle, though, others see Snape accurately this year,
or at least acknowledge the possibility that Snape deserves Dumbledore's
trust. When Harry overhears Snape offering to help Draco with Death
Eater work, Ron sums up what their allies are likely to think.

> "'Course, you know what they'll all say? Dad and Dumbledore and
> all of them? They'll say Snape isn't really trying to help Malfoy, he
> was just trying to find out what Malfoy's up to."
>
> [. . .] Harry turned to face him, frowning. "You think I'm right,
> though?"
>
> "Yeah, I do!" said Ron hastily. "Seriously, I do! But they're all

convinced Snape's in the Order, aren't they?" (*HP/HBP*, 328-9)

The one thing Harry can get people to acknowledge is that Draco is up to something and Snape knows it. The contradictory evidence regarding Snape's intentions means that it comes down to one thing: whether or not people trust in Dumbledore's judgment. Lupin lays out the equation succinctly.

> "Dumbledore trusts Severus, and that ought to be good enough for all of us."
>
> "But," said Harry, "just say—just say Dumbledore's wrong about Snape—"
>
> "People have said it, many times. It comes down to whether or not you trust Dumbledore's judgment. I do; therefore, I trust Severus." (*HP/HBP*, 332)

Lupin tells a skeptical Harry, "I neither like nor dislike Severus," mentioning that Snape relieved his suffering with Wolfsbane every month during Harry's third year.

> "But he 'accidentally' let it slip that you're a werewolf, so you had to leave!" said Harry angrily.
>
> Lupin shrugged. "The news would have leaked out anyway. We both know he wanted my job, but he could have wreaked much worse damage on me by tampering with the potion." (*HP/HBP*, 333)

The passage of three years has tempered Lupin's take on that year, but even he has bought the rumor that Snape coveted the Defense position. He knows better than to think about it too much, though. Lupin, too, is a spy for Dumbledore, and knows firsthand how Dumbledore uses rumors to provide cover. He speaks from an informed position when he suggests to Harry, "It might have been on Dumbledore's orders that Severus questioned Draco." (*HP/HBP*, 333)

Dumbledore and Snape have set up Snape's reputation to be dependent entirely on perceptions of Dumbledore's trust in him. With the endorsement of the DADA position protecting him, Snape has impunity to behave unpleasantly toward fellow members of the Order of the Phoenix. If they find him difficult, it underscores that Dumbledore must have reason to trust him.

Snape taunts Tonks cruelly about her Patronus when she uses it to communicate Order business. It has changed into an indistinct wolf shape, betraying that she is painfully in love with Lupin.

> "I think you were better off with the old one," said Snape, the malice in his voice unmistakable. "The new one looks weak."
>
> As Snape swung the lantern about, Harry saw, fleetingly, a look of shock and anger on Tonks's face. (*HP/HBP*, 160)

We know from Occlumency lessons that the hyper-alert Snape becomes uncontrollably agitated by—and for—"fools who wear their hearts proudly on their sleeves." (*HP/OotP*, 536) His jibe at Tonks is uncalled-for; it stands out, even for him. Perhaps the sight of a telling Patronus has unsettled him. Certainly, a wizard double agent must avoid any magic that could betray his true self. The only Order member that we know for certain has seen Snape's Patronus is Sirius, on the day he died.

Dumbledore has been telling Harry for six years that he trusts Snape, and for six years, Harry has been incredulous.

> "So, sir," said Harry, in what he hoped was a polite, calm voice, "you definitely still trust—?"
>
> "I have been tolerant enough to answer that question already," said Dumbledore, but he did not sound very tolerant anymore. "My answer has not changed." (*HP/HBP*, 359)

Dumbledore need not worry about the danger of Harry seeing through Snape's façade. It will not be difficult to break Harry's trust in Snape once Dumbledore can no longer vouch for him.

As for Snape's reputation with the Death Eaters, he is on solid ground. Voldemort trusts Snape, which puts his followers in the position of treachery if they disagree with his judgment. Nevertheless, Bellatrix is skeptical, but Snape shuts down her objections when he asks her to oversee his Unbreakable Vow to kill or help kill Dumbledore. Snape ensures that the Death Eaters hear and repeat the rumor of Dumbledore's greatest weakness: "He has to believe the best of people. I spun him a tale of deepest remorse when I joined his staff, fresh from my Death Eater days, and he embraced me with open arms—though, as I say, never allowing me nearer the Dark Arts than he could help."

(*HP/HBP*, 31) Snape and Dumbledore have primed the Death Eaters for the moment that Snape kills Dumbledore and claims he has been Voldemort's man all along.

The mystery of Snape's true motives

Rowling took care to write Snape's true motives as a mystery at the end of this book. In the two years between the publication of *Harry Potter and the Half-Blood Prince* and the final installment, *Harry Potter and the Deathly Hallows*, reader opinion was so divided about Snape's motives that conference panels and marketing campaigns debated the question of whether Snape supported Dumbledore, Voldemort, both, or neither. On the one hand, Snape used an Unforgivable Curse to kill Dumbledore. On the other hand, he protected Harry and guided him away from Dark Magic even while fighting him.

In *Half-Blood Prince*, the clues pointing to Snape's true protective motives can be found in the repeated instances of close calls and accidents that nearly turned tragic. Draco survived Harry's *Sectumsempra*. Katie Bell and Ron survived Draco's curses and poison. As Dumbledore said to Draco, "No harm has been done, you have hurt nobody, though you are very lucky that your unintentional victims survived. . . ." (*HP/HBP*, 591) But it would have taken very little for those incidents to end differently.

With close calls, as long as nobody dies, the attacker can walk away, free to resolve that they will not repeat the mistake. But sometimes attacks don't end well and there is no walking away from the aftermath. Harry was immediately aghast at the effects of *Sectumsempra*, showing that guilt from causing damage or death can be enormous, even if the attacker didn't know what they were doing.

Harry immediately regretted casting the spell "for enemies" that he picked up from the Half-Blood Prince's notes, even though Draco had been about to cast an Unforgivable on Harry. Not even his enemy deserved to suffer like that. But Harry does not want to admit that perhaps Hermione was right to be cautious about the Prince.

> "I wish I hadn't done it, and not just because I've got about a dozen detentions. You know I wouldn't've used a spell like that, not even on Malfoy, but you can't blame the Prince, he hadn't written 'try this out, it's really good'—he was just making notes for himself, wasn't he, not for anyone else. . . ." (*HP/HBP*, 530)

Ron, too, tries to rationalize that there was nothing really wrong with taking instructions from the Prince's book.

> "He was a genius, the Prince. Anyway . . . without his bezoar tip. . ." He drew his finger significantly across his own throat. "I wouldn't be here to discuss it, would I? I mean, I'm not saying that spell you used on Malfoy was great—"
>
> "Nor am I," said Harry quickly.
>
> "But he healed all right, didn't he? Back on his feet in no time."
>
> "Yeah," said Harry; this was perfectly true, although his conscience squirmed slightly all the same. "Thanks to Snape. . ." (*HP/HBP*, 539)

But we have seen the cost when things go wrong. Slughorn has lived in terror since Voldemort's return, understanding that his talk of Horcruxes helped create this monster. Dumbledore tells Harry, "You have no idea of the remorse Professor Snape felt when he realized how Lord Voldemort had interpreted the prophecy, Harry. I believe it to be the greatest regret of his life. . ." (*HP/HBP*, 549)

We don't know yet what Dumbledore was remembering when he drank the potion in the cave and sobbed, "It's all my fault, all my fault . . . Please make it stop, I know I did wrong, oh please make it stop and I'll never, never again. . ." (*HP/HBP*, 572) It is easy, though, to imagine Harry feeling the same anguish if *Sectumsempra* had killed Draco. Snape and Dumbledore both know that some forms of damage cause suffering that never ends. They would give their lives to protect their students from this pain.

Spinner's End

The first chapter of *Half-Blood Prince*, "The Other Minister," pulls back for a view from the office of the Muggle Prime Minister of Britain, showing the damage from Voldemort's war on the Muggle world. The second chapter, "Spinner's End," takes an extreme close-up view, winding its way into the very heart of the operation: the private home of Severus Snape, the one man who is pivotal to both Dumbledore's and Voldemort's sides of the war. These two chapters, set in these secret centers of power, establish the beginning of the endgame for Harry's fight against Voldemort and for the series itself.

Setting and characters

Narcissa Malfoy runs through a bleak Muggle neighborhood in a former mill town to the last house on a street called Spinner's End, shaking off the attempts of her older sister, Bellatrix Lestrange, to dissuade her. Snape is spending the summer here in his childhood home, along with Wormtail, whom Voldemort has placed there to assist him.

Even in a series famous for its allegorical or offbeat names, "Spinner's End" is unusually evocative. "Spinner" refers to the now-defunct Muggle industry in this working-class part of town; "End" reinforces awareness of the industry's decline, evident from the "boarded and broken windows" on the way to Snape's house. "Spinner" also evokes the Fates, who implacably spin, measure, and cut the threads of human lifespans. "Spinner" evokes the phrase "the distaff side," having to do with the feminine, maternal, or domestic side of life; the name may indicate that this would be a good place to find stories about mothers. Snape has been characterized as a spy and a spider throughout; at Spinner's End, Narcissa and Bellatrix are seeking him in the center of his web. Finally, "Spinner" suggests a male version of "spinster," Snape's single state as he approaches middle age.

We have seen magical spaces hidden in desolate Muggle surroundings before. Hogwarts is enchanted to look like "a moldering old ruin" to Muggle eyes. (HP/GoF, 166) Grimmauld Place is surrounded by Muggle houses with broken windows and heaps of rubbish. (HP/OotP, 158) The Ministry of Magic (HP/OotP, 125) and St. Mungo's (HP/OotP, 483) are also located in shabby Muggle areas. But there is nothing magical about the way Spinner's End repels visitors. This is where Snape comes from. There is no sign of parents, siblings, or any other family in his home. As far as we can tell, Snape has sole ownership of this house. Wealthy pureblood Narcissa Malfoy is usually a snob, but in her time of distress, she runs into Spinner's End without hesitation while Bellatrix grimaces and follows. For Narcissa, class distinctions, wealth, and blood status mean nothing anymore compared to the qualities in Snape that she needs: his cleverness, his long friendship with Lucius, Draco's respect for him, the trust he's earned from Voldemort. In crisis, she values him for his true self.

Narcissa wants Snape's help in subverting Voldemort's command for Draco to kill Dumbledore or die trying. She is not a Death Eater, but her husband, son, and sister are. What she wants would be treachery to the Dark Lord. Bellatrix argues that Snape cannot be trusted with keeping such a secret from Voldemort, but Narcissa's convoluted argument is that Voldemort trusts Snape, and therefore, Snape is trustworthy—a parallel to members of the Order reasoning that Dumbledore's trust in Snape ought to be enough guarantee. Bellatrix is Voldemort's most fanatical follower, but sisterly bonds seem to mean something to her as well, since she is trying to dissuade Narcissa instead of informing Voldemort about her directly.

Snape welcomes Narcissa sincerely and Bellatrix with a "slightly mocking smile," in acknowledgment of her distrust.

> They had stepped directly into a tiny sitting room, which had the feeling of a dark, padded cell. The walls were completely covered in books, most of them bound in old black or brown leather; a threadbare sofa, an old armchair, and a rickety table stood grouped together in a pool of dim light cast by a candle-filled lamp hung from the ceiling. The place had an air of neglect, as though it was not usually inhabited. (*HP/HBP*, 22)

We don't know if the house feels neglected because Snape does not usually live there or because he has just come from Hogwarts for the summer, but the furnishings suggest, unsurprisingly, a man who feels at home as long as he has books. We don't know the provenance of those old books. Perhaps they were family property from Snape's mother or father. Perhaps Snape acquired them as an adult. The age and state of the furniture suggest that the sitting room is the same as it was in Snape's childhood. Perhaps the candle-filled lamp is a recent switch to a light source that does not rely on Muggle utilities for power.

> "So, what can I do for you?" Snape asked, settling himself in the armchair opposite the two sisters.
>
> "We . . . we are alone, aren't we?" Narcissa asked quietly.
>
> "Yes, of course. Well, Wormtail's here, but we're not counting vermin, are we?"
>
> He pointed his wand at the wall of books behind him and with a bang, a hidden door flew open, revealing a narrow staircase upon which a small man stood frozen. (*HP/HBP*, 23)

The wall of books conceals a hidden door and a passageway: reading was child Snape's secret escape.

Wormtail is the final, least important character in this scene. What is *he* doing here?

> "Wormtail will get us drinks, if you'd like them," said Snape. "And then he will return to his bedroom."
>
> Wormtail winced as though Snape had thrown something at him.
>
> "I am not your servant!" he squeaked, avoiding Snape's eye.
>
> "Really? I was under the impression that the Dark Lord placed you here to assist me."
>
> "To assist, yes—but not to make you drinks and—and clean your house!" (*HP/HBP*, 23-4)

Assist Snape with what? If Snape is doing any Death Eater work that requires assistance, we never hear of it. It is difficult to imagine this self-sufficient, exacting man wanting to delegate sensitive work to someone he respects so little. Wormtail kept house for Voldemort at Riddle Manor; perhaps Voldemort has palmed him off on Snape for the same duties, as a mark of favor for Snape and a way to get rid of a despised hanger-on now that he has better followers. Of course, Wormtail can also keep an eye on Snape for Voldemort. But from the contemptuous way that Snape, Bellatrix, and Narcissa disregard Wormtail's presence, they seem unworried about their ability to block Wormtail from confidential discussion. Loathing of Wormtail is the one unanimous opinion that unites everyone in the series, be they Death Eater, Marauder, or even the author.

The loathing tells us the narrative purpose of Wormtail's inclusion in this scene. It is a replay of a pivotal moment in Snape's past, something he must and can change on his second chance. Snape and Wormtail were the two people who betrayed the Potters to Voldemort. Now they are faced with a similar situation. A woman is frantic to protect her son from Voldemort. Her older sister has her own twisted ideas about what should become of this son. Snape can choose to protect the child this time. Wormtail feels no regret and neither wants nor gets a second chance. He is banished from the room.

Snape vs. Bellatrix

Every one of Bellatrix's suspicions about Snape is correct, but she doesn't stand a chance against the defenses that Snape and Dumbledore have perfected to fool Voldemort. She bombards Snape with hostile questions, and Snape turns each one into an opportunity to catalogue her weaknesses and further his own agenda. At the end, she is no more convinced than before, yet thoroughly routed, while Snape merely looks "rather amused." (HP/HBP, 24)

Weaknesses:

#1: Bellatrix cannot admit that Voldemort has flaws

When she asks Snape questions ranging from his whereabouts when the Dark Lord fell to his reasons for letting Harry flourish at Hogwarts, Snape replies that Voldemort has asked him every one of these questions and been satisfied with the answers. Either Bellatrix should be satisfied as well or she is saying that Snape has fooled "the Dark Lord, the greatest wizard, the most accomplished Legilimens the world has ever seen." (HP/HBP, 26)

#2: She cannot criticize Lucius in front of Narcissa

Snape names several Death Eaters who, like him, did not search for Voldemort after his defeat, delicately listing Lucius last. As Lucius is currently in Azkaban, Bellatrix risks escalating tensions with an already distraught Narcissa if she criticizes Narcissa's husband.

#3: Snape has more to offer Voldemort than Bellatrix does

Snape provides Voldemort with practical information about Harry and Dumbledore, "a rather more useful welcome-back present than endless reminiscences of how unpleasant Azkaban is. . . ." (HP/HBP, 27)

#4: Bellatrix wants something from Voldemort. Snape doesn't

Bellatrix offers Voldemort her sacrifices as evidence of her devotion, which can only feed Voldemort's ego, not further his campaign. Unlike true Death Eaters, Snape wants absolutely nothing from Voldemort: not favor, not protection, not support for a racist agenda. This gives him greater freedom to focus on exactly what Voldemort wants.

#5: What kind of a Slytherin are you, anyway? What are you, a Hufflepuff?

Bellatrix criticizes Snape for staying at Hogwarts instead of going to jail for loyalty to Voldemort. Snape finds this criticism so absurd that his refutation is merely to repeat it.

> "Yes, Bellatrix, I stayed," said Snape, betraying a hint of impatience for the first time. "I had a comfortable job that I preferred to a stint in Azkaban. They were rounding up the Death Eaters, you know. Dumbledore's protection kept me out of jail; it was most convenient and I used it." (*HP/HBP*, 27)

#6: Bellatrix is competitive with all other Death Eaters

She cannot resist hearing that other Death Eaters have let down Voldemort. It distracts her with pleasure. Bellatrix asks Snape why he did not help Voldemort get the Sorcerer's Stone; Snape blames it on Quirrell's mediocrity. Bellatrix questions why Snape returned two hours late when Voldemort returned; Snape assures her that had he ever wished to ignore the summons, the strengthening Dark Mark would have given him plenty of time to plan an escape, as Karkaroff did.

#7: Bellatrix is losing favor with Voldemort while Snape is gaining

When she challenges the usefulness of Snape's contributions, Snape suggests that she doesn't know their extent because Voldemort no longer confides in her.

#8: Bellatrix failed to get the prophecy for Voldemort

All Snape has to do is remind her. While parrying Bellatrix's accusations, Snape spreads Dumbledore's misinformation and protects himself, as well.

Self-protections

#1: Snape wants to avoid committing evil

He argues that staying by Dumbledore's side, abstaining from the Death Eaters' violence, maintains his cover and access as a spy: "By allowing Dumbledore to think that I was only returning to the Dark Lord's side because I was ordered to, I have been able to pass information on Dumbledore and the Order of the Phoenix ever since!" (*HP/HBP*, 28)

#2: Snape takes credit for the Order's losses

Since Bellatrix believes herself no longer privy to Voldemort's secrets, she will not fact-check Snape's claims that his information led to the murder of Emmeline Vance or Sirius Black.

Lies:

#1: Dumbledore doesn't trust Snape with Defense Against the Dark Arts

"Seemed to think it might, ah, bring about a relapse . . . tempt me into my old ways." (HP/HBP, 27) Even if Snape dislikes Bellatrix, it must be a bit of a relief for him to be able to tell this old lie without having to suppress a wince at the listener's look of disgust.

#2: Only Voldemort must kill Harry

When Bellatrix asks why Snape has not killed Harry, he replies with a question: "Have you discussed this matter with the Dark Lord?" (HP/HBP, 30)

Harry is the only one who can defeat Voldemort, so he must be kept safe until they meet. Voldemort seems interested in killing Harry himself. It is in the interest of all of Voldemort's enemies to encourage this whim. Best that Bellatrix hear this from Voldemort herself. She will heed Voldemort where she would argue with Snape.

#3: Harry has no talent

Snape waxes most eloquent on this subject. His conviction makes this a masterpiece of a lie. Snape is well aware that Harry is outstanding at Defense Against the Dark Arts and has talents that Voldemort cannot detect, but his loathing of Harry is so heartfelt that it covers up the lie:

"Of course, it became apparent to me very quickly that he had no extraordinary talent at all. He has fought his way out of a number of tight corners by a simple combination of sheer luck and more talented friends. He is mediocre to the last degree, though as obnoxious and self-satisfied as was his father before him. I have done my utmost to have him thrown out of Hogwarts, where I believe he scarcely belongs. . . ." (HP/HBP, 31)

"More talented friends": so this is how he talks about Hermione when she's not around! It's a clever tactical move to shift credit for Harry's gifts to his Muggle-born friend, as Bellatrix and Voldemort are unable to believe that a Muggle-born can have any talent.

#4: Dumbledore has to believe the best of people

Snape tells Bellatrix about "Dumbledore's greatest weakness: He has to believe the best of people." (*HP/HBP*, 31) He's priming Bellatrix, too, to believe someday that Dumbledore was wrong to trust him.

Snape and Narcissa

Having immobilized Bellatrix with his logic, Snape turns his attention to Narcissa, who begs Snape to help her fight a secret plan that Voldemort has forbidden her to mention. She ignores Bellatrix's attempts to silence her. Bellatrix will not protect Draco against Voldemort. Snape might. Narcissa puts her trust in Snape.

Snape immediately protects Narcissa, checking to make sure they are unheard, telling her that he knows of the plan to stop her from divulging more. Narcissa's anguish affects Snape as nothing else has. His defenses are so perfected that Bellatrix's attacks are child's play to him, but empathy for a protective mother undoes him. He must avoid speech and eye contact with Narcissa while he figures out what he can offer without jeopardizing his plans: "Snape said nothing. He looked away from the sight of her tears as though they were indecent, but he could not pretend not to hear her." (*HP/HBP*, 33)

Narcissa appeals to him in three ways, two of which work on Snape.

> "Severus . . . please . . . You are, you have always been, Draco's favorite teacher. . . . You are Lucius's old friend. . . . I beg you. . . . You are the Dark Lord's favorite, his most trusted advisor. . . . Will you speak to him, persuade him—?" (*HP/HBP*, 33-4)

Snape is not acting when he says, with flat realism, "If you are imagining I can persuade the Dark Lord to change his mind, I am afraid there is no hope, none at all." (*HP/HBP*, 33) Snape has laid out the unvarnished truth: the only way to help Draco is by treachery against Voldemort. Narcissa's appeals to his bonds of sentiment have struck home. As a teacher and a family friend, he can protect this child. He can do better than he did for Lily Potter's child.

Narcissa makes the audacious proposal that Snape could kill Dumbledore, taking Draco's place: "You would succeed, of course you would, and he would reward you beyond all of us—" (*HP/HBP*, 34) Voldemort's esteem is something Snape wants, although not for himself, but to help his plot to undermine Voldemort. This could work. Once

Snape decides he can do it, he can meet Narcissa's eyes again. He needs only to double-check the details before committing. He speaks slowly, the way he does when he's thinking very quickly.

> Looking down into her tearstained face, he said slowly, "He intends me to do it in the end, I think. But he is determined that Draco should try first. You see, in the unlikely event that Draco succeeds, I shall be able to remain at Hogwarts a little longer, fulfilling my useful role as spy." (*HP/HBP*, 34)

Snape must buy time by convincing Narcissa to let him wait before killing Dumbledore for Draco. He must negotiate the most time possible for Dumbledore to stay alive and finish planning while putting Narcissa's mind at ease and protecting Draco from harm.

Bellatrix confirms for Snape that he is making the right decision when she says ruthlessly that Narcissa should be proud: "If I had sons, I would be glad to give them up to the service of the Dark Lord!" (*HP/HBP*, 35)

This is easy for Bellatrix to say, as she has no children. Yet if she did, she might very well sacrifice them to Voldemort. This is Snape's opponent in the fight for Draco's future. He has a chance to offer Draco the kind of defense against the Dark Arts that he did not receive at Draco's age.

Snape has to take more time to calculate when Narcissa begs him, on her knees, to make the Unbreakable Vow to protect Draco. He finds that even this will fall into line with the rest of his strategy. He can do this for her. It will help him, too.

> "The Unbreakable Vow?"
>
> Snape's expression was blank, unreadable. Bellatrix, however, let out a cackle of triumphant laughter.
>
> "Aren't you listening, Narcissa? Oh, he'll *try*, I'm sure. . . . The usual empty words, the usual slithering out of action . . . oh, on the Dark Lord's orders, of course!" (*HP/HBP*, 35)

Slithering out of action. Bellatrix has noticed that Snape has never done anything irrevocably evil to demonstrate his commitment to Voldemort's cause. This hints strongly that Snape has never cast an Unforgivable: an Imperius, a Cruciatus, a Killing Curse. We know from Bellatrix in *Order of the Phoenix* that Unforgivables only work if you really mean them: "You need to really want to cause pain—to enjoy it. . . ." (*HP/OotP*, 810) Snape, who never even attacked Sirius Black, would not want to cast an Unforgivable just to keep his spy cover, not if he could possibly find another way.

Snape ignores Bellatrix: "His black eyes were fixed upon Narcissa's tear-filled blue ones as she continued to clutch his hand." (*HP/HBP*, 36) Snape can look directly into the eyes of an anguished mother and show her his sympathy. He need Occlude nothing. It jeopardizes none of his plans if he adds protection of her near-grown child to the general protectiveness that he already provides to his Slytherin students and even to Potter. He has already dedicated himself to defending them against the Dark Arts. This costs him little more effort, but it brings Narcissa peace of mind, it puts the Malfoys in debt to him even greater than a life debt, it guarantees favor in Voldemort's eyes, and it yields the immensely satisfying bonus of shocking Bellatrix.

> "Certainly, Narcissa, I shall make the Unbreakable Vow," he said quietly. "Perhaps your sister will consent to be our Bonder."
>
> Bellatrix's mouth fell open. Snape lowered himself so that he was kneeling opposite Narcissa. Beneath Bellatrix's astonished gaze, they grasped right hands.
>
> "You will need your wand, Bellatrix," said Snape coldly.
>
> She drew it, still looking astonished.
>
> "And you will need to move a little closer," he said. (*HP/HBP*, 36)

Bellatrix is so shocked, she doesn't stop to reflect that she's about to commit avowed treachery to the Dark Lord. Surely this was not her intention when she set out for Spinner's End. She was trying to keep Narcissa from a plot against Voldemort, and now she's complicit in it herself. Snape gives her the opportunity to recall herself and back out. But she draws her wand. She moves in even closer: "She stepped forward so that she stood over them, and placed the tip of her wand on their linked hands." (*HP/HBP*, 36)

This is how Bellatrix falls into Snape's web.

Narcissa names three vows. Snape assents to them all.

> "Will you, Severus, watch over my son, Draco, as he attempts to fulfill the Dark Lord's wishes?" (*HP/HBP*, 36)

He accepts personal responsibility for an endangered young one. That is more than what a teacher would do. This is a vow that will change him.

> "And will you, to the best of your ability, protect him from harm?" (*HP/HBP*, 36)

He commits to taking action to protect Draco whenever Draco needs it. This will rewire his consciousness so that he is always aware of Draco, always primed to rush to his aid. This means he will never be truly at rest as long as both Draco and Dumbledore are alive. This will change him, day and night. This round-the-clock commitment to action makes him Draco's family.

> "And, should it prove necessary . . . if it seems Draco will fail . . ." whispered Narcissa (Snape's hand twitched within hers, but he did not draw away), "will you carry out the deed that the Dark Lord has ordered Draco to perform?" (*HP/HBP*, 36)

The twitch of the hand could mean anything. It could mean that Snape doesn't want to kill Dumbledore. That he flinches at the depth of commitment. That the thought of watching Draco attack Dumbledore and stepping in at the precise moment of failure overwhelms him with tension. But he chooses to leave his hand in Narcissa's. He will never again be the uncertain man who flinched under the gaze of Aurors or Death Eaters. He agrees to kill for Draco, or give his life, or take Draco's place, the way Lily did for Harry.

Three times, Snape says to Narcissa, "I will." This life bond is the closest that Severus Snape will ever come to a wedding. What Narcissa has done for him with the Unbreakable Vow is beyond measure. Until this vow, Snape has never been the most important person to anyone in his adult life. But now someone's entire happiness depends upon his survival and success. In the moments when his courage fails him at the thought of killing Dumbledore, it will help to remember that he must stay strong for Narcissa. It strengthens him. He is no longer alone.

Snape has had the thankless work of protecting Harry Potter, a child he can't stand, who acknowledges Snape's efforts with only hostility. Now, he can protect a child he likes for the sake of a father who respects him and a mother who knows the enormity of what she's asking him. The gratification he generates from protecting Draco will give him more momentum to extend the same protection to Harry. Thanks to Narcissa Malfoy, Snape's job has just gotten easier.

The Chosen One's Broken Nose

Snape heads into the school year knowing he has limited time to cram Defense Against the Dark Arts instruction into his students, since most of them will surely never listen to him again once he kills Dumbledore. He has to teach them whatever he thinks would be most helpful to them in war, based on what he knows of the Death Eaters' plans. As soon as the students get there, he must prevent Draco from hurting people and he must prevent Harry from provoking Draco to do so.

Unfortunately, he's already too late. Harry gets on the Hogwarts Express but doesn't get off. Snape must have flooded with adrenaline at the news. Death Eaters? Voldemort? Is Snape going to have to kill Dumbledore already? Has the war come to the Hogwarts Express?

No, nothing like that. Auror Tonks finds the Chosen One stuck on the train: invisible, voiceless, and immobilized with a broken nose, trying and failing to summon his wand by saying the spell in his head.

Tonks sends a message explaining what happened. Not full-scale war, then, but a boy lashing out because his father is in prison and another boy foolish enough to get caught trailing him. So much drama and the year hasn't even begun. As Snape says to Harry, "We haven't even started pudding." (*HP/HBP*, 161)

Tonks fixes Harry's nose, though his face is still covered in blood, and they walk in the dark to the Hogwarts gates.

> A lantern was bobbing at the distant foot of the castle. Harry was so pleased to see it he felt he could even endure Filch's wheezy criticisms of his tardiness and rants about how his timekeeping would improve with the regular application of thumbscrews. It was not until the glowing yellow light was ten feet away from them, and Harry had pulled off his Invisibility Cloak so that he could be seen, that he recognized, with a rush of pure loathing, the uplit hooked nose and long, black, greasy hair of Severus Snape. (*HP/HBP*, 159-60)

When Snape feels fear and then relief for someone else, he often expresses it as anger. He cares and he will rescue people; the glowing yellow light is his promise of safety. He tells Tonks, "Potter is quite—

ah—safe in my hands." (*HP/HBP*, 160) But he is his nastiest self in his anger. Harry thinks that "Snape had come to fetch him for this, for the few minutes when he could needle and torment Harry without anyone else listening." (*HP/HBP*, 161) That is not quite right. Snape came to defend him in case there were any other surprise attacks on the Chosen One. The opportunity to needle Harry is merely a bonus.

Snape's Defense Against the Dark Arts Classroom

After all this buildup, we finally get to see what it's like when Snape teaches Defense Against the Dark Arts.

> Snape had imposed his personality upon the room already; it was gloomier than usual, as curtains had been drawn over the windows, and was lit by candlelight. New pictures adorned the walls, many of them showing people who appeared to be in pain, sporting grisly injuries or strangely contorted body parts. Nobody spoke as they settled down, looking around at the shadowy, gruesome pictures. (*HP/HBP*, 177)

It's not clear whether there's any need to close the curtains and use candlelight, or whether Snape simply cannot resist a touch of drama. It's good that he commands student attention, though, because his curriculum is going to be "viciously difficult." (*HP/HBP*, 448)

As he did on the first day of Potions class in Harry's first year, Snape begins by casting a spell with his words, enchanting his students into a magical understanding of the discipline they're about to learn. They are wizards and they have been given the gift of power beyond what ordinary humans can command. Snape addresses not the grubby teens sitting before him but the magic in them, which he respects and would like them to respect, too.

> "The Dark Arts," said Snape, "are many, varied, ever-changing, and eternal. Fighting them is like fighting a many-headed monster, which, each time a neck is severed, sprouts a head even fiercer and cleverer than before. You are fighting that which is unfixed, mutating, indestructible." (*HP/HBP*, 177-8)

This is the opposite approach from Snape's tactic with the Death Eaters. To them, he continually underplays Harry's talents or Dumbledore's potency, leading them to a sense of false superiority. But he is warning his students not to underestimate Dark wizards. Rote tricks will not defeat them. To fight them, one must understand how they think. It will not work to try to eradicate them and be done.

> "Your defenses," said Snape, a little louder, "must therefore be as flexible and inventive as the arts you seek to undo." (*HP/HBP*, 178)

Undo. That is a clue to Snape's approach to the Dark Arts. Those who know how damage was done, plus have the extra push that comes of wanting to combat evil instead of being tempted by it, can reverse Dark Magic. Not everyone can take this approach, especially if they have not done many Dark things themselves. But this is Snape's way, and we know he is better at reversing Dark Magic than anyone else at Hogwarts.

> "What is the advantage of a nonverbal spell?"
>
> Hermione's hand shot into the air. Snape took his time looking around at everybody else, making sure he had no choice, before saying curtly, "Very well—Miss Granger?"
>
> "Your adversary has no warning about what kind of magic you're about to perform," said Hermione, "which gives you a split-second advantage."
>
> "An answer copied almost word for word from *The Standard Book of Spells, Grade Six*," said Snape dismissively (over in the corner, Malfoy sniggered), "but correct in essentials. Yes, those who progress to using magic without shouting incantations gain an element of surprise in their spell-casting." (*HP/HBP*, 178-9)

"Shouting incantations"—this is reminiscent of an earlier putdown from Snape, the lament that many students are unimpressed by Potions because that discipline involves "little foolish wand-waving." (*HP/SS*, 137) Once again, Snape reveals, in his insulting way, that he values self-sufficiency in magic, power generated from the person's inner resources alone without depending on anything external that could give the person away.

Snape sets the class to practicing nonverbal spells.

> Typically, ten minutes into the lesson Hermione managed to repel Neville's muttered Jelly-Legs Jinx without uttering a single word,

a feat that would surely have earned her twenty points for Gryffindor from any reasonable teacher, thought Harry bitterly, but which Snape ignored. (*HP/HBP*, 179)

Why is Snape ignoring Hermione this time?

We don't know what kind of answer Snape was hoping for, but it was not the textbook answer that Hermione gave, which focused on only one limited area and closed down further discussion. But we can see how her reply could put him in no mood to acknowledge her. She's going about this in completely the wrong way. A split-second advantage is not always going to be enough to protect her in the coming war. If she had thought this one through from experience, she could have recognized the greater potential of nonverbal spells and understood why this was Snape's very first lesson in his long-desired Defense class.

Miss Granger, you should know this one

What is the advantage of a nonverbal spell?

- If you're lying on the floor of the Hogwarts Express covered in blood, you can Summon your wand without moving your mouth.
- If you're a Death Eater and a Muggle-born Silences you in the Department of Mysteries (*HP/OotP*, 792), you can still use a Dark curse on her that takes ten different potions to cure. (*HP/OotP*, 847) By the way, thank you for those, Professor Snape.
- If the Minister of Magic and the High Inquisitor of Hogwarts are trying to terrorize a student into betraying an underground organization, you can modify the student's memory without them noticing. (*HP/OotP*, 621)
- If you're a house-elf—or any magical creature with no political power, *no voice*—you can still perform wondrous magic without words.
- If you're hiding from someone who wants to kill you, you can do magic without giving away your location.
- If you're trying to protect someone else, you can make yourself invisible and cast protective magic without giving yourself away.

In the few months before he makes most of them hate him, Snape is trying to teach the students how to stay powerful when they are voiceless or silenced. Hermione is a Muggle-born and the lead strategist in Harry's fight against Voldemort. She's going to need to know how to hide. To cast magic to protect herself, *and others*, without giving herself away. If she doesn't learn nonverbal magic, she's as good as dead.

The same goes for Harry's other best friend, who is having more trouble.

> Ron, who was supposed to be jinxing Harry, was purple in the face, his lips tightly compressed to save himself from the temptation of muttering the incantation. Harry had his wand raised, waiting on tenterhooks to repel a jinx that seemed unlikely ever to come.
>
> "Pathetic, Weasley," said Snape, after a while. "Here—let me show you—"
>
> He turned his wand on Harry so fast that Harry reacted instinctively; all thought of nonverbal spells forgotten, he yelled, *"Protego!"*
>
> His Shield Charm was so strong Snape was knocked off-balance and hit a desk. (*HP/HBP*, 179-80)

Oh, dear. Well, at least Harry's reflexes are in good order and his Shield Charm is strong.

Snape is genuinely trying to teach, but after their history together, it's no wonder that Harry is too jumpy to learn from him.

> "He tried to jinx me, in case you didn't notice!" fumed Harry. "I had enough of that during those Occlumency lessons! Why doesn't he use another guinea pig for a change? What's Dumbledore playing at, anyway, letting him teach Defense? Did you hear him talking about the Dark Arts? He loves them! All that *unfixed, indestructible* stuff—" (*HP/HBP*, 180)

It takes Hermione to point out that Snape is saying the same thing Harry always says: that Defense Against the Dark Arts is not "just memorizing a bunch of spells" but thinking quickly and trusting your gut. (*HP/HBP*, 181) Hermione has already learned from Snape's critique of her earlier answer. One benefit of Snape generally ignoring her is that unlike Harry, she's not too jumpy to learn from him. Hermione quickly becomes proficient in nonverbal magic.

Snape's curriculum is the opposite of Umbridge's. He wants the students to be able to defend themselves against likely dangers, such as the Imperius Curse, Inferi, the Cruciatus Curse, and dementors. (*HP/HBP*, 459-61) Harry expects a low mark on one essay "because he had disagreed with Snape on the best way to tackle dementors." (*HP/HBP*, 448)

Presumably, Harry argues in favor of the Patronus method. It is effective, though difficult, and it can protect others who can't defend themselves. The only other method we have seen so far, in the series, is the Animagus escape that Sirius pulled off, but that is too difficult to be a good option. We never learn how Snape disagrees with Harry, but we can guess based on what we know of him. He might well argue that there is no *best* way, that it depends upon the situation. Perhaps, since dementors feed on happy thoughts, it is possible to evade them through Occlumency. Harry might well object that such an approach doesn't repel dementors or protect others; it might even strike him as selfish or cowardly. But unlike Harry, Snape knows that sometimes the way to help others the most is to stay unseen. Patronuses give away too much. They betray your location, your identity, and your heart. In war, sometimes it is necessary to keep those things hidden.

The Half-Blood Prince: Potions

Harry and Ron arrive at Professor Slughorn's Potions classroom without books, since they had not expected to study sixth-year Potions with Snape. Slughorn forages in a cupboard until he finds "two very battered-looking copies of *Advanced Potion-Making* by Libatius Borage." (*HP/HBP*, 184)

In Snape's Potions classroom, as we have seen, Snape used to put directions on the board himself rather than having the students brew from the textbook. Slughorn, however, requires his students to use the textbook. Harry finds that the previous owner of his used book had amended the textbook so heavily "that the margins were as black as the printed portions." (*HP/HBP*, 189) The previous owner's absorption in the subject was equal to the textbook author's. He tries out the amended directions and finds that they always yield much better results than the textbook; the previous owner was already advancing the field as a student.

Harry's stellar work wins him Slughorn's prize of Felix Felicis, a potion guaranteeing good luck, which Draco wanted desperately to win. A delighted Slughorn attributes Harry's success to heredity: "Good lord, it's clear you've inherited your mother's talent. She was a dab hand at Potions, Lily was!" (*HP/HBP*, 191) This is the first time Harry has learned any details about his mother's life as a student, apart from the glimpse in Snape's Pensieve memory. It immediately raises unanswered questions about how Lily's skills compared with Snape's. They would both have been top students in the same year for Potions, in direct competition.

The longer Harry follows the previous owner's instructions, the more Slughorn fawns on him. Harry knows he is an impostor, earning credit he doesn't deserve, but Slughorn makes it difficult for him to come clean about the source of his success.

Meanwhile, for the first time in her Potions studies, Hermione's results are weaker than Harry's, even though she's following the textbook perfectly. This puts her in a miserable temper. She's envious, but worse than that, in Hermione's worldview, Harry isn't learning. He's following better instructions without understanding the theory and wouldn't be able to transfer the concepts on his own to other potions.

Ginny, too, is incredulous that Harry would take instructions from a mysterious book after his experience with Tom Riddle's diary. Hermione casts a revealing spell on the book that confirms that it is nothing more than an old textbook containing student notes. The only identifier is the inscription "This Book is the Property of the Half-Blood Prince," written in the same "small, cramped handwriting" as the rest of the notes. (*HP/HBP*, 193)

From that moment until the day of Dumbledore's death, Harry is intrigued by the Half-Blood Prince without suspecting that it was Snape. Could Harry and teen Snape have been friends? He certainly admires the Prince's mind. Copying off the Prince's work brings even better results in Potions than copying Hermione, whose strengths in Potions seem to be theory and procedure, not experimentation.

Hermione is delighted when Slughorn challenges the students to invent a difficult antidote in class: "'It's a shame that the Prince won't be able to help you much with this, Harry,' she said brightly as she straightened up. 'You have to understand the principles involved this time. No shortcuts or cheats!'" (*HP/HBP*, 375)

In desperation, Harry searches the Half-Blood Prince's notes for something, anything, that might prevent him from being revealed as a fraud.

And there it was, scrawled right across a long list of antidotes:

> *Just shove a bezoar down their throats.*
>
> Harry stared at these words for a moment. Hadn't he once, long ago, heard of bezoars? Hadn't Snape mentioned them in their first-ever Potions lesson? *"A stone taken from the stomach of a goat, which will protect from most poisons."*
>
> It was not an answer to the Golpalott problem, and had Snape still been their teacher, Harry would not have dared do it, but this was a moment for desperate measures. (*HP/HBP*, 377)

Just shove a bezoar down their throats. Even as a teen, Snape could infuse all his irritable genius into seven grumpy words, his aggrieved impatience with the stupidity of the world at large and the dunderheads in particular who managed to get themselves poisoned.

Bezoars. Harry vaguely recalls bezoars from that dreadful first Potions class, forgetting entirely that Snape spent a good portion of Harry's fourth year trying and failing to teach him about bezoars.

Harry takes the gamble and pretends to Slughorn that the bezoar was his idea all along, counting on the politics of favoritism to help him get away with it. Snape, like Hermione, would not have permitted "shortcuts or cheats"; we don't even see Draco try it. In Slughorn's class, though, being the teacher's pet is legal tender.

> Slughorn looked down at it for a full ten seconds. Harry wondered, for a moment, whether he was going to shout at him. Then he threw back his head and roared with laughter.
>
> "You've got nerve, boy!" he boomed, taking the bezoar and holding it up so that the class could see it. "Oh, you're like your mother. . . . Well, I can't fault you. . . . A bezoar would certainly act as an antidote to all these potions!" (*HP/HBP*, 378)

To Hermione's disgust, Harry's gamble is a wild success. Slughorn warns that because bezoars "don't work on everything, and are pretty rare, it's still worth knowing how to mix antidotes," then grants ten points to Gryffindor for "sheer cheek." (*HP/HBP*, 378)

And then later that year, Ron drinks poison and Harry is able to save his life.

> "Blimey, it was lucky you thought of a bezoar," said George in a low voice.

"Lucky there was one in the room," said Harry, who kept turning cold at the thought of what would have happened if he had not been able to lay hands on the little stone. (*HP/HBP*, 400)

Snape's hatefulness, from the moment Harry stepped into Potions class, prevented Harry from absorbing any of his expertise in the subject. Slughorn isn't reaching Harry, either. The Half-Blood Prince turns out to be Harry's best Potions teacher, after all. Harry is fortunate to have access to teen Snape's cleverness minus the hostility, although it's a pity for Hermione that once again, via proxy and a sort of time travel, Snape is paying attention to Harry and ignoring her. It's a pity, as well, that Voldemort and Dumbledore required Snape to pose as a teacher. This gifted misanthrope might have been happier in a career as a trailblazing inventor who didn't have to deal with *people* all day long.

The Half-Blood Prince: Invented Spells

As long as Harry sticks to the Half-Blood Prince's improvements to Libatius Borage's potions, he's on safe ground. But "there was barely a page on which the Prince had not made additional notes, not all of them concerned with potion-making." (*HP/HBP*, 194-5) Once Harry starts exploring spells the Prince invented himself, he gets into ambiguous territory.

> The more Harry pored over the book, the more he realized how much was in there, not only the handy hints and shortcuts on potions that were earning him such a glowing reputation with Slughorn, but also the imaginative little jinxes and hexes scribbled in the margins, which Harry was sure, judging by the crossings-out and revisions, that the Prince had invented himself. (*HP/HBP*, 238)

Imaginative. Few moments in Rowling's story sparkle with such admiration as Harry eagerly discovering the Prince's creativity. In all the series, the word "imaginative" occurs just this once, a high compliment to the mind of teen Snape.

Rowling deftly introduces a current of growing unease with the Prince's spells.

There had been a hex that caused toenails to grow alarmingly fast (he had tried this on Crabbe in the corridor, with very entertaining results); a jinx that glued the tongue to the roof of the mouth (which he had twice used, to general applause, on an unsuspecting Argus Filch). . . (*HP/HBP*, 238)

The toenail hex is amusing, no worse than the usual tentacles or jelly legs, and it was Crabbe, so who cares . . . right? Filch can be awful, but . . . should Harry have jinxed an unsuspecting Squib? In front of applauding students? Twice?

Harry finds an intriguing spell that the Prince developed painstakingly, judging by the many revisions:

Levicorpus (nvbl) (*HP/HBP*, 238)

He's had little success with nonverbal spells in Snape's class, but he tries his hand at this one, thinking that "the Prince had proved a much more effective teacher than Snape so far."

> Pointing his wand at nothing in particular, he gave it an upward flick and said *Levicorpus!* inside his head.
>
> "Aaaaaaaargh!"
>
> There was a flash of light and the room was full of voices: Everyone had woken up as Ron had let out a yell. Harry sent *Advanced Potion-Making* flying in panic; Ron was dangling upside down in midair as though an invisible hook had hoisted him up by the ankle.
>
> "Sorry!" yelled Harry, as Dean and Seamus roared with laughter, and Neville picked himself up from the floor, having fallen out of bed. "Hang on—I'll let you down—"
>
> He groped for the potion book and riffled through it in a panic, trying to find the right page; at last he located it and deciphered one cramped word underneath the spell: Praying that this was the counter-jinx, Harry thought *Liberacorpus!* with all his might.
>
> There was another flash of light, and Ron fell in a heap onto his mattress. (*HP/HBP*, 239)

Harry and Ron shout down Hermione when she suggests that Harry be more cautious with the Half-Blood Prince's spells. Harry doesn't stop using *Levicorpus*; we see him cast it as an instinctive reaction, "without conscious thought" (*HP/HBP*, 393), when Ron attacks him under influence of a love potion. Ron rationalizes *Levicorpus* as "just a laugh," but Harry remembers with excitement that his father used *Levicorpus* on Snape—and, with a sinking feeling, that Death Eaters used it on Muggles at the Quidditch World Cup.

He retorts to Hermione, though, that the Half-Blood Prince couldn't have been a budding Death Eater or he wouldn't have been "boasting" about being half-blood. (*HP/HBP*, 241) It doesn't occur to him that the Prince might have come from a background where clinging to his half-blood status was a way to keep up his hopes.

Harry checks hopefully with Lupin, but no, pureblood James was definitely not the Half-Blood Prince, even if he did use *Levicorpus*.

> "Oh, that one had a great vogue during my time at Hogwarts," said Lupin reminiscently. "There were a few months in my fifth year when you couldn't move for being hoisted into the air by your ankle." (*HP/HBP*, 336)

On Lupin's suggestion, Harry checks the date on the book: nearly fifty years old. That doesn't help Harry, but the reader can guess that the Half-Blood Prince might have been using a parent's old book. Certainly, if Snape perfected *Levicorpus* in time to use it before fifth-year O.W.L.s, he was mastering and revising the N.E.W.T.-level *Advanced Potion-Making* precociously, well before his sixth year.

By this point, the book's silence around the relationship between teen Snape and Lily is so conspicuous that it aches. If the annotations in *Advanced Potion-Making* chronicle Snape's fifth year, they are still speaking. They are both clearly stars at Potions. Did they work together? Was one of them more gifted than the other at Potions? We don't find out. We have already seen that James and Sirius were considered the best in their year without mention of how Snape compared, but how did Snape compare to Slughorn's favorite? We get an answer from a drunk Slughorn at his Christmas party.

> "But I don't think I've ever known such a natural at Potions!" said Slughorn, regarding Harry with a fond, if bloodshot, eye.
> "Instinctive, you know—like his mother! I've only ever taught a few with this kind of ability, I can tell you that, Sybill—why even Severus—"

> And to Harry's horror, Slughorn threw out an arm and seemed to scoop Snape out of thin air toward them. (*HP/HBP*, 319)

"Even" Severus. Slughorn had acknowledged Snape as the top student in his year, then, more gifted at Potions than the instinctive Lily Evans, although not a favorite, lacking the cheekiness necessary to elevate a student without social connections to that elite. That might actually have come as a relief to teen Snape.

> "Stop skulking and come and join us, Severus!" hiccuped Slughorn happily. "I was just talking about Harry's exceptional potion-making! Some credit must go to you, of course, you taught him for five years!"
>
> Trapped, with Slughorn's arm around his shoulders, Snape looked down his hooked nose at Harry, his black eyes narrowed.
>
> "Funny, I never had the impression that I managed to teach Potter anything at all." (*HP/HBP*, 319)

It's true enough that Harry has learned best from Snape when the lessons have been refracted through a third party. Lockhart took credit for the club that taught Harry *Expelliarmus*. The Half-Blood Prince has finally taught him about bezoars. It's rather like surviving the basilisk's glare through a camera lens or mirror. It's always been fraught when these two look at each other, especially after the eye contact of the Occlumency lessons.

> "Well, then, it's natural ability!" shouted Slughorn. "You should have seen what he gave me, first lesson, Draught of Living Death—never had a student produce finer on a first attempt, I don't think even you, Severus—"
>
> "Really?" said Snape quietly, his eyes still boring into Harry, who felt a certain disquiet. The last thing he wanted was for Snape to start investigating the source of his newfound brilliance at Potions. (*HP/HBP*, 319)

Readers are divided on whether Snape arranged to have his old Potions book fall into Harry's hands or whether it was coincidence. Snape's use of Legilimency here suggests coincidence: that he did not know Harry had the book, but now he suspects.

Of course, Harry does better at Potions when Snape isn't around, as he found during the previous year's O.W.L. practical exam.

> With Snape absent from the proceedings he found that he was much more relaxed than he usually was while making potions. . . Harry corked his sample flask feeling that he might not have achieved a good grade but that he had, with luck, avoided a fail. (*HP/OotP*, 716)

Harry does get a good grade—"Exceeds Expectations"—but Snape knows Harry's aptitude for potions is not the kind that would suddenly take him to the top of the class once free of a mean teacher. In Defense Against the Dark Arts, he knows Harry does have that kind of gift. He saw 13-year-old Harry produce a Patronus more powerful than most adults could; he's been on the receiving end of Stinging Hexes and Legilimency from Harry during Occlumency lessons; he's just been knocked off balance by Harry's Shield Charm. In contrast, Harry is not the kind of potioneer who could use the Libatius Borage textbook and beat Snape's first classroom attempt, including his careful innovations, at the Draught of Living Death. Something's not adding up.

Protecting Draco

Snape's investigations into Harry's potions success are interrupted when Filch catches Draco lurking in a corridor and drags him into the party by the ear. Draco tells the embarrassing lie that he was hoping to gate-crash the party. Harry notes that Draco looks ill, with "dark shadows under his eyes and a distinctly grayish tinge to his skin," and Snape is looking at him "as though both angry and . . . was it possible? . . . a little afraid?" (*HP/HBP*, 321)

Snape takes Draco for a private word and an eavesdropping Harry learns that Snape, too, believes Draco is behind the near death of Katie Bell. But Draco, unlike Harry, is able to Occlude Snape from confirming his suspicions.

> "—[D]on't look at me like that! I know what you're doing, I'm not stupid, but it won't work—I can stop you!"
>
> There was a pause and then Snape said quietly, "Ah . . . Aunt Bellatrix has been teaching you Occlumency, I see. What thoughts are you trying to conceal from your master, Draco?"

"I'm not trying to conceal anything from *him*, I just don't want *you* butting in!" (*HP/HBP*, 322)

Unlike Harry, who studied Occlumency unwillingly, Draco is an effective Occlumens: he has thoughts he wants to protect. Snape must recognize some telltale detail in Draco's Occlumency technique that identifies his teacher. Even if Bellatrix couldn't refute Snape's arguments in Spinner's End, she doesn't trust Snape at all. Bellatrix is a dangerous opponent in the fight for Draco's future. She doesn't have a son to offer to Voldemort's service, so she's offering Narcissa's.

Snape reveals the extent to which he is worried for Draco.

> "Listen to me," said Snape, his voice so low now that Harry had to push his ear very hard against the keyhole to hear. "I am trying to help you. I swore to your mother I would protect you. I made the Unbreakable Vow, Draco—" (*HP/HBP*, 323)

Perhaps it will eventually sink in for Draco that a teacher thinks he matters enough to be worth dying for. It's the highest form of life debt: *I would die for you and your loved ones.*

When Draco rejects Snape's protection, Snape tries to provide some practical advice, at least. He warns that it was foolish to wander alone, without backup.

> "I would've had Crabbe and Goyle with me if you hadn't put them in detention!"
>
> "Keep your voice down!" spat Snape, for Malfoy's voice had risen excitedly. "If your friends Crabbe and Goyle intend to pass their Defense Against the Dark Arts O.W.L. this time around, they will need to work a little harder than they are doing at pres—" (*HP/HBP*, 323-4)

On top of everything else, Snape has been giving Crabbe and Goyle detention. It is one thing for Snape to look out for clever Draco Malfoy, with his "Outstanding" in Potions and his prefect-worthy grades. But Crabbe and Goyle have always struggled academically and now, destabilized by the risks to their fathers, they're unlikely to absorb even the most basic Defense Against the Dark Arts. They're being groomed for Voldemort, but Snape can't give up on them. They're his students.

This was foreshadowed before the start of term, when Harry,

awaiting his O.W.L. results, wondered, "What happens if we fail?" and Hermione replied, "We discuss our options with our Head of House, I asked Professor McGonagall at the end of last term." (*HP/HBP*, 100-1)

Professor McGonagall has been Snape's ally in trying to protect the at-risk students from themselves this year. If they have to give multiple detentions to keep the students out of trouble, that's what the two of them will do. She's been giving Draco detention and keeping her eye on him. (*HP/HBP*, 255) When Snape punishes Harry's *Sectumsempra* with detention that keeps him out of Quidditch matches, McGonagall approves "wholeheartedly." (*HP/HBP*, 529) McGonagall has always disciplined students from her own House as severely as others, but now Snape is doing the same.

When McGonagall barks at Draco to pay attention during Apparition class instead of arguing with Crabbe, Snape looks annoyed, "though Harry strongly suspected that this was less because of Malfoy's rudeness than the fact that McGonagall had reprimanded one of his House." (*HP/HBP*, 382) Given Snape's anxiety for Draco this year, though, it's more likely that he wanted Draco to focus on learning the survival skills that he will need no matter what side he chooses.

> "What does it matter?" said Malfoy. "Defense Against the Dark Arts—it's all just a joke, isn't it, an act? Like any of us need protecting against the Dark Arts—"
>
> "It is an act that is crucial to success, Draco!" said Snape. "Where do you think I would have been all these years, if I had not known how to act?" (*HP/HBP*, 324)

Draco's naïveté is frightening. He seems to believe that the Dark Mark will confer invincibility on him if he can just get into Voldemort's favor, and it would only alienate Draco for Snape to try to disillusion him at the moment. Snape's comment about acting is one of his basic tenets for survival, something he wants all his students to learn, but that's not his primary reason for saying this to Draco now. He just wants to say things that have a chance of reaching Draco without engaging the fight that Draco is spoiling to start. If Draco is in love with his self-image as Voldemort's rising star, Snape can at least be a useful role model for how to protect the self while undercover.

Snape wants his students to learn non-aggression. They don't need to understand. They can just learn it by rote so that maybe, when they're in crisis and acting on instinct, defensive magic will be among the spells they'll cast "without conscious thought," as Harry has begun to cast *Levicorpus*.

This is how Snape uses his teaching position as Defense Against the Dark Arts Master. The things that young people let slip under duress may not even be things they believe. They may simply be repeating things they learned in childhood before they were mature enough to understand and choose wisely. But words—and spells are words, words that sometimes have effects that the caster didn't intend—can cause the same damage whether or not they're spoken in full knowledge. Some damage can never be undone and the regret will not ease, even if the words were spoken *in innocence*. Draco is almost of age, but as Narcissa said, he is too young to understand what Voldemort will do to him—too innocent. Snape, a teacher, has the opportunity to ingrain automatic defenses in Draco while he is still innocent and not fully able to choose his own path wisely.

Should a near-adult teen be mature enough to understand the consequences of their evil deeds? Perhaps, but the practical truth is that many are not. Nor are many adults, but they don't have the benefit of teachers to train them in defensive magic. Should teens be held fully responsible for the consequences of their evil deeds? Whether they should or not, some consequences are not negotiable; they will pay.

One way or another, Snape did not realize that calling Lily "Mudblood" would lead to the loss of her friendship and, later, her life. It may seem absurd that anyone would not *realize* such an obvious thing; it may seem like making excuses for that person. But considering Draco's situation, there is no question: the stakes are too high to argue about excuses. Every attempt must be made to reach him, to save him, before he kills innocent others in a hopeless quest for an illusory guarantee of safety.

It is not a matter of whether a young Death Eater is good enough to deserve the effort or whether they should simply be discarded as hopeless causes. It is a matter of preventing as much damage as possible and protecting people so they can *become* mature and deserving, as anyone can.

Adult Snape is the opposite of innocent. His guilt and subsequent remorse make him *experienced*, able to understand the danger that Draco is in, already pledged to Voldemort, able to keep working with Draco and not be repelled by the knowledge that Draco will never be free of the Dark Mark. He's the only adult at Hogwarts with a Dark Mark, the only one who can travel with Draco across that dividing line and back and have a chance of still protecting him. He has done Dark Magic and lived to regret it.

This is what makes him the staff expert on Dark Magic. He knows how it feels to cast it, to mean it, to want to cause harm, and then to wish with all his being that he could undo the damage, to wish he could give his life if it would turn back time so he could change the past. Only someone who has felt both what it takes to cast Dark Magic successfully *and* the greater urge to reverse it can undo Dark Magic. This is why Professor McGonagall specifically tells the students to take cursed objects to Snape (*HP/HBP*, 252) and what Dumbledore means when he explains, "Professor Snape knows much more about the Dark Arts than Madam Pomfrey, Harry." (*HP/HBP*, 259)

Snape's rare power to undo Dark curses is one of the reasons Dumbledore trusts him so completely. The remorse necessary to effect such powerful magic cannot be faked. Snape could not have saved Dumbledore's life if he had not wished it with all his being, as Dumbledore describes it:

> "The ring, Harry. Marvolo's ring. And a terrible curse there was upon it too. Had it not been—forgive me the lack of seemly modesty—for my own prodigious skill, and for Professor Snape's timely action when I returned to Hogwarts, desperately injured, I might not have lived to tell the tale." (*HP/HBP*, 503)

Dumbledore sets Snape to watch over Draco out of respect for Snape but also because of his own regrets and guilt. Dumbledore failed to reach student Tom Riddle before he became irrevocably evil:

> "Did I know that I had just met the most dangerous Dark wizard of all time?" said Dumbledore. "No, I had no idea that he was to grow up to be what he is. However, I was certainly intrigued by him. I returned to Hogwarts intending to keep an eye upon him, something I should have done in any case, given that he was alone and friendless, but which, already, I felt I ought to do for others' sake as much as his." (*HP/HBP*, 276)

Dumbledore is concerned for the safety of others around Draco, too, this year. But he learned from Tom Riddle that some students are too isolated to respond to adults who can't understand them. Dumbledore couldn't have reached Tom Riddle; the one with the power to reach him had not been born yet. Dumbledore can't reach Draco, nor is it safe to try when Voldemort is regularly invading Draco's mind. But Snape has been a Death Eater; Snape may be able to reach him.

There is another layer of regret and guilt to Dumbledore's order. He failed Snape, as the two of them recalled in their arguments after the escape of Sirius Black. Snape, who entered Hogwarts as a first-year knowing more curses than most seventh-years, could have used someone to keep an eye on him. Though not as far gone as first-year Tom Riddle, he had tendencies similar to Dumbledore's description of Tom: "His powers, as you heard, were surprisingly well-developed for such a young wizard and—most interestingly and ominously of all—he had already discovered that he had some measure of control over them, and begun to use them consciously." (*HP/HBP*, 276)

It is no wonder that Snape is feeling the strain of being the *only* one who can help Draco, the *only* one who can fight some forms of Dark Magic, the *only* one who can retain Voldemort's trust while taking his place at Dumbledore's right hand. In some ways, it's a bit similar to being the Chosen One, although Harry gets credit for his sacrifices and the blessing of a clean conscience. Snape's job depends upon his guilty past and upon the secrecy that ensures his sacrifices will never be seen.

Hagrid lets slip to Harry that Snape has argued with Dumbledore.

> "Well—I jus' heard Snape sayin' Dumbledore took too much fer granted an' maybe he—Snape—didn' wan' ter do it anymore—"
>
> "Do what?"
>
> "I dunno, Harry, it sounded like Snape was feelin' a bit overworked, tha's all—anyway, Dumbledore told him flat out he'd agreed ter do it an' that was all there was to it. Pretty firm with him. An' then he said summat abou' Snape makin' investigations in his House, in Slytherin." (*HP/HBP*, 405-6)

Hagrid tries to tell Harry not to read too much into the argument, for all the good that does. But Hagrid does get across that he trusts Snape. Snape has never given him reason not to.

Sectumsempra

Harry continues to track Draco Malfoy and finds him weeping in Moaning Myrtle's bathroom. Draco looks into a mirror and sees Harry over his shoulder. The ensuing battle is exactly what Snape has been dreading all year. Harry tries *Levicorpus*, but Draco blocks it and tries to cast the Cruciatus Curse on Harry—an Unforgivable that is probably on his mind after seeing other Death Eaters use it. Harry retaliates with *Sectumsempra*, a curse that the Half-Blood Prince had marked "For enemies," which Harry has never tested.

Sectumsempra, it turns out, is a vicious curse that cuts flesh with Dark Magic.

> Blood spurted from Malfoy's face and chest as though he had been slashed with an invisible sword. He staggered backward and collapsed onto the waterlogged floor with a great splash, his wand falling from his limp right hand.
>
> "No—" gasped Harry.
>
> Slipping and staggering, Harry got to his feet and plunged toward Malfoy, whose face was now shining scarlet, his white hands scrabbling at his blood-soaked chest.
>
> "No—I didn't—"
>
> Harry did not know what he was saying; he fell to his knees beside Malfoy, who was shaking uncontrollably in a pool of his own blood. Moaning Myrtle let out a deafening scream: "MURDER! MURDER IN THE BATHROOM! MURDER!" (*HP/HBP*, 522-3)

Harry's shock is instant, his remorse complete. He didn't mean to hurt Draco this way. *Not even my enemy deserves this.* He hadn't known what he was doing. He just said the first thing that came to his mind, "without conscious thought," when he felt threatened.

> The door banged open behind Harry and he looked up, terrified: Snape had burst into the room, his face livid. Pushing Harry roughly aside, he knelt over Malfoy, drew his wand, and traced it over the deep wounds Harry's curse had made, muttering an incantation that sounded almost like song. The flow of blood seemed to ease; Snape wiped the residue from Malfoy's face and repeated his spell. Now the wounds seemed to be knitting. (*HP/HBP*, 523)

What is Snape chanting to heal Draco's wound? Harry can't understand the words yet. He's too innocent. He's never yet had to grieve the harm done to someone entrusted to his care. He hasn't yet felt that he failed to protect someone vulnerable or young, or that the harm stemmed from his own weakness.

The words to Snape's phoenix song might have gone something like this:

I am sorry I did this, so long ago. I am sorry I brought it into the world for others to use without knowing how it would hurt you. I am sorry you were so hurt by this. You didn't deserve this. I stopped doing this a long time ago, but as long as I live, I will track down all the damage I caused. If I could suffer this in your place, I would. Take my remorse. Let it re-integrate your wounds. I will sing to you until it stops. I was supposed to protect you. I will always protect you. Thank goodness it is not too late.

Few moments in the series are as starkly beautiful as the tableau of Snape singing shut Draco's *Sectumsempra* wounds, performing magic that nobody else in the world could cast, suffusing the song with all his grief and regret that his long-ago evil is still doing harm in the world, still hurting this child who has spent all year trying to kill people and yet doesn't deserve this because nobody deserves this. Draco has been pushing Snape away all year, descending deeper into horror, yet when he is in danger, Snape's protective response is absolute: *I came as soon as I could. You'll be all right. I've got you. I'm here.* This is a merciful gift to Snape, a second chance to make right the damage he caused.

> When Snape had performed his countercurse for the third time, he half-lifted Malfoy into a standing position.
>
> "You need the hospital wing. There may be a certain amount of scarring, but if you take dittany immediately we might avoid even that. . . . Come. . . ."
>
> He supported Malfoy across the bathroom, turning at the door to say in a voice of cold fury, "And you, Potter . . . You wait here for me."
>
> It did not occur to Harry for a second to disobey. He stood up slowly, shaking, and looked down at the wet floor. There were bloodstains floating like crimson flowers across its surface. (*HP/HBP*, 523)

Snape hasn't known a moment's peace since he heard that Draco broke Harry's nose on the Hogwarts Express, waiting for something like this to happen. But he probably didn't expect to be undoing a Dark curse from *Harry*. Snape, who can identify Draco's teacher from a moment of Occlumency, knows with heart-sinking certainty where Harry learned *Sectumsempra*.

We can excuse our younger selves. We can claim, "That was a long time ago." We can argue that no one got hurt in the end. We can push guilt to the backs of our minds or cupboards, flush cursed diaries down the toilet, or tamper with our memories. But once we release Dark Magic into the world, in the moments when we "really want to cause pain," it is beyond our control. (*HP/OotP*, 810)

Snape returns to deal with Harry. Harry tells him immediately that he didn't know what the spell would do, but that's not Snape's concern.

> "Apparently I underestimated you, Potter," he said quietly. "Who would have thought you knew such Dark Magic? Who taught you that spell?"
>
> "I—read about it somewhere."
>
> "Where?"
>
> "It was—a library book," Harry invented wildly. "I can't remember what it was call—"
>
> "Liar," said Snape. Harry's throat went dry. He knew what Snape was going to do and he had never been able to prevent it. . . .
>
> The bathroom seemed to shimmer before his eyes; he struggled to block out all thought, but try as he might, the Half-Blood Prince's copy of *Advanced Potion-Making* swam hazily to the forefront of his mind. (*HP/HBP*, 524)

Sectumsempra isn't in a library book. Snape knows Harry is telling the truth about reading it instead of learning from another person, since he didn't even know what the spell would do. As far as Snape knows, there's only one place that spell has ever been written down. Harry hides the book from Snape, but they both know he has it. The whole school hears what happened. With McGonagall's full support, Snape gives Harry detention every Saturday through the end of the year. His detentions keep Harry from Quidditch games and cut into his dates with Ginny, driving home the point: these are the kinds of joys he nearly forfeited. Had Snape not rescued Draco, Harry's life would be very different now. The penance he does with Snape ensures that he will never be able to deny to himself the seriousness of what almost happened. He is thoroughly sorry and then it is over, lesson learned, with gratitude for the close call. This is another version of the quick action that Snape took with Draco to prevent permanent damage, and it is merciful as well as angry.

Dumbledore and Snape: Endgame

All these years, Dumbledore has been careful not to tell Harry exactly who overheard Professor Trelawney's prophecy about the Dark Lord. Unfortunately, he couldn't secure the weakest spot: Trelawney herself. Harry pieces it together from Trelawney's drunk comments and enters the state of rage he always feels when people deliberately withhold information pertaining to his family, the only birthright he cares about. A powerful picture forms in Harry's mind: "Snape and Peter Pettigrew together had sent Voldemort hunting after Lily and James and their son. . . ." (*HP/HBP*, 545)

Harry confronts Dumbledore, who goes pale and considers what he can possibly tell Harry without jeopardizing the precarious endgame he and Snape have planned.

> "Professor Snape made a terrible mistake. He was still in Lord Voldemort's employ on the night he heard the first half of Professor Trelawney's prophecy. Naturally, he hastened to tell his master what he had heard, for it concerned his master most deeply. But he did not know—he had no possible way of knowing—which boy Voldemort would hunt from then onward, or that the parents he would destroy in his murderous quest were people that Professor Snape knew, that they were your mother and father—" (*HP/HBP*, 549)

Harry reviles the notion that Snape was sorry about his father's death. Dumbledore tries to let Harry know that there was more to the story, but there are too many secrets Dumbledore must keep. He cannot name names.

> "But *he's* a very good Occlumens, isn't he, sir?" said Harry, whose voice was shaking with the effort of keeping it steady. "And isn't Voldemort convinced that Snape's on his side, even now? Professor . . . how can you be *sure* Snape's on our side?"
>
> Dumbledore did not speak for a moment; he looked as though he was trying to make up his mind about something. At last he said, "I

am sure. I trust Severus Snape completely." (*HP/HBP*, 549)

Harry thinks Dumbledore is saying Snape felt the kind of regret that Harry has just escaped regarding Draco: the unintended death of an enemy. Certainly, if that is the extent of Snape's burden around Harry's parents' deaths, then combined with Snape's animosity toward Harry, there is room for doubt about Snape's true feelings. Dumbledore must think carefully about what he can tell Harry, and the reader does not yet know all the details. Telling Harry too much can put Snape at risk with Voldemort, who must not know that Snape's remorse is real. Finally, Dumbledore can only settle for the line he has taken all along about Snape's trustworthiness: Harry must take it on faith.

But when Dumbledore takes Harry on their evening mission to find one of Voldemort's Horcruxes, Harry *sees* some things about both Dumbledore and Snape that Dumbledore cannot risk saying directly.

Foreseeing trouble during Dumbledore's absence, Harry instructs Ron and Hermione to watch Draco and Snape and tells them to split his remaining Felix Felicis potion with Ginny. Felix Felicis helped Harry get the crucial information about Horcruxes from Slughorn; this evening, it will save the lives of his friends. This protection has come from the Half-Blood Prince, whose notes told Harry how to brew the potion that won Felix Felicis as a prize.

Dumbledore takes Harry to the cave where Voldemort hid part of his soul. Harry witnesses the potency of Dumbledore's magic.

> Dumbledore approached the wall of the cave and caressed it with his blackened fingertips, murmuring words in a strange tongue that Harry did not understand. Twice Dumbledore walked right around the cave, touching as much of the rough rock as he could, occasionally pausing, running his fingers backward and forward over a particular spot, until finally he stopped, his hand pressed flat against the wall.
>
> "Here," he said. "We go on through here. The entrance is concealed."
>
> Harry did not ask how Dumbledore knew. He had never seen a wizard work things out like this, simply by looking and touching; but Harry had long since learned that bangs and smoke were more often the marks of ineptitude than expertise. (*HP/HBP*, 558)

But Harry *has* seen this before. Snape sang together Draco's wounds with words Harry did not understand, using the part of himself that has known Dark Magic to detect Dark Magic. In these final hours before the fight against Voldemort passes from Dumbledore's leadership to Snape's, we see that Snape's magic and Dumbledore's are of a similar potent strain. Snape has succeeded in teaching Harry a few things: he has been trying since the first day of Potions class to impress upon his students a respect for quiet expertise.

Dumbledore summons an invisible boat to take Harry and him across the lake in the cave.

> "How did you know that was there?" Harry asked in astonishment.
>
> "Magic always leaves traces," said Dumbledore, as the boat hit the bank with a gentle bump, "sometimes very distinctive traces. I taught Tom Riddle. I know his style." (*HP/HBP*, 563)

This, too, Harry has seen from Snape. He detected traces of Bellatrix's magic in Draco's Occlumency. No wonder Dumbledore and Snape have been so cautious about what they share with anyone whose mind Voldemort is likely to scan. Had Dumbledore reached out directly to Draco this year, Voldemort would have known.

At the center of the lake, Dumbledore drinks a potion that puts him in flashback to his greatest regrets. Harry doesn't know it yet, but he's witnessing Dumbledore's anguish over causing the unintended death of a loved one, a child under his care. This is closer to what Dumbledore cannot tell Harry about what motivates Snape. When Dumbledore cries out "it's my fault, hurt me instead" (*HP/HBP*, 572), it's something that Snape would understand.

The potion incapacitates Dumbledore. Harry gets him back to Hogwarts and tries to go for Madam Pomfrey, but Dumbledore insists that it can only be Snape: "Tell him what has happened and bring him to me. Do nothing else, speak to nobody else, and do not remove your Cloak." (*HP/HBP*, 583) There must be plans that Dumbledore and Snape have shared with no one else, not even McGonagall or the rest of the Order.

But before the invisible Harry can run for Snape, Draco Malfoy bursts onto the scene and disarms Dumbledore with *Expelliarmus*. Dumbledore immobilizes Harry and talks to Draco, who cannot bring himself to kill Dumbledore.

Draco cast *Expelliarmus*. He could have, should have, attacked, but he disarmed, instead, and then attacked no further. The effort Snape has poured into this boy for the past six years has been worth it. He will not split his soul by killing. Covertly, against the efforts of Lucius, Bellatrix, and Voldemort, Snape has taught Draco non-aggression. He has fulfilled two of his three vows to Narcissa: he has watched over Draco and protected him from harm. Perhaps Draco's acute suffering and gratitude from his near-death due to *Sectumsempra* and the remorse that Snape poured into him to knit his wounds make it harder for Draco to truly want to cause such pain in another person, even an enemy.

When Dumbledore tells Draco that he ordered Snape to keep an eye on him, Draco retorts that Snape has been following a vow to Narcissa, not Dumbledore's orders. Is it possible that Dumbledore does not know about Snape's Unbreakable Vow? We don't know for sure, but it works either way.

Someday, perhaps, Draco will understand everything Snape has done for him. But until then, judging by what Draco says to Dumbledore, it's a good thing that Snape has long practice in receiving no recognition for his efforts:

> "He's been offering me plenty of help—wanting all the glory for himself—wanting a bit of the action—'What are you doing?' 'Did you do the necklace, that was stupid, it could have blown everything—' But I haven't told him what I've been doing in the Room of Requirement, he's going to wake up tomorrow and it'll all be over and he won't be the Dark Lord's favorite anymore, he'll be nothing compared to me, nothing!"
>
> "Very gratifying," said Dumbledore mildly. "We all like appreciation for our own hard work, of course." (*HP/HBP*, 588)

Dumbledore offers to send Draco and his parents into hiding. Draco lowers his wand, about to stop fighting, when Death Eaters arrive on the scene and urge Draco to kill Dumbledore.

> "Draco, do it or stand aside so one of us—" screeched the woman, but at that precise moment, the door to the ramparts burst open once more and there stood Snape, his wand clutched in his hand as his black eyes swept the scene, from Dumbledore slumped against the wall, to the four Death Eaters, including the enraged werewolf, and Malfoy.

"We've got a problem, Snape," said the lumpy Amycus, whose eyes and wand were fixed alike upon Dumbledore, "the boy doesn't seem able—"

But somebody else had spoken Snape's name, quite softly.

"Severus . . ." (*HP/HBP*, 595)

The moment has arrived. Snape's Time-Turner journey is complete. This is his second chance. He has been a double agent for years, working to protect Harry Potter. But if he kills Dumbledore—if he can kill his friend and mentor, the one living person who knows the full truth about the good self he's been hiding under his spy façades—if he can bring himself to break his last remaining mirror, committing to live the rest of his dangerous life being thought a murderer and traitor—then he will be upholding his vow to protect Draco in addition to Harry Potter. He will be able to save more than one innocent life.

> Snape said nothing, but walked forward and pushed Malfoy roughly out of the way. The three Death Eaters fell back without a word. Even the werewolf seemed cowed.
>
> Snape gazed for a moment at Dumbledore, and there was revulsion and hatred etched in the harsh lines of his face.
>
> "Severus . . . please . . ."
>
> Snape raised his wand and pointed it directly at Dumbledore.
>
> *"Avada Kedavra!"*
>
> A jet of green light shot from the end of Snape's wand and hit Dumbledore squarely in the chest. (*HP/HBP*, 595-6)

We are told repeatedly that the Killing Curse doesn't work unless you *mean* it. It has no counter-curse, but you need full power and intention to kill with it. Barty Crouch, Jr. tells a class of fourth-years that they could all cast *Avada Kedavra* on him together and he probably wouldn't get so much as a nosebleed. (*HP/GoF*, 217) Slughorn tells Tom Riddle that murder is the supreme act of evil: "Killing rips the soul apart." (*HP/HBP*, 498)

When *Harry Potter and the Half-Blood Prince* was first published, before the series concluded, some read this scene and concluded that Snape had been Voldemort's man all along. Some concluded the opposite. But whatever Snape was thinking—whether his "revulsion and hatred" were for the act or for Dumbledore himself—by casting the Killing Curse successfully, he has just ripped apart his soul.

All of Snape's actions that follow show him behaving protectively.

The first thing he does after Dumbledore dies is seize Draco "by the scruff of the neck," like a puppy, and rush him out of the castle. (HP/HBP, 597) He calls for the other Death Eaters to stop fighting, as well, and come with them. Harry hears "the hated voice shout, *It's over, time to go!*" (HP/HBP, 598) With that *Avada Kedavra*, Snape has killed all of Harry's sentiments toward him except hatred.

Harry chases Snape to the gates of Hogwarts, trying to Stun him. Snape yells at Draco to Disapparate, then turns to face Harry. Snape blocks Harry's attempt at the Cruciatus Curse so hard that he knocks Harry backward off his feet. A Death Eater sets Hagrid's hut on fire with Fang trapped inside. Snape blocks a second attempt at Cruciatus with a sneer.

> "No Unforgivable Curses from you, Potter!" he shouted over the rushing of the flames, Hagrid's yells, and the wild yelping of the trapped Fang. "You haven't got the nerve or the ability—"
> (HP/HBP, 602)

This is how Snape has always talked to Harry, teaching him non-aggression accompanied by insults and loathing. Snape has just cast an Unforgivable Curse and knows how bitterly it cost him. Harry wouldn't be able to do it based on vengeance alone; it took Snape greater emotions than that to pull it off, and it ripped his soul apart. Everyone deserves, if at all possible, to remain too innocent to cast an Unforgivable.

Snape refuses to attack Harry. All he does is block, expending almost no effort. At this moment, Snape is fueled by grief for the friend he just killed and protectiveness toward Draco. This makes him vastly more powerful than Harry, who is fueled by vengefulness. Harry calls him a coward for not fighting back, which is absurd when Snape so clearly overpowers him.

> "Coward, did you call me, Potter?" shouted Snape. "Your father would never attack me unless it was four on one, what would you call him, I wonder?"
>
> "*Stupe—*"

"Blocked again and again and again until you learn to keep your mouth shut and your mind closed, Potter!" sneered Snape, deflecting the curse once more. "Now *come*!" he shouted at the huge Death Eater behind Harry. "It is time to be gone, before the Ministry turns up—" (*HP/HBP*, 603)

Even on the run, Snape takes care of the Order. He gives Harry one last lesson on dueling. He thinks of a good excuse to call off the Death Eater attacking Hagrid's house.

"*Impedi—*"

But before he could finish this jinx, excruciating pain hit Harry; he keeled over in the grass. Someone was screaming, he would surely die of this agony, Snape was going to torture him to death or madness—

"No!" roared Snape's voice and the pain stopped as suddenly as it had started; Harry lay curled on the dark grass, clutching his wand and panting; somewhere overhead Snape was shouting, "Have you forgotten our orders? Potter belongs to the Dark Lord—we are to leave him! Go! Go!" (*HP/HBP*, 603)

A Cruciatus Curse hits Harry. He thinks it's from Snape, but Snape calls off whoever cast it and gets them away before they can do further damage. Harry tries to attack Snape with *Sectumsempra* and *Levicorpus*. Snape blocks him again and comes to stand over him, his face "suffused with hatred."

"You dare use my own spells against me, Potter? It was I who invented them—I, the Half-Blood Prince! And you'd turn my inventions on me, like your filthy father, would you? I don't think so . . . *no!*"

Harry had dived for his wand; Snape shot a hex at it and it flew feet away into the darkness and out of sight. (*HP/HBP*, 604)

Harry is disarmed. What is Snape going to do to him?

"Kill me then," panted Harry, who felt no fear at all, but only rage and contempt. "Kill me like you killed him, you coward—"

> "DON'T—" screamed Snape, and his face was suddenly demented, inhuman, as though he was in as much pain as the yelping, howling dog stuck in the burning house behind them—"CALL ME COWARD!" (*HP/HBP*, 604)

Many people read this line from Snape as rage at being called a coward: perhaps he was taunted as a coward by bullies too many times. Perhaps after making the brave choice to kill his dying friend and accept a life of being vilified, it's unbearable to be taunted so wrongly. Perhaps this sentence is primarily about the mortal panic of feeling trapped in a world that's going up in flames, as unable to articulate his pain as a beast (Justice). Certainly, Snape must be feeling all of these torturous things. But the long pause within the sentence suggests another reading as well.

Harry has just accused him of killing James. Until now, Snape didn't know that Harry learned who overheard Trelawney's prophecy. Harry had only found out earlier that evening, before the cave, before the Inferi, before the Killing Curse. Snape and Dumbledore have hidden this from Harry for years, and Harry has just informed Snape that he now knows.

Harry did not say "James." He said "Kill me like you killed him." They were speaking of James, but "him" could also mean killing Dumbledore, the act that is tearing apart Snape's soul, the act that turned him from being the traitor *responsible* for James and Lily's deaths into an actual killer. Snape's guilt over the deaths of Lily and James has distorted his perceptions of Harry every day for the past six years, and now, minutes after killing Dumbledore, Harry's words slam him with a renewed realization of the enormity of that guilt.

"DON'T—" he screams. But what can he say? Don't *what?* Don't call him a murderer? He will never again be able to deflect that guilt. From now on, he *is* a murderer, has chosen to be one in order to protect others, and the life that lies ahead of him will require more courage than anything he has yet imagined.

Snape's pain, the demented screaming, isn't primarily about Snape hating to be called a coward. It's his pain at causing the death of James: like Harry when he saw what *Sectumsempra* did to Draco, Snape had never thought that James deserved to *die.* It's his pain at causing the death of innocent Lily, who had defended him when no one else had, and his guilt at having to look at James and Lily's orphaned child for six years. It's the same pain that reduced Slughorn to begging Harry to stop talking to him about how Lily died. It's Dumbledore screaming in his potion-induced flashback about the wrong he's done, no more able to escape the anguish in his mind than Fang is able to escape a burning house. Snape and Dumbledore have killed and died in order to protect Draco and Harry from ever experiencing these pains.

In his defensive shame, for the only time this evening, Snape lashes out magically at Harry.

> And he slashed at the air: Harry felt a white-hot, whiplike
> something hit him across the face and was slammed backward into
> the ground. Spots of light burst in front of his eyes and for a
> moment all the breath seemed to have gone from his body, then he
> heard a rush of wings above him and something enormous
> obscured the stars. Buckbeak had flown at Snape, who staggered
> backward as the razor-sharp claws slashed at him. (*HP/HBP*, 604)

Even this proud magical beast cuts at Snape's flesh with his claws for lashing out, finally pushed beyond his limits after this night of superhuman restraint and protectiveness toward everybody except himself. The only person who could have appreciated Snape's self-control on this night is now dead. There is no time yet to grieve; Snape must bring Draco back to his mother, intercede on Draco's behalf when Voldemort punishes him for failing to kill Dumbledore, and accept Voldemort's congratulations for doing the deed himself. His difficulties have just begun.

With his *Avada Kedavra*, Snape kills not only his dying headmaster but, more painfully, the thriving trust he's built with his colleagues, especially McGonagall.

Hagrid's first, disbelieving response is the accurate one: "What musta happened was, Dumbledore musta told Snape ter go with them Death Eaters," Hagrid said confidently. "I suppose he's gotta keep his cover." (*HP/HBP*, 607)

McGonagall recalls Dumbledore's certainty that Snape's repentance was genuine. She blames herself for sending Flitwick for Snape's help, even though she had every reason to believe Snape would be as steadfast as he had been for the past 15 years as her colleague.

> "I'd love to know what Snape told him to convince him," said
> Tonks.
>
> "I know," said Harry, and they all turned to look at him. "Snape

passed Voldemort the information that made Voldemort hunt down my mum and dad. Then Snape told Dumbledore he hadn't realized what he was doing, he was really sorry he'd done it, sorry that they were dead." (*HP/HBP*, 616)

In all the turmoil, Harry doesn't recall that in fact, Dumbledore never divulged how Snape convinced him. He repeats only as much as Dumbledore did tell him, newly sensitized to the model of remorse that he has come to understand after Draco's close call with *Sectumsempra*: regret at the unintended death of an enemy.

Hermione, who has always tended to be sympathetic to Snape, is blaming herself as well. At Harry's instruction, she and Luna were standing guard outside Snape's office when Flitwick came to request Snape's help.

> "And then we heard a loud thump and Snape came hurtling out of his room and he saw us and—and—"
>
> "What?" Harry urged her.
>
> "I was so stupid, Harry!" said Hermione in a high-pitched whisper. "He said Professor Flitwick had collapsed and that we should go and take care of him while he—while he went to help fight the Death Eaters—" (*HP/HBP*, 619)

Tonks recalls that when Snape led Draco away, she and Lupin assumed the two of them were not with the Death Eaters: "'We just let them pass,' said Tonks in a hollow voice." (*HP/HBP*, 621)

The self-trust in Snape's former allies is one of the saddest casualties of Snape's Killing Curse. After this, they question themselves. They had been so *sure*. They had built up affection and a history of successful collaboration. Of course they trusted Snape. He was meticulous about retaining their trust until the last possible moment so he could depend upon it to protect students: Hermione and Luna in Flitwick's office, safe passage for Draco.

When Snape spoke to Hermione and Luna outside his office, they believed him because he must have communicated with them in absolute sincerity: that would have been the only safe strategy with this particular pair of students, one of whom has always understood him too well for comfort and the other who sees through disguises as though they aren't there. Lupin and Tonks must have seen the solicitude with which Snape ushered Draco away from the battle. That protective sentiment would have been unmistakable. Their confusion now is reminiscent of the public attitude toward Sirius Black when he was sent to Azkaban. Either they were right to trust him before, or—and this seems as though it must be the case, because Snape killed Dumbledore—they actually were wrong all along, and none of them had ever really known Severus Snape.

The Name of the Half-Blood Prince

What does it mean that the Half-Blood Prince, imaginative potioneer and dodgy inventor, turns out to have been another name for teen Snape?

All year long, Hermione has insisted angrily that the Half-Blood Prince might have been a girl, impervious to Harry's argument that the term "Prince" ruled it out. But Hermione is on to something, too, and she's the one whose research reveals the whole picture.

> "Right!" said Hermione, red patches blazing in her cheeks as she pulled a very old piece of newsprint out of her pocket and slammed it down on the table in front of Harry. "Look at that! Look at the picture!"
>
> Harry picked up the crumbling piece of paper and stared at the moving photograph, yellowed with age; Ron leaned over for a look too. The picture showed a skinny girl of around fifteen. She was not pretty; she looked simultaneously cross and sullen, with heavy brows and a long, pallid face. Underneath the photograph was the caption: EILEEN PRINCE, CAPTAIN OF THE HOGWARTS GOBSTONES TEAM. (*HP/HBP*, 537)

The photo is from the same time period as the textbook, but Harry doesn't believe this girl has anything to do with the Half-Blood Prince.

> "The truth is that you don't think a girl would have been clever enough," said Hermione angrily.
>
> "How can I have hung round with you for five years and not think girls are clever?" said Harry, stung by this. (*HP/HBP*, 538)

Hermione's accusation of sexism is skewed by her envy of the Half-Blood Prince's cleverness, but she's pointed in the right direction. Researching only the patronymic line misses half the story. It's not always about the name of the father. Unlike Muggle Britain, what we see of wizarding Britain in these seven books indicates that *all* wives take their husbands' surnames (and all the marriages we see are between a woman and a man). The mother's name can be obscured within a generation, as we see with Merope Gaunt, who named her son after her father and her husband, eliding her own identity as completely as she could. Yet the key to understanding Voldemort in this volume has been his mother's story. The mother's name and story are key to understanding Snape. The author is using loud silence to tell the reader that the missing story of Harry's mother will turn out to be key, as well.

After Snape flees Hogwarts with Draco in the chapter called "Flight of the Prince," Hermione finds a *Prophet* announcement of Eileen Prince marrying Tobias Snape and giving birth to a—

> "—murderer," spat Harry.
>
> "Well . . . yes," said Hermione. "So . . . I was sort of right. Snape must have been proud of being 'half a Prince,' you see? Tobias Snape was a Muggle from what it said in the *Prophet*."
>
> "Yeah, that fits," said Harry. "He'd play up the pure-blood side so he could get in with Lucius Malfoy and the rest of them. . . . He's just like Voldemort. Pure-blood mother, Muggle father . . . ashamed of his parentage, trying to make himself feared using the Dark Arts, gave himself an impressive new name—*Lord* Voldemort—the Half-Blood *Prince*—how could Dumbledore have missed—?" (*HP/HBP*, 637)

In his towering hatred of Snape, Harry willfully misinterprets the evidence and likens teen Snape to Voldemort. There is no evidence about whether Eileen Prince was half-blood or pure-blood, no evidence that teen Snape ever told anyone else the name he inscribed in his schoolbook. The Prince's book, like Riddle's diary, preserves a memory of a student's personality, but the portrait that emerges from the Half-Blood Prince's book is very different. He is not grandiose or manipulative. He is retaliatory, not aggressive. He is gifted, resentful, judgmental, bitter, private. He does not expect anyone ever to read this book and find it of value. He expects it to remain unseen.

Harry tells Ron and Hermione that Snape knew Harry had the Prince's book, probably when Slughorn talked about Harry's Potions brilliance but definitely by the time Harry used *Sectumsempra*.

"But why didn't he turn you in?"

"I don't think he wanted to associate himself with that book," said Hermione. "I don't think Dumbledore would have liked it very much if he'd known." (*HP/HBP*, 638)

Snape did not arrange to have the book fall into Harry's hands; he genuinely left it behind with the other supplies while moving classrooms, in the rush of activity between the battle at the Ministry of the previous June and his first day teaching Defense Against the Dark Arts. It's understandable enough that an adult would not want to show anyone else the diary of his miserable teens, but this book chronicled his transformation into the Dark Magic-obsessed young man who betrayed Lily Evans and eventually let her die. He would have wanted to put it from his mind, as Slughorn did with his own memory of catastrophic bad judgment.

But the problem with books is that once they are out in the world, their original authors cannot control them. There is no controlling who sees them, how they use what they read, how they judge the authors based on the stagnant information that stays fixed no matter how much the authors themselves have changed. Voldemort let his diary out into the world to harm others. When Snape recognized that his textbook was doing the same, though, he did not treat it as a Horcrux—he did not separate it from his own soul to harm others. In his horror, he did his best to track it down, claim responsibility for the contents, name himself as the author, and warn others not to use the Dark Magic he invented. Like Slughorn, he was able to make amends: he healed Draco's *Sectumsempra* wounds and he taught better spells to both Draco and Harry.

Just as Hermione, a gifted girl, is open to considering that "Prince" might be a girl's name, she has a different perspective, as a Muggle-born, on why Snape might have been proud to be "half a Prince." There are several ways to be a half-blood. Harry and Dumbledore, for example, each had one Muggle-born parent, but both of these Muggle-born parents were full witches. Tobias Snape was a Muggle, not a Muggle-born wizard. Harry associates his magical identity with both of his parents. Teen Snape, however, probably associated his magical gifts entirely with the parent who nurtured his learning, giving him her own books when they could not afford new ones for him. It would have made sense for him to name his magical scholar self after his matrilineage.

Hermione understands the feeling of secret intellectual hopes coming true, living in a Muggle world that doesn't understand her while dreaming of a magical world where she can exercise her gifts with no limits except her own imagination. While Harry, too, lived with an extreme Muggle/magical divide, his sort of giftedness didn't drive him to the intensely lonely autodidactism that drove child Hermione and child Snape to memorize their textbooks before the first day of school.

Harry is also forgetting a piece of evidence that Hermione doesn't have. The memories he saw of teen Snape hint strongly at wife abuse, the father shouting at the cowering mother while the small child cried. Any survivor of an abusive childhood can identify with the Half-Blood Prince's tendencies toward contempt and vengeance. But Harry didn't have to change his name to formalize his disavowal of the Dursleys. The abuse he endured from the Dursleys wasn't gendered. Snape ultimately kept his patronymic, perhaps knowing that he could claim it entirely as his own within the magical world, but we see from the record that he considered another option as a teen.

What can we guess about Eileen Prince as a mother? We know she raised her son in Muggle poverty, judging from the used textbook and the neighborhood of Spinner's End. Snape is not materialistic; magical artifacts or trappings of luxury hold no sway over him; she did not raise him to covet worldly goods, perhaps helping him see value in intellectual riches instead. She was president of a social club: she associated Hogwarts with friendship. She would have passed that on to her son as his birthright.

Whatever their relationship became later, she probably married Tobias Snape for love. The power imbalance between a witch and a Muggle makes that likely. Did she love her son? The evidence suggests that she did. Snape's powers of protective care toward the young are tremendously, if capriciously, developed. More resoundingly, Snape, the emotionally stunted man who cannot contemplate romance without snarling, is able to look deeply in Narcissa Malfoy's eyes when she's in mortal anguish about her son. He can withstand her degree of emotion and meet it in full.

The "Prince" portion of "Flight of the Prince" refers to the strength that Snape got from his mother. The "Flight" portion refers to a different matronymic: the author's. J.K. Rowling's mother's birth name was Anne Volant (McGinty). Anne Volant Rowling named her two children Joanne and Dianne, and called them Jo and Di. They had their mother's given name as part of their own identities. *Volant* is the French word for "flying." Rowling famously wrote her love and grief for her late mother into every aspect of the *Harry Potter* series, which celebrates flying in every volume, from brooms to hippogriffs to motorcycles. The word "flight" can mean the act of *fleeing*, or it can mean the act of *flying*. In this chapter, it means both. To flee is not an act of cowardice if it is done to take a child to safety. Snape's "Flight of the Prince" is about the ascendancy of the protective magic he got from his mother. Starting from this chapter, that's the aspect of Snape that will remain dominant for the rest of his life.

We see that "Flight" has two meanings, then. What about "Prince"? Harry takes it to mean the son of a king, perhaps awaiting his chance to take the throne. But it is also a reference to the very Slytherin-esque treatise *The Prince* by Niccolò Machiavelli, the 16th-century Italian strategist who used the term "prince" to mean a political ruler. *The Prince* contains his advice for how leaders can remain in power during times of treachery and war—in order to best protect their people.

The tenets set forth in *The Prince* provide clues for how to interpret Snape's motivations for the end of *Half-Blood Prince* and, even more, the entirety of the following year in *Deathly Hallows*. Rowling confirms the connection between Snape and Machiavelli by naming her character after this book not once, but twice. Not only does Snape call himself the Half-Blood "Prince," but in *The Prince*, Machiavelli praises a "ferocious," "shrewd" emperor named Severus who killed a rival named Albinus (Machiavelli, 67). Rowling's combination of the name "Severus," with its implications of *severity* and *severing*, with "Snape," which sounds like *snipe* or *snip*, creates a brilliantly unpleasant picture of a character who will be ferocious and shrewd about snipping the thread of another prince's lifespan.

All of *Harry Potter and the Half-Blood Prince* is a study of the ambiguous distinctions that qualify some magic as "Dark." Machiavelli theorized:

> Those cruelties are well used (if it is permitted to speak well of evil) that are carried out in a single stroke, done out of necessity to protect oneself, and then are not continued, but are instead converted into the greatest possible benefits for the subjects. Those cruelties are badly used that, although few at the outset, increase with the passing of time instead of disappearing. (Machiavelli, 34)

According to Machiavelli's definition, then, Dark Magic is intentional harm, not perpetrated in self-defense, that becomes more destructive over time. A single stroke of cruelty, converted into the greatest possible benefits for the subjects—such as killing a dying man in order to shield a minor from a tyrant—could, perhaps, be considered a cruelty well used, not Dark Magic.

Machiavelli also gives possible insight into the argument between Snape and Dumbledore that Hagrid overheard in the forest.

> And so it is necessary that he should have a mind ready to turn itself according to the way the winds of Fortune and the changing circumstances command him. . . . He should not depart from the good if it is possible to do so, but he should know how to enter into evil when forced by necessity. (Machiavelli, 61)

Being a double agent means Snape is always poised to do potentially distasteful things in order to maintain his cover. But perhaps Hagrid was hearing the cry of a double agent being ordered to do something that goes further into evil than he thinks he can withstand. We will find out more in *Deathly Hallows* about how Snape converted his evil act from this volume into the greatest possible benefits for his subjects.

By the end of *Half-Blood Prince*, Snape has accomplished much that he set out to do at the beginning of the year.

He has upheld his vow to Narcissa: He protected Draco, prevented Draco (and Harry) from killing or permanently harming anyone, and eventually killed Dumbledore in Draco's stead.

He has kept Dumbledore alive as long as possible, then derived protection for others from Dumbledore's death.

He has taught Draco enough non-aggression so that Draco cast *Expelliarmus* against Dumbledore instead of a Killing Curse. This made the time and room for Dumbledore to show that he believes Draco is worth saving, Draco's parents are worth saving, and Dumbledore would give his life to keep Draco from harm.

He has made room for Harry to have some empathy for Draco: His quick intervention with both Draco and Harry after Harry cast *Sectumsempra* gave Harry the room to feel sorry and to know that there are some things he would not wish on his worst enemy. His teaching of *Expelliarmus* to both boys enabled Harry, under his Invisibility Cloak, to

witness how Draco speaks to his intended victim when they come face
to face.

> Harry had not spared Malfoy much thought. His animosity was all
> for Snape, but he had not forgotten the fear in Malfoy's voice on
> that tower top, nor the fact that he had lowered his wand before the
> other Death Eaters arrived. Harry did not believe that Malfoy
> would have killed Dumbledore. He despised Malfoy still for his
> infatuation with the Dark Arts, but now the tiniest drop of pity
> mingled with his dislike. Where, Harry wondered, was Malfoy
> now, and what was Voldemort making him do under threat of
> killing him and his parents? (HP/HBP, 640)

**Snape has drawn some of Harry's ire away from Draco and toward
himself,** which will be essential for both Harry and Draco to survive
their coming battles. Snape can take Harry's ire better than Draco can.

He has earned the respect of the Death Eaters so they will not
question him in the future when he acts to protect the students of
Hogwarts.

**And he has killed all the trust and faith his colleagues ever had in
him** by killing the one remaining person who knew his true self.

At Dumbledore's funeral, Harry believes that he goes into his future
completely unprotected: "The last and greatest of his protectors had died,
and he was more alone than he had ever been before." (HP/HBP, 645)
But that is only true of Snape, not of Harry. Snape will still protect Harry
Potter and all the other people that he can, but it will be from a distance
and they must not know.

No longer does the story show Snape as an ugly man. The usual
gratuitous descriptors of his ugliness—the mentions of the hooked nose
and the greasy hair during standard exposition—are now gone from the
narrative. Rowling writes him with stark realism when he is being brave:
when he pulls up his sleeve to show his Dark Mark, when he sings shut
Draco's wounds, when his eyes sweep the scene and he kills his mentor.
He is heroic then, harshly beautiful as he does magic that no one else can
do.

SEVERUS SNAPE
AND THE DEATHLY HALLOWS, PART 1

In Dumbledore's will, he bequeaths Harry a Golden Snitch (*HP/DH*, 134), a winged orb bearing a mysterious inscription:

I open at the close.

When Harry is about to die, it cracks open for him and yields memories of love that give him the strength to meet death.

But just like prophecies, magical bequests don't have to be transmitted within enchanted orbs. They are just words, after all, words that can be spoken to a person who then becomes their keeper. Unbeknownst to Harry, Dumbledore also bequeaths him a final message that he entrusts to Snape with instructions to deliver the message only when Harry is close to defeating Voldemort. Snape must stay alive long enough to deliver the message then and no sooner. He must remain tightly Occluded until he meets with Harry.

Then he, too, can open at the close.

There are other mysteries in *Harry Potter and the Deathly Hallows*, but the revelation of Snape's motives is the key to them all. After a buildup of a million words, Rowling finally shows us Snape as he truly is, the full story of how he became the right-hand man of two opposing generals and what was in his heart the entire time.

Plot

The book opens with something we have never seen before: Snape in action as a Death Eater, sitting at Voldemort's right hand at the full assembly, giving intelligence that raises him above other Death Eaters. Voldemort tortures Charity Burbage, teacher of Muggle Studies. Her dying words are the same as Dumbledore's: "Severus . . . please." Snape locks eyes with her but remains "quite impassive" as Voldemort kills her (*HP/DH*, 12).

And then he is absent from the book for nearly 500 pages. In a book that's 759 pages long, Snape appears through page 12 and then does not make another direct appearance until page 500. We see and hear of him indirectly, alone at the top of his tower at Hogwarts while Harry, Ron and Hermione go underground. He is there as Voldemort's puppet, running the school as a Death Eater dystopia. Nobody alive knows that he is covertly devoting his entire existence to helping Harry bring down Voldemort and protecting as many students as he can along the way.

What can we gather about Snape during those almost 500 pages of absence? We see Harry putting his lessons to the test. We see him indirectly through newspaper headlines, the portrait of Phineas Nigellus Black, and his Patronus. We see him in his absence from Grimmauld Place.

During those 500 pages, we learn of new mysteries underpinning Harry's quest. What are the Deathly Hallows? Why is the Tale of the Three Brothers significant? What does it mean to be a Master of Death?

At the heart of the book is the silver doe. Rowling uses imagery from the Arthurian tradition, the white hind that signals adventure in the forest, to lead Harry to the sword in the lake that goes only to the worthy. We have been wondering what Snape's Patronus is. When it appears, at the book's midpoint, it is the light that Harry has needed. Voldemort cannot touch this. It provides the guidance that Dumbledore doesn't. There is comfort in this light, which takes the image of Lily Potter, the mate to James Potter's silver stag. Snape and Harry have been strengthened by love from the same person. The silver doe tells us: follow the mother's story.

We see Snape again, finally, when Voldemort comes to Hogwarts and Snape lets him in at the gate. From then on, it's a race for Snape to find Harry and get him the final message. He reveals himself to McGonagall in his search for Harry, but he has destroyed her trust. McGonagall, Flitwick, and Sprout attack him and rather than fight them, he crashes through the window and takes flight, abandoning his post as Headmaster. He has a message to deliver. He leaves Hogwarts in good hands.

Voldemort believes, mistakenly, that he will become invincible by killing Snape. He orders his snake to kill Snape with a venomous bite. Snape is trying to stanch the wound to live long enough to find Harry when Harry, Ron, and Hermione find him. He is able to transmit a series of memories to Harry before dying. The memories are the key to everything Snape has done, and they strengthen Harry with the magic from his mother that he needs to defeat Voldemort.

Snape's Year in Overview

Viewed from a distance this year, Snape is a monolith, an impenetrable column of black robes and marble. Two major elements of Snape characterization are gone forever: his sardonic humor and his ugliness. There is no point in his being sardonic: he has no desire to joke with Voldemort or his deputies, the Carrows. His former colleagues hate him. His Slytherins are no longer unpopular students who need to be heartened with waspish humor; they are the favored ones, being trained into junior tyrants. Dumbledore is dead.

Snape's personal dislike of Harry

Now that Snape is separated from Harry, he is no longer ugly. His face is described as "thin" in this book, rather than hook-nosed and sneering. (HP/DH, 597) It is partly that we are not seeing him through Harry's eyes and partly that he no longer has the irritation of Harry's presence in his classroom to provoke him to ugly behavior. But mostly, Snape is no longer ugly because he is doing the kind of life-or-death work that transforms his appearance from ugly to stark. No one but the Dark Lord has power over him. Everyone else sees the authority and forbidding intelligence that emanates from him throughout this sleepless year.

Snape's hostility to the Defense teacher

Voldemort has placed siblings Alecto and Amycus Carrow at Hogwarts to teach Death Eater doctrine. Amycus, as Neville Longbottom explains to Harry, "teaches what used to be Defense Against the Dark Arts, except now it's just the Dark Arts." (HP/DH, 573) The Carrows require students to practice the Cruciatus Curse on classmates. Some of Snape's Slytherins, such as Crabbe and Goyle, are among those who embrace this sadistic new order, and he is powerless to dissuade them while he is masquerading as a headmaster who is sympathetic to the Carrows' doctrine.

Neville tells Harry that some students staged guerrilla protests against Snape and the Carrows: "We used to sneak out at night and put graffiti on the walls: *Dumbledore's Army, Still Recruiting*, stuff like that. Snape hated it." (HP/DH, 575)

The Carrows punish protesters with torture. The best Snape can do about it is divert detentions Hagrid rather than the Carrows, at least until

Hagrid gets caught throwing a "Support Harry Potter" party. Hagrid manages to flee Hogwarts, suggesting that Snape may have obstructed attempts to take him into custody. (HP/DH, 442) For Snape, with his hypersensitive protective reactions, standing by while adults torture children requires the utmost in self-control. But he can't betray his true sentiments or he will be killed and replaced by someone worse.

Snape's reputation

Dumbledore and Snape were completely successful in their years-long defamation campaign. Everyone believes that Dumbledore was mistaken to trust Snape and Snape has returned to practicing the Dark Arts, if indeed he ever stopped. McGonagall is bitterly convinced of his betrayal, and Flitwick duels him with the cry, "You'll do no more murder at Hogwarts!" (HP/DH, 599) If Snape ever feels tempted to protest to these good people that their old faith in him was not misplaced, he can remember what happened when Dumbledore succumbed to the flaw in the plan, the affection that makes it difficult to be ruthless. Dumbledore flinched at telling Harry the truth and Sirius died for it. Snape cannot permit such a lapse when so much is at stake.

The mystery of Snape's true motives

We see a few clues to Snape's true motives before the climactic reveal of his memories in Chapter 33, "The Prince's Tale."

Harry (HP/DH, 90), Ron, Hermione (HP/DH, 163), and Lupin (HP/DH, 204) expect him to attack Grimmauld Place or tell other Death Eaters how to enter the Secret-Kept location, but this never happens. (HP/DH, 201)

Harry guesses that it must have been Snape who ransacked Grimmauld Place and took half of a letter and photo from Lily to Sirius, but he has so little to support this line of thought that he drops it. (HP/DH, 177)

Harry and Ron are too convinced of Snape's evil to figure out whose Patronus helped them in the forest. The reader, however, knows that Snape can cast a Patronus, which we have never seen, and that Rowling has repeatedly underscored the importance of the mother's story while revealing almost nothing about Lily's friendships. Snape must have been careful to avoid letting Hermione see the silver doe. She was the last to lose faith in him, and he has never been able to evade her understanding for long.

Severus Snape and the Deathly Hallows

The final installment of the series introduces an entirely new storyline: the Deathly Hallows. In the wizarding fairy tale "The Tale of the Three Brothers," Death once gave gifts to three brothers: an unbeatable wand, a stone that can bring back the dead, and his own cloak of invisibility. According to the tale, the person who can unite these three Hallows is the Master of Death.

A few believers, including Dumbledore, know these relics are real. Dumbledore won the Elder Wand by defeating Grindelwald. The Resurrection Stone is in the ring that Voldemort turned into a Horcrux, not knowing it was a Hallow. The Cloak of Invisibility is the very one that Harry inherited from his father.

Those who seek these objects out of greed sometimes pay dearly. The Elder Wand often changes hands by murder. Dumbledore lost a hand and shortened his life in his eagerness to seize the ring. Like other powerful objects, such as the Sorcerer's Stone, the Deathly Hallows are subject to one of Rowling's cardinal rules: they belong to those who seek them not for gain, but to protect others.

At different points in his life, Snape is each of the brothers in the tale. In youth, he was combative. After Lily died, he wanted to join her in death. But for his second chance in life, he has been keeping his true self hidden, not for personal gain but in order to protect others. According to Dumbledore, that is the essence of the Cloak of Invisibility, "the true magic of which, of course, is that it can be used to protect and shield others as well as its owner." (*HP/DH*, 716)

Dumbledore left Harry very little information about the Deathly Hallows, worried that they might tempt Harry away from hunting Horcruxes. He told Snape nothing at all about them, but for different reasons.

Dumbledore withheld information from Snape that might prove fatal to him if Voldemort read it in his mind. But he also knew that Snape would have no use for the information because he is not greedy for magical relics. This most unmaterialistic of men is a believer in wandless magic, nonverbal magic, magic that relies on the self alone. All manner of magical treasure passes through Snape's hands during his year as Headmaster, including the sword of Gryffindor, but he covets none of it. We will see, in this volume, the ways in which Snape casts exactly the same magic promised by the Deathly Hallows, proving himself a Master of Death, without the need for wand or Hallow or anything but the strength of his mind.

Defense Against the Dark Arts: Lessons Snape Taught Harry

Machiavelli, spycraft, and covert operations

Dumbledore's last words, just before Snape killed him, were "Severus . . . please . . ." (*HP/HBP*, 595)

In the opening chapter of *Deathly Hallows*, Voldemort tortures a Muggle Studies teacher in front of the assembled Death Eaters: Charity Burbage, Snape's colleague at Hogwarts. Her crime was writing "an impassioned defense of Mudbloods in the *Daily Prophet*." (*HP/DH*, 11-2) As Voldemort revolves her in mid-air, she begs Snape for help: "Severus . . . please . . . please . . ." (*HP/DH*, 12) Snape meets her eyes but offers no response as Voldemort kills her.

Snape, newly promoted to Voldemort's right-hand man, soon to be Hogwarts headmaster, cannot do anything for Charity. To show sympathy for her would only be to draw Voldemort's murderous attention to himself as well, possibly losing Muggle-born students yet another ally. Snape can only follow this precept of Machiavelli's from *The Prince*:

> One must understand this: a prince, and especially a new prince, cannot observe all those things for which men are considered good, because in order to maintain the state he must often act against his faith, *against charity*, against humanity, and against religion. (Machiavelli, 61, *emphasis mine*)

Unlike Charity, who spoke out in defense of others and paid the price, Snape has a long-term strategy to defeat Voldemort, which sometimes requires him to witness evil without speaking out.

> A man who wishes to profess goodness at all times will come to ruin among so many who are not good. Therefore, it is necessary for a prince who wishes to maintain himself to learn how not to be good, and to use this knowledge or not to use it according to necessity . . . For there is such a distance between how one lives and how one ought to live, that anyone who abandons what is done for what ought to be done achieves his downfall rather than his preservation. (Machiavelli, 53)

How do we know that Snape was suppressing sympathy for Charity in this scene? How do we know he wasn't indifferent or glad for her death? Because she called upon Snape with the same loaded words that Dumbledore used: "Severus, please." Something similar happens later in this book, when Snape escapes confrontation by crashing through a window and McGonagall repeats Harry's accusation from the previous year: "Coward!" (*HP/HBP*, 604 and *HP/DH* 599) These are words that people say to Snape when he's being most tested. In this scene, Rowling shows only how Snape appears to Voldemort. But by pointing us toward Machiavelli once again with the name "Charity," she tells us that Snape, a "new prince," is acting against his own beliefs.

Similarly, Harry is helpless to protect Kreacher when Death Eaters breach the security of Grimmauld Place.

> What if the Death Eaters tortured the elf? Sick images swarmed into Harry's head and he tried to push these away too, for there was nothing he could do for Kreacher: He and Hermione had already decided against trying to summon him; what if someone from the Ministry came too? (*HP/DH*, 278)

Even Harry, with his "saving-people-thing," must learn that sometimes it is necessary to do nothing or appear callous when harm befalls a friend.

Harry gets a brief but jolting insight into how it feels to live Snape's life when he encounters Arthur Weasley while disguised as a Voldemort sympathizer: "It was very strange to have Mr. Weasley glare at him with that much dislike." (*HP/DH*, 254) He wants to give Mr. Weasley a warning, but Mr. Weasley views him with so much hostility that Harry cannot be sure his warning has done any good.

> "Arthur," Harry interrupted, "you know you're being tracked, don't you?"
>
> "Is that a threat, Runcorn?" said Mr. Weasley loudly.
>
> "No," said Harry, "it's a fact! They're watching your every move—"
>
> The lift doors opened. They had reached the Atrium. Mr. Weasley gave Harry a scathing look and swept from the lift. Harry stood there, shaken. He wished he was impersonating somebody other than Runcorn. . . . The lift doors clanged shut. (*HP/DH*, 256)

Harry now has an experience comparable to Snape fighting through layers of hostility to teach him Occlumency or warn Sirius that Lucius Malfoy recognized him on the train platform. Snape earned some of that distrust with his own native charm. A great deal of it, though, was a necessary result of his strategic cover as a double agent, and it severely compromised Snape's ability to communicate with the people he was trying to help.

Harry, Ron, and Hermione learn the importance of sticking close to the truth when lying for cover. Ron figures that when Xenophilius Lovegood was trying to detain them to hand them over to Death Eaters, everything Lovegood was saying was probably true: "It's a damn sight harder making stuff up when you're under stress than you'd think. I found that out when the Snatchers caught me. It was much easier pretending to be Stan, because I knew a bit about him, than inventing a whole new person." (*HP/DH*, 426)

Ron's explanation sheds more light on Snape's ability to convince Voldemort of his loyalty. Whenever Voldemort practiced Legilimency on Snape, Snape could summon his feelings of dislike for Harry or Sirius to the fore, and they would certainly be convincing. It was both useful and convenient that Snape had no particular urge to push himself toward a more mature perspective on either of them. The unevolved tenacity of his schoolboy grudge served a purpose in protecting them all.

Harry learns, too, what it takes to cast an Unforgivable in order to protect others. We know that for Unforgivables to work, the caster really has to *mean* them. At Gringotts Bank, Harry commits an Unforgivable crime against a goblin who has never done anything to deserve it: "Harry raised the hawthorn wand beneath the cloak, pointed it at the old goblin, and whispered, for the first time in his life, *'Imperio!'*" (*HP/DH*, 531) He knows there is no other way he can reach the Horcrux stored in the Lestrange vault. The ends will have to justify the means; he can settle his conscience later. According to Machiavelli, it is vital for a prince to be able to do this:

> And so it is necessary that he should have a mind ready to turn itself according to the way the winds of Fortune and the changing circumstances command him. . . He should not depart from the good if it is possible to do so, but he should know how to enter into evil when forced by necessity. (Machiavelli, 61)

The same thing is happening to Draco under Voldemort's tyranny. He is being forced to cast the Cruciatus Curse against fellow Death Eaters under threat of punishment if he disobeys. Harry sees Draco's "gaunt, petrified face" and feels "sickened by what he had seen, by the use to which Draco was now being put by Voldemort," understanding that Draco is obeying against his will in order to protect himself and the rest of his family. (*HP/DH*, 174-5) This moment of sympathy for Draco will someday help Harry understand how Snape brought himself to cast the Killing Curse at Dumbledore.

Expelliarmus and the Elder Wand

During the air battle between Death Eaters and the seven Harrys, Harry uses only defensive spells against the people trying to kill him, in the style of fighting he learned from Snape and Dumbledore: spells to block or protect against the aggression of others rather than initiating new attacks. But in an air battle, even a Stunning Spell can be murder if it causes someone on a broom to fall from the sky.

> Harry sent Stunning Spell after Stunning Spell back at their pursuers, barely holding them off. He shot another blocking jinx at them: The closest Death Eater swerved to avoid it and his hood slipped, and by the red light of his next Stunning Spell, Harry saw the strangely blank face of Stanley Shunpike—Stan—
>
> *"Expelliarmus!"* Harry yelled.
>
> "That's him, it's him, it's the real one!" (*HP/DH*, 59)

When Harry recognizes Stan Shunpike, he downgrades his defenses to something that might disarm Stan but not kill him. This leads to an all-out argument with Lupin about battle tactics.

> "They recognized you? But how? What had you done?"
>
> "I . . ." Harry tried to remember; the whole journey seemed like a blur of panic and confusion. "I saw Stan Shunpike. . . . You know, the bloke who was the conductor on the Knight Bus? And I tried to Disarm him instead of—well, he doesn't know what he's doing, does he? He must be Imperiused!"
>
> Lupin looked aghast.
>
> "Harry, the time for Disarming is past! These people are trying to

capture and kill you! At least Stun if you aren't prepared to kill!"

"We were hundreds of feet up! Stan's not himself, and if I Stunned him and he'd fallen, he'd have died the same as if I'd used Avada Kedavra!" (*HP/DH*, 70)

Recognizing Stan made the difference for Harry: *I know you. I know the* real *you. I refuse to attack you. You do not deserve to die like this.* Sparing the life of your attacker because you know them is a powerful magic with potent, unpredictable results. Lupin is completely opposed, but Snape's teachings, plus years of his own battle experience, leave Harry in no doubt that this is his magic of choice.

> "Expelliarmus is a useful spell, Harry, but the Death Eaters seem to think it is your signature move, and I urge you not to let it become so!"
>
> Lupin was making Harry feel idiotic, and yet there was still a grain of defiance inside him.
>
> "I won't blast people out of my way just because they're there," said Harry. "That's Voldemort's job." (*HP/DH*, 71)

It may seem surprising that Lupin, the kind teacher, is more militant than Snape the spiteful classroom bully. But Lupin and Sirius were once prepared to kill Wormtail execution-style, out of vengeance, in front of three unwilling teenage witnesses. Snape is the one who sentenced Harry to endless detentions to drum it into him that aggression can cause irreparable harm. Lupin might have been aghast at Harry's *Expelliarmus*, but Snape would have understood it as confirmation that his teachings have taken effect.

This awareness of disarmament as a greater power than aggression helps us understand what Grindelwald said to Voldemort in the topmost cell at Nurmengard: *"You will not win, you cannot win! That wand will never, ever be yours—"* (*HP/DH*, 472)

How does Grindelwald know this? Grindelwald tells Voldemort, *"There is so much you do not understand. . . ."* (*HP/DH*, 469)

There is something Voldemort does not understand, but Harry does: "Deeper and deeper Harry sank into the grave, and he knew where Voldemort had been tonight, and whom he had killed in the topmost cell of Nurmengard, and why. . . ." (*HP/DH*, 479)

The allegiance of the Elder Wand goes to whoever wields the more powerful magic in a duel. The last person to use the Elder Wand was Dumbledore, but he defeated and imprisoned Grindelwald rather than kill him. In Voldemort's mind, that means ownership of the wand may not have passed to Dumbledore and might still pass to whoever killed Grindelwald. Voldemort doesn't understand that Dumbledore used the same magic on Grindelwald that Harry used on Stan Shunpike: Disarmament, not attack. *I know you. I know the* real *you. I refuse to attack you. You do not deserve to die like this.* The recognition of human worth in an opponent creates magic that wasn't there before. It is more complex magic than a simple Killing Curse, lingering and unpredictable.

Dumbledore and Draco raised this magic together in their face-off at the tower. Draco disarmed Dumbledore rather than attacking, and once Dumbledore was wandless, cast no further spells against him. Dumbledore neither counterattacked nor defended himself, taking that time, unbeknownst to Draco, to freeze Harry in place. Draco learned that Dumbledore thought him and his family worth protecting—worth dying for. That magic joined with Snape's grief and healing magic after Draco's *Sectumsempra* wounds to create a young Death Eater who felt too much connection to others to be a killer.

Draco had overpowered the greatest wizard of the age using *Expelliarmus*, the defensive spell that Snape taught Draco and Harry to use against each other so they could hate without harm. The Elder Wand recognized this magic in Draco as akin to Dumbledore's in strength and willingly changed allegiance.

At Malfoy Manor, Harry disarms Draco by wresting three wands out of his hand: Draco's, Bellatrix's, and Wormtail's. Wormtail's he gives to Ron, who sheltered Wormtail unwittingly for years. Harry escapes to Shell Cottage, buries Dobby, and wants to inscribe Dobby's headstone.

> He then felt in his pocket for a wand.
>
> There were two in there. He had forgotten, lost track; he could not now remember whose wands these were; he seemed to remember wrenching them out of someone's hand. He selected the shorter of the two, which felt friendlier in his hand, and pointed it at the rock. (*HP/DH*, 481)

Draco's wand turns out to work well for Harry, "at least as well as Hermione's had done." (*HP/DH*, 520) The wand recognizes Harry's and Draco's magic as equivalent. This wand has cast *Expelliarmus* at a wizard of great power and then been taken in a disarming move by a wizard whose signature magic is *Expelliarmus*. It is an easy transfer of wand allegiance from Draco to Harry, prompted in large part by a recognition of interchangeability.

Voldemort understands none of this. He steals the Elder Wand from Dumbledore's tomb but finds that it works no better for him than his own wand or Lucius Malfoy's, both of which have failed to kill Harry Potter. In that case, then, he thinks perhaps Dumbledore had its allegiance after all, since killing Grindelwald doesn't seem to have conferred greater power to Voldemort. Robbing Dumbledore's tomb doesn't seem to have done the trick, either. A logical solution occurs to Voldemort, which he explains to Snape.

> "The Elder Wand cannot serve me properly, Severus, because I am not its true master. The Elder Wand belongs to the wizard who killed its last owner. You killed Albus Dumbledore. While you live, Severus, the Elder Wand cannot be truly mine."
>
> "My Lord!" Snape protested, raising his wand.
>
> "It cannot be any other way," said Voldemort. "I must master the wand, Severus. Master the wand, and I master Potter at last." (*HP/DH*, 656)

Voldemort kills Snape for possession of the Elder Wand.

That's not how it was supposed to go.

In the "King's Cross" chapter, in the dialogue with Dumbledore that took place in his head, Harry thinks about what Dumbledore might have planned.

> "Poor Severus . . ."
>
> "If you planned your death with Snape, you meant him to end up with the Elder Wand, didn't you?"
>
> "I admit that was my intention," said Dumbledore, "but it did not work as I intended, did it?"
>
> "No," said Harry. "That bit didn't work out." (*HP/DH*, 721)

What did Dumbledore hope would happen, then?

We know that in the Final Battle, when Harry and Voldemort cast *Expelliarmus* and *Avada Kedavra* at each other, the Elder Wand goes "spinning through the air toward the master it would not kill." (*HP/DH*,

743-4) Dumbledore wanted the Elder Wand to recognize the mercy and regret in Snape's Killing Curse and transfer allegiance to Snape, quietly. He knew he could trust Snape to be a good custodian of the Elder Wand, since Snape's signature magic is purely defensive: when he has to force himself to attack or use Dark Magic, it's only in order to protect others, then immediately dropped.

Dumbledore expected Voldemort might violate his tomb and take the wand. He had hoped that any spell Voldemort cast against Snape with it would fail because the Elder Wand would not kill its master, especially if its master counteracted with purely defensive magic, as Harry did and Snape surely would have.

Dumbledore also knew he could trust Snape to be the rightful owner of the Elder Wand because with all powerful magical objects, Snape handles them without greed, not for personal gain but to protect others. In his third year, Harry saw that his Invisibility Cloak, one of the Deathly Hallows, worked perfectly for Snape because Snape was using it in the belief that he would protect children from murderers. Dumbledore, in contrast, says he once borrowed the Cloak from Harry's father "out of vain curiosity, and so it could never have worked for me as it works for you, its true owner." (*HP/DH*, 720) The sword of Gryffindor cannot be owned but presents itself of its own volition to worthy Gryffindors, yet it permitted Snape to handle it.

Dumbledore planned not to tell Snape about the Elder Wand for two reasons: it wouldn't be safe and it wouldn't be necessary. He didn't want Voldemort to learn of Snape's ownership through Legilimency and kill him. He also knew Snape would be a worthy owner, a Master of Death, whether or not he was conscious of owning a Deathly Hallow. In the "King's Cross" chapter, the Dumbledore in Harry's vision says he has found that "perhaps those who are best suited to power are those who have never sought it." (*HP/DH*, 718)

But the flaw in the plan was that Dumbledore didn't foresee Draco casting *Expelliarmus*, choosing the spell Snape ingrained into him rather than the violence his father or Voldemort would have encouraged. Dumbledore had never been able to turn either Tom Riddle or Snape away from Dark Magic when they were students, but he lived long enough to see that Snape's teaching reached Draco.

With *Expelliarmus*, Draco's hawthorn wand conquered the Elder Wand. This makes it doubly safe for Harry to risk using the same hawthorn wand to cast *Expelliarmus* at Voldemort in their final battle. Harry has learned that it doesn't matter much what wand he uses to fight

Voldemort. His holly and phoenix wand recognized Voldemort, "a man who was both kin and mortal enemy, and it regurgitated some of his own magic against him," even when Voldemort used Lucius Malfoy's wand during the flight of the Seven Harrys. (*HP/DH*, 711) The wand that Harry won from Draco would recognize Voldemort as well, whatever wand Voldemort used. In the "King's Cross" chapter, Dumbledore confirms it for Harry:

> "He killed me with your wand."

> "He *failed* to kill you with my wand," Dumbledore corrected Harry. (*HP/DH*, 712)

Voldemort cannot kill Harry with *any* wand because in order for the Killing Curse to work, the caster has to *mean it*, and Voldemort doesn't realize that he identifies with Harry too much, sees too much of Harry's humanity, to kill him the same way he has killed others. But just in case, Harry—and the author—derive some support from the connection that the hawthorn wand and the Elder Wand now have. The Elder Wand has submitted to disarmament from the hawthorn wand once before. Harry is conscious of drawing on that parallel history as he casts his signature magic using Draco's wand (*emphasis mine*).

> Harry heard the high voice shriek as he too yelled his best hope to the heavens, pointing **Draco's wand**:

> *"Avada Kedavra!"*

> *"Expelliarmus!"* (*HP/DH*, 743)

All of Snape's labors were worth it. The subterfuge of Dueling Club under Lockhart, the manipulations to teach Harry and Draco to cast *Expelliarmus* against one another, the Unbreakable Vow, the healing of Draco's *Sectumsempra* wounds, the detentions to turn Harry away from Dark Magic, and the murder of Dumbledore in Draco's place: it all paid off. Using nothing but a teenager's wand and *Expelliarmus*, Draco and Harry brought down the most powerful wizards of their age and survived. Both of them had cast the Cruciatus and Imperius curses, sometimes of their own volition and sometimes to protect others. But as he vowed to Narcissa and, posthumously, Lily, Snape's efforts ensured that both Draco and Harry turned away from killing and kept their souls intact.

Connections and Occlumency

Throughout *Deathly Hallows*, Harry gains mastery over his scar connection to Voldemort's mind. The greater Voldemort's panic, and the fewer Horcruxes that remain, the less he can Occlude Harry from his thoughts.

A similar connection opens up between Snape and Hermione. As soon as she reads that he's become headmaster of Hogwarts, Hermione realizes that he can spy on them through the portraits of Phineas Nigellus Black, Slytherin former headmaster and Sirius Black's great-great-grandfather. (*HP/DH*, 225)

> The painted image of Phineas Nigellus Black was able to flit between his portrait in Grimmauld Place and the one that hung in the headmaster's office at Hogwarts: the circular tower-top room where Snape was no doubt sitting right now, in triumphant possession of Dumbledore's collection of delicate, silver magical instruments, the stone Pensieve, the Sorting Hat and, unless it had been moved elsewhere, the sword of Gryffindor. (*HP/DH*, 228)

Hermione shoves the Grimmauld Place portrait into her bag so Phineas Nigellus cannot spy on them. Hermione's workspace, her portable headquarters, anchors one end of the connection. Snape's private workspace anchors the other. After six years of ignoring Hermione's raised hand, Snape is no longer in control of their interactions. Hermione takes out the portrait whenever it pleases her, blindfolding Black for good measure, and shoves it back into the depths when his questions annoy her. Snape cannot use this conduit to glean or transmit information unless Hermione wants something from him and initiates communication.

Dealing with Phineas Nigellus Black is rather like having Snape around. He is snide, waspish, and quick to take offense. But as the portrait of Armando Dippet says, portraits of former headmasters are "honor-bound to give service to the present headmaster of Hogwarts." (*HP/OotP*, 473) After the first time Hermione blindfolds him, he declares he will never return, but that decision is not his to make.

Through this connection, Snape learns that Harry, Ron, and Hermione are alive. In return, they learn that Dumbledore used the sword of Gryffindor to kill a Horcrux, that Dumbledore's Army is still active, that Snape sends them to Hagrid for detentions, and that Ginny has been banned from Hogsmeade visits. Anytime Phineas Nigellus asks for hints about their location, Hermione puts the painting away, but Snape manages to get them some information and assurance that Ginny is safe.

While Hermione controls this mediated communication with Snape, Harry is gaining mastery over his mental connection with Voldemort. Through much of this year, he cannot blot out Voldemort's thoughts. But once he, Ron, and Hermione are captured by Snatchers, their mortal danger pushes him to learn how to stay present: "Harry's scar was exquisitely painful, but he struggled with all his strength against the pull of Voldemort's thoughts: It had never been so important to remain in his own right mind." (HP/DH, 452)

Harry finds a few things that help him resist. One is adrenaline: "it was easier, as his fear mounted, to block out Voldemort's thoughts, though his scar was still burning." (HP/DH, 457) Another is empathy for endangered loved ones: "He felt Voldemort's fury, but as Hermione screamed again he shut it out, returning to the cellar and the horror of his own present." (HP/DH, 469) Grief, he finds, works best of all.

Harry has lost loved ones before, but his grief for Dobby is something specific and new.

> His scar burned, but he was master of the pain; he felt it, yet was apart from it. He had learned control at last, learned to shut his mind to Voldemort, the very thing Dumbledore had wanted him to learn from Snape. Just as Voldemort had not been able to possess Harry while Harry was consumed with grief for Sirius, so his thoughts could not penetrate Harry now, while he mourned Dobby. Grief, it seemed, drove Voldemort out . . . though Dumbledore, of course, would have said that it was love. . . . (HP/DH, 478)

Until now, Harry has only lost human guardians who died protecting him: his parents, Sirius, Dumbledore. Dobby's small size, his restricted status and social power, his devotion to Harry as a champion, and the purity of his courage in choosing to rebel all contribute to a quality of protective sorrow and awe in Harry's grief for him. Harry feels *responsible* for Dobby. Many children have not yet experienced this feeling. The understanding that it brings Harry takes him another step across the divide into adulthood. He would be better able, now, to understand Dumbledore's difficulty in telling Harry some bald truths, or Snape's words in healing Draco's *Sectumsempra* wounds, or even, perhaps, the recognition of Harry's unfair burdens that has kept Snape working to protect Harry despite years of dislike.

This protective grief is something entirely outside of Voldemort's experience or understanding, invisible to him and safe from him. Voldemort knows that protective love makes people easy to manipulate when their loved ones are threatened, but he doesn't understand that this love is so nourishing that it can block out emotions that help Dark Magic thrive, such as self-doubt, fear, or obsession. It is during this rush of protective, loving grief, digging Dobby's grave, that Harry comes to understand how the Elder Wand works and why it belongs to him whether or not he ever holds it in his hand.

> The steady rhythm of his arms beat time with his thoughts. Hallows . . . Horcruxes . . . Hallows . . . Horcruxes . . . Yet he no longer burned with that weird, obsessive longing. Loss and fear had snuffed it out: He felt as though he had been slapped awake again. (*HP/DH*, 479)

This is one reason why Snape doesn't covet magical objects. Loss and fear have taught him to be concerned with protecting others, not aggrandizing himself. If magical treasures can be won by being worthy—for example, by choosing to disarm rather than attack—then one can be worthy of them without expending energy pursuing material objects.

Once Harry decides to trust his hunch not to pursue the Elder Wand, he has to endure the feeling of inaction and his knowledge that Dumbledore's tomb is being shamefully desecrated: "He could not remember, ever before, choosing *not* to act." (*HP/DH*, 502) It's one of his first encounters with the kind of self-control that Snape exhibited in showing no reaction to the torture of Charity Burbage. When something even greater is at stake, focusing on the urgency of that protectiveness can help to seal off private emotions so they remain inviolable.

Harry manages to close down his visions of Voldemort until he talks to Ollivander and Griphook, Ron and Hermione. When it's finally safe for him to give in to the visions of Voldemort's surroundings, he sees the same light that he saw at the beginning of his sixth year, coming late to school after being attacked on the Hogwarts Express: "Voldemort was at the gates of Hogwarts; Harry could see him standing there, and see too the lamp bobbing in the pre-dawn, coming closer and closer." (*HP/DH*, 499)

Snape is coming to let Voldemort in. After nearly 500 pages of absence, he reenters the story. Now that Harry has learned Occlumency, now that Voldemort fears contact with Harry's mind and isn't aware that Harry can see his thoughts, it is safe for Snape and Harry to connect again. Snape cannot be certain that Harry has mastered Occlumency, but he knows that Voldemort will never again read Harry's thoughts, and he knows what it looks like in Harry's mind when Harry reads Voldemort's thoughts. He must suspect that when Voldemort looks at him, Harry might see him, too. The light coming closer and closer is to welcome in Harry as well as Voldemort. Harry and Snape have closed in on Voldemort from either side. From this moment, Voldemort is doomed.

Dementors

In his sixth year, Harry expected low marks on a Defense Against the Dark Arts assignment "because he had disagreed with Snape on the best way to tackle dementors" (*DH/HBP*, 448). Like Snape's lessons about bezoars, none of Snape's information about dementors got through to Harry, sabotaged by Snape's long history of tormenting Harry in class. Harry sticks to the Patronus method he learned from Professor Lupin, which is beautifully suited to Harry's strengths but is only one strategy, not the "flexible and inventive" array of approaches that Snape advises for effective Defense Against the Dark Arts (*DH/HBP*, 178).

We never learn what Snape considered the best way to tackle dementors, but assuming that Harry argued for the Patronus method, we can guess at Snape's possible objections.

The Patronus method is not an option for any situation requiring stealth. Harry realizes this when he's in the Ministry of Magic underneath the Invisibility Cloak, trying to retrieve the locket Horcrux from Dolores Umbridge. Umbridge has brought in Muggle-borns for interrogation and surrounded them with dementors, which affect Harry as well. Harry cannot cast a Patronus without revealing himself. The best he can do is "think of Hermione and of Ron, who needed him." (*HP/DH*, 257) This method cannot protect anyone else from the dementors, but it keeps Harry safe until he can do more.

Patronus method is an elite-level spell. Even a gifted witch like Hermione has trouble casting it (*HP/DH*, 263); Lupin told Harry, "Many qualified wizards have difficulty with it." (*HP/PoA*, 237) Furthermore, the effects of trauma can hinder the ability to cast a Patronus, as Harry learns while wearing the locket Horcrux. (*HP/DH*,

286) Snape would not have recommended such an inaccessible spell for basic defense.

In great enough numbers, dementors can overpower even the strongest Patronus. When Harry imagines rescuing people from Azkaban, he realizes that "dementors in those numbers would be virtually unassailable." (*HP/DH*, 435)

The Patronus method gives away too much. A spy like Snape would not recommend a defense method that would reveal the caster's identity or what is closest to the caster's heart. There is no disguising a Patronus. When Harry repels dementors in Hogsmeade, Death Eaters identify his stag immediately. (*HP/DH*, 556)

By the time of the Final Battle, Harry discovers two more ways to handle dementors, and we see evidence that Snape probably used these tactics to seal his own mind against them.

The Resurrection Stone gives Harry one way. The almost solid forms of Lily, James, Sirius, and Lupin keep him company on his walk toward death. These are the parents and family friends whose care instilled love in him so that he could have the kind of joy in life that can produce a Patronus. Not everyone is fortunate enough to have such riches. Not everyone is unfortunate enough to lose many of their loved ones so early. These intense memories of beloved caretakers are the sort of emotion that Patronuses are made of. Just thinking about them is protection enough.

> "Stay close to me," he said quietly.
>
> And he set off. The dementors' chill did not overcome him; he passed through it with his companions, and *they acted like Patronuses to him*, and together they marched through the old trees that grew closely together, their branches tangled, their roots gnarled and twisted underfoot. (*HP/DH*, 700, *emphasis mine*)

Memories of these loved ones keep Harry safe from dementors on his walk toward death. On his return, when he feigns death and Hagrid carries him from the forest to the castle, Harry passes the dementors again. This time, he is protected from them in a different way.

> And now a chill settled over them where they stood, and Harry heard the rasping breath of the dementors that patrolled the outer

trees. They would not affect him now. *The fact of his own survival burned inside him, a talisman against them,* as though his father's stag kept guardian in his heart. (*HP/DH,* 728, *emphasis mine*)

Harry knows he is a survivor; that gives him strength. But more than that, he knows that he gave himself up not for his own gain—not killed while trying to escape, as Voldemort claimed—but to protect others, to stop Voldemort from killing them. (*HP/DH,* 731) In King's Cross, he had a choice: he could "go on," remain at peace, or he could head "back to pain and the fear of more loss" because there was a chance he could finish Voldemort for good. (*HP/DH,* 722) He chose to return for a second chance in order to protect others. These choices give Harry protective magic that is made of the same stuff as Patronuses, but stronger: the knowledge that others, both friends and enemies, are precious enough that Harry would give his life for them, as others gave their lives for him.

In the chapters "The Silver Doe," "The Elder Wand," and "The Prince's Tale," we see that both of these tactics are known to Snape.

Snape draws strength from the memory of a loved one always but keeps the image internal, introjecting rather than projecting it. This prevents him from protecting others by scattering dementors, but he is a spy; his life's work is to protect others on a grand scale by remaining hidden for the long term, even if that means forgoing immediate action. Part of remaining hidden is keeping his true self secret. There are very few people whom Snape can trust with the sight of his Patronus.

He also knows that he has chosen both life and death to protect others, not for his own gain. The final book shows us that Snape was once ready to die to ease his own pain, but he accepted the offer of a second chance in order to protect someone else, difficult as that was guaranteed to be. When he does accept death, again, it is not for personal gain but to protect others. These convictions mean that Snape always knows why he is alive and what is important to him. The emotional connections necessary for a Patronus are not only available to those who remember receiving love. Those who choose to live to protect others create in themselves the same defensive strength.

The Silver Doe

At Harry's darkest hour, near the midpoint of the book, Snape comes to Harry in his purest form: completely unknowable, invisible except for his Patronus.

Three days after their disastrous Christmas Eve trip to Godric's Hollow, Harry and Hermione still don't know how to find the sword of Gryffindor. Ron has abandoned them, Harry's wand is broken beyond repair, and they've just learned that in his youth, Dumbledore wanted to join Grindelwald in subjugating Muggles. Harry wonders how he can have faith in Dumbledore anymore. Even the forest, where Harry is keeping watch alone while Hermione sleeps, is in darkness: "The night reached such a depth of velvety blackness that he might have been suspended in limbo between Disapparition and Apparition." (HP/DH, 365)

That's when Snape sends his Patronus to lead Harry to the sword of Gryffindor, which he has submerged at the bottom of a frozen pool. The Patronus first appears as a bright silver light, like the lantern bobbing closer to Harry when Snape lets him into Hogwarts at the beginning of his sixth year.

The reader has known since *Order of the Phoenix* that Snape can cast a Patronus, but Rowling has carefully waited until this moment to reveal its form:

> It was a silver-white doe, moon-bright and dazzling, picking her way over the ground, still silent, and leaving no hoofprints in the fine powdering of snow. She stepped toward him, her beautiful head with its wide, long-lashed eyes held high.
>
> Harry stared at the creature, filled with wonder, not at her strangeness, but at her inexplicable familiarity. He felt that he had been waiting for her to come, but that he had forgotten, until this moment, that they had arranged to meet. (HP/DH, 366)

The doe compels Harry with her radiant goodness. She leads him to the pool with the sword.

> Deeper and deeper into the forest she led him, and Harry walked quickly, sure that when she stopped, she would allow him to approach her properly. And then she would speak and the voice would tell him what he needed to know.
>
> At last, she came to a halt. She turned her beautiful head toward him once more, and he broke into a run, a question burning in him, but as he opened his lips to ask it, she vanished. (HP/DH, 366-7)

Harry never guesses whose Patronus this is. The doe's silence keeps this luminous moment firmly in the magical, her image rich in allusions but eluding definition, ruling out nothing. This is nonverbal magic.

A doe, the adult female counterpart to the stag Patronuses of James and Harry, suggests Lily. But ever since his third year, when he wanted to believe it was his father who cast the stag Patronus he saw, Harry has known that Patronuses come from the living. He knows this is not from his mother. Yet he, and the reader, know from Tonks's experience that Patronuses can reflect a person's love. No wonder the doe is familiar to Harry. As Dumbledore once told him, "Magic always leaves traces." (HP/PoA, 563) No matter what strife there has been between Harry and Snape, they have loved and been loved by the same person. They both contain traces of Lily's magic.

Is it unusual that Snape's Patronus is feminine? It may seem that Patronuses usually represent the caster's self, including gender. However, the only Patronuses we see with specified genders are the doe and the two Potter stags. Gender is not mentioned for any other Patronus—not Kingsley's lynx, not Dumbledore's phoenix, not Hermione's otter—even if we might imagine these Patronuses speaking in the gendered voices of their casters. The doe Patronus must have spoken to Sirius in Snape's voice, a thought that seems comical and incongruous. It seems probable, though, that it was in Snape's low, urgent registers rather than the sneer with which he usually addressed Sirius. The mindset for casting a Patronus emphasizes love, and Snape's Patronus in particular points toward his better nature.

Snape's Patronus takes the form of a feminine counterpart to the Patronus of his enemy and his enemy's son. Some readers find this odd, pathetic, or creepy. Is Rowling suggesting that Snape would actually be a compatible mate for James or Harry? That's not the story she's telling here, although authors of fanfiction have written beautiful and imaginative explorations of this idea. Is he stuck in the past or unhealthily obsessed with a dead woman? This reading is understandable, but his actions during his final year suggest someone very much focused on the present. Rather, the image of the silver doe points us toward a variant of the trope of courtly love.

The white hind or hart—the Muggle version of a silver doe—is a mainstay of Arthurian legend. The elusive white hind was a magical creature whose appearance indicated the way to a wondrous adventure. Rowling's allusion to the white hind directs us to other elements of Arthurian story tradition as well, such as chivalry and courtly love.

Courtly love, which features in Arthurian legend and many other traditions, is the unrequited love of a knight for an idealized, unattainable woman, often married to another man. In the lady's honor, the knight strives to accomplish chivalrous deeds and become pure of heart. Chivalry—the most complex of the quintessential Gryffindor traits—is the choice of the privileged to undergo personal risk to help the less privileged, prompted only by goodness and not reward. Chivalrous knights often carried a "favor" from their lady, a small object such as jewelry, that they promised to return after their labors. This promise would give them a surge of extra determination to remain alive and safe.

Snape's Patronus shows that he holds in his heart an image of a woman whose friendship and love helped form the best part of his nature. During this year when nobody knows Snape's true self, Snape cannot depend upon external recognition of his nearly superhuman efforts. He can turn to his memories of Lily's friendship as a guide: he can atone for his betrayal that resulted in her death by becoming, in the second part of his life, someone who would be able to meet the gaze of a person like Lily without shame.

It is not exactly courtly love that Rowling is portraying with Snape's Patronus. Lily is unattainable to Snape not because of her marriage or station but because Snape's choices killed her. He is not deluded; he is not somehow trying to win posthumous favor; if anyone knows that the dead remain dead, it is Snape. He is simply reminding himself how to live so he can make the best of a great gift: the chance to do things over again, not to undo the past, not to gain reward, but only to do good and save innocent lives. We will see later that he does carry with him a favor of sorts, but it is not to guarantee his own safety. This is Rowling's original variation on the power of love to give strength.

After the doe leads Harry into the forest, she vanishes. Harry finds the sword of Gryffindor at the bottom of a frozen pool, recalling Arthurian legends of enchanted swords in lakes that can be retrieved only by the worthy. The sword looks like a "great silver cross," recalling the Christian treasures that often figured in Arthurian quests. (*HP/DH*, 367) In the wizarding world, though, you don't have to be extraordinary to be worthy of this sword. You just have to be a Gryffindor.

> What was it, Harry asked himself (walking again), that
> Dumbledore had told him the last time he had retrieved the sword?
> *Only a true Gryffindor could have pulled* that *out of the hat.* And what
> were the qualities that defined a Gryffindor? A small voice inside

> Harry's head answered him: *Their daring, nerve, and chivalry set*
> *Gryffindors apart.* (*HP/DH*, 368)

In his second year, when Harry prayed for help fighting Tom Riddle and the basilisk, Fawkes brought him the Sorting Hat. He jammed the hat onto his head and the sword of Gryffindor thudded out of it. (*HP/CoS*, 319) The Sorting Hat had looked into his mind and seen that Harry's temperament is best suited to a surge of adrenaline or chivalry in times of crisis: that's what makes him a Gryffindor. Rufus Scrimgeour said that "the sword may present itself to any worthy Gryffindor." (*HP/DH*, 129) That characteristic Gryffindor surge of energy is what summons the sword in particular, as opposed to a magical object that might enhance one's wisdom, loyalty, or cunning.

That would be why Snape placed the sword at the bottom of a frozen pool in late December, then. It recalls the story of Excalibur and the Lady of the Lake, but it also ensures that Harry would produce enough adrenaline when diving to make him unmistakably recognizable to the sword as a Gryffindor.

Reluctantly, Harry concedes that he is going to have to jump into the frozen pool to demonstrate his Gryffindor daring and nerve: "Where 'chivalry' entered into this, he thought ruefully, he was not entirely sure, unless it counted as chivalrous that he was not calling for Hermione to do it in his stead." (*HP/DH*, 369)

Harry "gathered all his courage, and dived." (*HP/DH*, 370) But Snape's plan hadn't accounted for the adverse effect that the locket Horcrux—which intensifies the trauma that Harry has suffered from Voldemort's attacks—would have on Harry's courage, since Snape doesn't know about the Horcruxes. It turns out to be Ron's chivalry that gets the sword out of the pool.

Ron's return to hunt Horcruxes alongside Harry and Hermione is chivalry. As a pureblood, he has the privilege of walking away from the fight against Voldemort in a way that Harry and Hermione do not. His choice to return is conscious chivalry on top of his original motives of friendship and justice. Jumping into the pool to help Harry, unhindered by the kind of trauma that burdens Harry, is his chivalrous first act upon returning.

Snape would have known, through Phineas Nigellus Black's reports, that Ron was no longer with Harry and Hermione. He would also have seen Ron searching for Harry and Hermione in the forest earlier that day. The silver doe led Ron to Harry as well as leading Harry to the sword.

> "I did think I saw something move over there, but I was running to the pool at the time, because you'd gone in and you hadn't come up, so I wasn't going to make a detour to—hey!"
>
> Harry was already hurrying to the place Ron had indicated. The two oaks grew close together; there was a gap of only a few inches between the trunks at eye level, an ideal place to see but not be seen. (*HP/DH*, 372)

Snape stayed long enough to see Harry's near drowning, Ron's rescue, and the retrieval of the sword. He left before witnessing what they used the sword to destroy. Neither Ron nor Harry can figure out who cast the silver doe.

The Snape-Shaped Hole

There comes a time when the narrative of the Death Eater headmaster cannot contain Snape anymore.

All year, Snape has playacted the faithful Death Eater. But once he learns that Harry has entered Hogwarts and Voldemort is coming, his job as headmaster comes second. What matters now is that he fulfills Dumbledore's order to get a final message to Harry. He must stay alive at all costs until he succeeds. Once he's done that, he will have fulfilled the terms of his second chance at life.

Harry, under his invisibility cloak, is walking with McGonagall in Hogwarts when they hear the quiet footsteps of someone joining them.

> She halted, raised her wand ready to duel, and said, "Who's there?"
>
> "It is I," said a low voice.
>
> From behind a suit of armor stepped Severus Snape. (*HP/DH*, 597)

For the first time in a year, Snape steps out from behind his ironclad defenses and declares his true identity in low tones meant only for McGonagall, who had been his delightfully acerbic colleague and teaching partner for so many years. When speaking to her, he stops Occluding. It is as if he is taking off his own invisibility cloak.

> Hatred boiled up in Harry at the sight of him: He had forgotten the details of Snape's appearance in the magnitude of his crimes, forgotten how his greasy black hair hung in curtains around his

> thin face, how his black eyes had a dead, cold look. He was not
> wearing nightclothes, but was dressed in his usual black cloak, and
> he too was holding his wand ready for a fight. (*HP/DH*, 597)

Seeing Snape's humanity and bodily existence up close reignites Harry's visceral hatred. When Snape has been described in this volume without Harry's point of view, there has been no focus on greasy hair or dead-looking eyes; these are artifacts of Harry's revulsion. But Harry no longer dwells on Snape's sallow skin or hooked nose, which have made him seem more like a cartoon villain. The mentions here of his greasy hair, thin face, and cold eyes emphasize that he has been living under enormous strain. Of course he is dressed for a fight, not in his grotesquely comical gray nightshirt as he was years ago. The sight of Snape hasn't been very funny lately, and he probably hasn't had a night's rest in . . . years.

He scans the air around McGonagall "with an air of hardly noticing what he was doing," as though he knows Harry is there. (*HP/DH*, 598) His state of high alertness has brought him to the same degree of wizardry as Dumbledore, able to sense magic that is undetectable to others.

> "I was under the impression," said Snape, "that Alecto had
> apprehended an intruder."
>
> "Really?" said Professor McGonagall. "And what gave you that
> impression?"
>
> Snape made a slight flexing movement of his left arm, where the
> Dark Mark was branded into his skin.
>
> "Oh, but naturally," said Professor McGonagall. "You Death Eaters
> have your own private means of communication, I forgot."
> (*HP/DH*, 597)

The trust of Minerva McGonagall must have been one of Snape's most painful sacrifices. Rowling's choice to have him indicate his Dark Mark with a gesture rather than acknowledge it with words makes him seem suddenly younger and vulnerable. The flexing of an arm reminds us of his physical existence again; it's a gesture both masculine and intimate. He is less the imposing Death Eater here than a lone man, not yet middle-aged, wanting the comfort, just for a moment, of his former friend thinking about how it's felt for him to know every pulse of evil for the past several years in his very flesh.

But it's too late. Her trust is dead. When Snape looks directly into her eyes and asks about Harry, McGonagall hears this as a threat and attacks to kill.

> Professor McGonagall moved faster than Harry could have believed: Her wand slashed through the air and for a split second Harry thought that Snape must crumple, unconscious, but the swiftness of his Shield Charm was such that McGonagall was thrown off balance. (*HP/DH*, 598)

Flitwick and Sprout join McGonagall in fighting Snape. He refuses to fight back; he only defends. They attack him with fire, which he turns into a serpent; a swarm of daggers, which sink into the suit of armor he forces in front of him; the armor itself, using his defenses against him until he struggles free and destroys it. He cannot remain at Hogwarts without getting hurt or hurting his colleagues.

Once again, in order to protect others, it is time for him to take flight: to smash through a classroom window and literally *fly* to the edges of the Hogwarts grounds, fly as Voldemort did, without broom or thestral, while McGonagall cries after him, "Coward! *COWARD!*" (*HP/DH*, 599)

There is no way for McGonagall to know why Snape is fleeing. At this point, his entire being is focused on being a vessel for a message, like a human version of the crystal orbs made to hold prophecies, fragile and brittle.

McGonagall assumes that Voldemort taught Snape to fly: "he seems to have learned a few tricks from his master." (*HP/DH*, 599) She tells the other Heads of House that Snape is "taking a short break" as she points out "the Snape-shaped hole in the window." (*HP/DH*, 600)

The "Snape-shaped hole": one last bit of narrative bullying of Snape, describing his ordeals in a mocking tone that shows him in an absurd, repulsive light. Does the shattered glass in the classroom window really show a perfect silhouette of this unsympathetic character, greasy hair and all?

The story that Harry and McGonagall believe to be Snape's cannot contain Snape anymore. There is no exit possible for Snape that would allow him to take peaceable leave of his former colleagues and survive to deliver the message to Harry. Over seven volumes and a million words, Rowling has carefully balanced a portrait of an almost unknowable man whose every action could be interpreted as protective or wicked. He has played both sides expertly for so long. Does he even *have* an authentic self anymore? Or is the person known as Severus Snape just an absence, an outline into which others project their assumptions of who he is?

Harry tells the rest of the Order that "Snape's run for it" (*HP/DH*, 603) and McGonagall tells the assembled students that Snape has, "to use the common phrase, done a bunk"—he has abdicated his duties as headmaster. (*HP/DH*, 609) Rowling confirmed in interview that "Snape had effectively abandoned his post" (The Leaky Cauldron 2007). But Snape left the school in care of the Heads of House before he left to fight Voldemort, much as Dumbledore did the year before when he asked Harry, "Do you think that I have once left the school unprotected during my absences this year?" (*HP/HBP*, 550) Snape knows that McGonagall, Flitwick, Sprout, and Slughorn will protect the students with their lives.

"Look . . . at . . . me. . . ."

Once Voldemort realizes that Harry is hunting Horcruxes, he begins keeping Nagini near him in an enchanted sphere. As more of his soul is destroyed, the small remaining portion of his soul depends more heavily on Harry. The diminishment of his soul and his rising panic make it easier for Harry to control their mental connection. Harry sees Voldemort call Snape to him in the Shrieking Shack. He, Ron, and Hermione must destroy Nagini, so they go to the Shrieking Shack, too, using the tunnel entrance.

For the third time, the Shrieking Shack is a place of mortal peril for Snape. Voldemort explains that he believes Snape to be the master of the Elder Wand and therefore must be killed in order for the wand to give Voldemort its proper allegiance.

Snape is barely listening: "And for a moment Harry saw Snape's profile: His eyes were fixed upon the coiling snake in its enchanted cage." (*HP/DH*, 654)

Harry, watching from the tunnel under his Invisibility Cloak, closes his eyes in pain when he feels one of Voldemort's stabs of rage in his scar—and in closing his eyes, Harry's vision shifts to Voldemort's point of view, looking directly into Snape's face.

Snape offers to bring Harry to Voldemort; three times, he asks permission to do so and is denied. The only time he takes his eyes off the snake is when Voldemort reveals that he plundered Dumbledore's grave to steal the Elder Wand.

> And now Snape looked at Voldemort, and Snape's face was like a death mask. It was marble white and so still that when he spoke, it was a shock to see that anyone lived behind the blank eyes. (*HP/DH*, 655)

With the words "death mask" and "marble white," Rowling alludes to Dumbledore in his white marble tomb. If Snape's eyes are shockingly blank, at least in Voldemort's view, he must be Occluding Voldemort with all of his might. Grief strengthens Occlumency and drives out Voldemort; Snape is grieving Dumbledore and the violation of his grave.

On Voldemort's orders, Nagini gives Snape a fatal bite. Snape falls to the floor, blood gushing from his neck, "a foot in a black boot trembling on the floor." (*HP/DH*, 657) Nagini and Voldemort leave the Shrieking Shack and Harry enters it:

> He did not know why he was doing it, why he was approaching the dying man: He did not know what he felt as he saw Snape's white face, and the fingers trying to staunch the bloody wound at his neck. Harry took off the Invisibility Cloak and looked down upon the man he hated, whose widening black eyes found Harry as he tried to speak. Harry bent over him, and Snape seized the front of his robes and pulled him close. (*HP/DH*, 657)

Why does Harry approach him? To Snape's dying breath, Harry hates him. But he approaches because in Snape's final moments, alone with a genocidal madman, the only thing he asked for, three times, was permission to look for Harry. He didn't ask for his life, only Harry. Dumbledore once told Harry that "help will always be given at Hogwarts to those who ask for it." (*HP/CoS*, 264) Harry heard Snape's dying wish and granted it.

Readers often wonder: What would have happened if Harry hadn't appeared just before Snape died? Was it only coincidence that Snape was able to deliver the final message? Or did Snape make the choice to grasp the front of Harry's robes rather than save himself (Justice, 232-8)? Snape was "trying to staunch the bloody wound at his neck" until Harry appeared; he was trying to live long enough to find Harry. When Harry appeared, he took his fingers off the wound.

How was Snape planning to counter a fatal bite? If his fingers managed to halt the blood loss, what was he going to do? Did the master potioneer and Slytherin strategist carry a potion with him that would put a stopper in death? It seems likely; certainly, it seems prudent. Perhaps Snape had no concerns about carrying this potion on his person at all times because he knew nobody would look for it: he lived an intensely lonely life his final year, surrounded by people but with little genuine contact. The foot in a black boot, trembling, is a stark reminder that behind the imposing façade, Snape has been just one man with a life as fragile and human as any other, so callously ended by Voldemort.

What death-stoppering potion might he have carried? The Elixir of Life would have done the trick, but it seems probable, in accordance with the laws of Rowling's world, that Dumbledore would not have asked the Flamels to brew stores of it for anyone but themselves to administer. It might have been whatever Snape used to revive Dumbledore after he picked up the cursed ring. If Snape was carrying a potion that we have seen before within the books, though, a likely candidate would be the one that "completely cured" Arthur Weasley of Nagini's near-fatal bite, which Molly Weasley described at Grimmauld Place—to a room that included Snape—as "an antidote to whatever that snake's got in its fangs." (*HP/OotP*, 522) The Order knew that Voldemort relied heavily on Nagini. It would have been foolish not to set aside a store of that antidote.

Once Harry approaches Snape, he takes off his Invisibility Cloak, paralleling Snape stepping out from behind a suit of armor earlier. It must seem a wonder to Snape that the person he needs to see is materializing before his eyes, an answer to his prayers. These adversaries, who have long viewed each other through prejudices and disguises, can finally view each other as they really are. There is no need for Snape to hide any thoughts from Harry; after all, he no longer fears Voldemort killing him.

He cannot hide thoughts anymore, anyway. So close to death, he is unable to Occlude:

> Something more than blood was leaking from Snape. Silvery blue, neither gas nor liquid, it gushed from his mouth and his ears and his eyes, and Harry knew what it was, but did not know what to do—
>
> A flask, conjured from thin air, was thrust into his shaking hands by Hermione. (*HP/DH*, 657)

Hermione has always been ready to be the vessel that receives Snape's thoughts. She knows precisely what Snape needs; the flask she conjures is even the perfect size.

> Harry lifted the silvery substance into it with his wand. When the flask was full to the brim, and Snape looked as though there was no blood left in him, his grip on Harry's robes slackened.
>
> "Look . . . at . . . me. . . ." he whispered.
>
> The green eyes found the black, but after a second, something in the depths of the dark pair seemed to vanish, leaving them fixed, blank, and empty. The hand holding Harry thudded to the floor, and Snape moved no more. (*HP/DH*, 657-8)

Look at me.

With those words, Rowling completes the incantation for the stupendous magic she has cast over seven books with her creation of Severus Snape. Everything about Snape is contained in those three words. The spy who longed for nothing more than *to be seen*. The double agent who killed the mentor who was the last person to see his true self. The ugly boy who grew up into a man so ugly that students couldn't look upon him without revulsion. The master of Occlumency who was sealed shut so tightly, his eyes looked dead. The Master of Death who didn't need a cloak to be invisible, completing his second chance at life, removing his disguise and meeting Death as a friend.

Many critics have written eloquently about Rowling's allusions to Dante and Beatrice in Snape's death scene, including John Granger in his essay "Snape's Green-Eyed Girl: Dante, Renaissance Florence, and the Death of the Potions Master" (Granger, 131-150). As Granger points out, "The Prince's Tale," the chapter in which Harry views Snape's memories of Lily, is Chapter 33 of *Deathly Hallows*, in homage to the 33 cantos of each section of *The Divine Comedy*. Dante's dead beloved and spiritual guide, Beatrice, had green eyes like the eyes that Harry inherited from Lily. At the end of his earthly labors, Snape might well have wanted to gaze into Lily's eyes, in Harry's face, as he moved on.

Rowling crafted many other facets into this death scene, as well. Hilary K. Justice reads "Look . . . at . . . me. . . ." not as a plea but as an imperative (Justice). As Justice shows, Harry has just seen Snape choose to die, taking his hands off his wound, in order to give Harry his memories, and the sight of this choice propels Harry to view the memories immediately before resuming the fight against Voldemort. Snape's choice to help Harry rather than use his last moments to save his own life echoes Dumbledore's choice to protect Harry rather than counter Draco's *Expelliarmus*: "Dumbledore had wordlessly immobilized Harry, and the second he had taken to perform the spell had cost him the chance of defending himself." (*HP/HBP*, 584)

Snape has carried memories of Lily's love within him through unspeakable peril, impervious to the world's greatest Legilimens, locked as inexorably as the room in the Department of Mysteries that, according to Dumbledore, "contains a force that is at once more wonderful and more terrible than death, than human intelligence, than forces of nature." (*HP/OotP*, 843) The door cannot be forced. But when Snape and Harry see each other for who they truly are, this is the key. The locked door swings open. Through the shared gaze, Snape transmits to Harry his memories of Lily's love, Harry's birthright. Like the Snitch that contains the Resurrection Stone, Snape opens at the close, memories pouring out of him. At such a moment of uncontrollable emotion, when he meets Harry's eyes, he *cannot* see only Lily's eyes and not Harry. He sees Lily *in* Harry in a way he has always willfully refused to see before, the eyes that look like hers in the face that resembles James, combined in someone altogether different whom Snape is dying to protect.

"Look . . . at . . . me. . . ." means that Snape feels finished with the work of his second chance at life. He deprived Harry of Lily's love years ago, dedicated the second half of his life to returning it, and it is done. He can take off his cloak of invisibility and meet Death as a friend now. He can say *look at me* because he finally meets the standard he set for himself: if he were to see Lily Potter now, he would be able to meet her gaze without shame at last. He has done all he can do to atone.

SEVERUS SNAPE

AND THE DEATHLY HALLOWS, PART 2

"The Prince's Tale," Chapter 33 of *Harry Potter and the Deathly Hallows*, is the emotional climax of all of Harry's preparations to face Voldemort, giving him the last piece he needs before testing himself against the tyrant. The twenty memories that Snape passed to Harry are more than just the final message that Dumbledore charged Snape with delivering. They contain everything Snape couldn't tell Harry during his life, including the reasons for his secrecy. They contain, among other things, an apology. They deliver some gifts that only Snape could give. Most of all, they return to Harry his maternal inheritance, which Snape had in his keeping until the moment it was safe to pass it on.

The stories in the Prince's Tale could fill a book in themselves, and indeed, for many readers fascinated by the character of Snape, this one chapter *is* the richest payoff of *Deathly Hallows*. We meet, at last, the true Severus Snape, and this sheds light retrospectively on events of the whole series, going back to before Harry's birth. The writing is dense with emotion but delicate and sardonic as well, raw at times, and it answers the question the series has been asking with increasing urgency: *What is the mother's story?* So much about Snape has to do with a mother's story, whether his own, Harry's, Draco's, or the author's.

This chapter shows us what other two memories Snape removed into the Pensieve during Occlumency lessons. It provides hints about how Snape learned to fly. We see why Dumbledore trusted Snape. The memories fill in the Snape-shaped hole in the story that he created by crashing through the window, the first breach in the Battle of Hogwarts, when he was no longer able to uphold defense of the school and dedicated his full efforts only to reaching Harry. We find out where Snape came from and what motivated all his actions.

Harry remains by Snape's side after his death until he hears Voldemort's declaration of a truce: Voldemort plans to wait one hour for

Harry to give himself up, after which he intends to enter battle and slaughter everyone who has helped Harry. Harry, Ron, and Hermione hurry back to the castle. Hermione, always the most attuned to Snape, stops to glance at Snape's body before leaving. (HP/DH, 660) She will not forget about him.

Hermione and Ron join the mourners in the Great Hall, but Harry cannot endure the sight of his dead and injured friends:

> Harry reeled backward from the doorway. He could not draw breath. He could not bear to look at any of the other bodies, to see who else had died for him. He could not bear to join the Weasleys, could not look into their eyes, when if he had given himself up in the first place, Fred might never have died. . . . He yearned not to feel. . . He wished he could rip out his heart, his innards, everything that was screaming inside him. . . . (HP/DH, 661-2)

Harry runs to the Pensieve in the headmaster's office, thinking wryly, "Nothing that even Snape had left him could be worse than his own thoughts." (HP/DH, 662) What he finds, though, is that Snape left him thoughts that speak directly to his own. Snape, too, once yearned not to feel because of the weight of others' deaths and could not endure the sight of the survivor, the orphan boy who reminded him of his guilt.

The memories Snape bequeaths to Harry:
1. Snape's first meeting with Lily and Petunia
2. Snape and Lily talking in a small thicket of trees
3. Platform 9 ¾
4. The Hogwarts Express
5. The Sorting
6. Snape and Lily arguing about Dark Magic
7. Snape's Worst Memory
8. Snape's apology to Lily
9. Snape's request of Dumbledore
10. Snape's second chance from Dumbledore
11. Harry's first year
12. The Yule Ball
13. Dumbledore's request of Snape
14. The argument in the forest
15. The final message to Harry
16. Advice from Dumbledore's portrait

17. Confunding Mundungus Fletcher

18. The flight of the Seven Harrys

19. Remorse

20. The sword of Gryffindor

Snape's Memories

#1: Snape's first meeting with Lily and Petunia

Harry dives into the Pensieve and falls headlong into a warm, sunlit scene, a playground near the childhood homes of Snape, Lily, and Petunia. Even Snape was a small child once.

> Two girls were swinging backward and forward, and a skinny boy was watching them from behind a clump of bushes. His black hair was overlong and his clothes were so mismatched that it looked deliberate: too short jeans, a shabby, overlarge coat that might have belonged to a grown man, an odd smocklike shirt. (*HP/DH*, 663)

The first sight of child Snape starts an avalanche of realizations and connections for Harry. Yes, this is going to be about Lily. So Snape knew Petunia. Snape looked ludicrous in his clothing, but not the way wizards often do in Muggle garb; more the way Harry did at the same age, neglected, wearing Dudley's cast-off clothes. He wasn't an attractive child. Beauty was one of the inequalities between Snape and Lily. He was an outsider and a spy, even then.

> Harry moved closer to the boy. Snape looked no more than nine or ten years old, sallow, small, stringy. There was undisguised greed in his thin face as he watched the younger of the two girls swinging higher and higher than her sister. (*HP/DH*, 663)

Undisguised greed: beyond hunger, beyond yearning. A sense of desire and entitlement for things that belong by rights to others. It's the same "greedy expression" that was on Voldemort's face when he first saw Hufflepuff's cup (*DH/HBP*, 436). Child Lily had something that Snape coveted.

The very first memory solves the mystery of Snape's flight, mere hours after Harry, and the reader, first learned of Snape's ability.

> "Lily, don't do it!" shrieked the elder of the two.

> But the girl had let go of the swing at the very height of its arc and
> flown into the air, quite literally flown, launched herself skyward
> with a great shout of laughter, and instead of crumpling on the
> playground asphalt, she soared like a trapeze artist through the air,
> staying up far too long, landing far too lightly. (*HP/DH*, 663)

Quite literally flown. Lily was pure magic. Nobody taught her this; she
developed this rare skill by prolonging the joy of soaring on a swing,
teaching herself the wandless, nonverbal magic of how to reproduce
flight at will. That's where Snape first saw flight. This shows us one of
the ways the author imagines her late mother as a child, too, the girl with
the surname Volant, *flying*.

Harry got his flying ability from both sides, then. James was a
brilliant flyer, but Lily was something else entirely. All that time, while
James and Harry received plaudits for their broom-flying skills, Snape
had known of something even more wondrous.

McGonagall assumed that Snape learned flight from Voldemort. But
we know that cannot be true: everything she believed about Snape at that
moment was heartbreakingly wrong. Voldemort never shares knowledge
that he believes makes him exceptional; he even thinks he's the only one
ever to discover the Room of Requirement, known to everyone from
house-elves to Sybill Trelawney. (*HP/DH*, 641) He would never reward
a Death Eater with special knowledge, anyway. Voldemort believes that
punishment works better than reward.

Did Snape and Lily fly together as children? Perhaps he flew as a
child and then stopped. Perhaps he lost the ability or will after Lily died,
a dreadfully sad thought; or perhaps he continued as an adult without
Lily, which is sadder still and seems less likely. It's even possible, though
unlikely for such an avid learner, that Snape never flew at all until the
moment he broke through the window and called on his memories of
Lily to help him remain airborne.

In the memory, worried, envious Petunia scolds Lily for flying, but
Lily giggles, "Tuney, look at this. Watch what I can do." (*HP/DH*, 663)

Look at me. What children say when delighted by their growing
powers. Perhaps Snape did learn flying from Lily and when he mastered
the skill, said joyfully, *Look at me.*

Lily shows Petunia more magic.

Lily had picked up a fallen flower from the bush behind which

> Snape lurked. Petunia advanced, evidently torn between curiosity and disapproval. Lily waited until Petunia was near enough to have a clear view, then held out her palm. The flower sat there, opening and closing its petals, like some bizarre, many-lipped oyster. (*HP/DH*, 663-4)

Petunia asks, with longing, "How do you do it?" (*HP/DH*, 664)

No wonder Snape died in order to leave Harry this memory. *Look how magical your mother was.* Lily's magic was ecstatic: flight, the breath of flowers, female sexuality in its purest form.

The sight raises such exhilaration in child Snape that he forgets his self-consciousness and the need to hide. Nothing matters more than wanting to bring self-knowledge and revelation to the beautiful creature who is the same age as he is, has the same powers, will surely understand and love him. Snape has the correct answer and that overrides all. He forgets that introducing himself will bring the same discord that his presence always does.

> "It's obvious, isn't it?" Snape could no longer contain himself, but had jumped out from behind the bushes. Petunia shrieked and ran backward toward the swings, but Lily, though clearly startled, remained where she was. Snape seemed to regret his appearance. A dull flush of color mounted the sallow cheeks as he looked at Lily. (*HP/DH*, 664)

Decades later, when Hermione levitates out of her seat with the desire to speak, Snape cannot even look at her. The unguarded enthusiasm of innocent children simply begs to be savaged, and Petunia tears into Snape, putting him in his place with her Muggle mockery of his poverty and strange appearance. It's brave Lily who saves the moment, standing her ground. She makes it okay for him to tell her she's a witch.

She doesn't like the term this first time she hears it. Snape tries to run after her but keeps his "ridiculously large coat" on, his defenses up: "He flapped after the girls, looking ludicrously batlike, like his older self." (*HP/DH*, 664-5) The girls leave and "Harry, the only one left to observe him, recognized Snape's bitter disappointment, and understood that Snape had been planning this moment for a while, and that it had all gone wrong. . . ." (*HP/DH*, 665)

How different his mother's experience was from the first time Harry learned he was a wizard. Harry's announcement came crashing unstoppably through the cracks in grim reality as he knew it, pursuing him to rescue him. Lily's came quietly in her safe space, an odd, fey little person emerging from the greenery to tell her that the beautiful gifts she enjoyed every day marked her as special and strange.

#2: Snape and Lily talking in a small thicket of trees

Snape and Lily have become friends. Harry sees them speaking in idyllic privacy.

> He was now in a small thicket of trees. He could see a sunlit river glittering through their trunks. The shadows cast by the trees made a basin of cool green shade. Two children sat facing each other, cross-legged on the ground. Snape had removed his coat now; his odd smock looked less peculiar in the half light. (*HP/DH*, 665-6)

This has the feel of a sacred grove, a place where the two children are equal and Snape feels safe enough to remove his defenses. Snape teaches Lily about the culture of the magical world: the Ministry, childhood magic, wands, Azkaban, dementors. The children confide in each other. Some of the most beautiful aspects of Snape come alive in this space.

Petunia has been telling Lily that Hogwarts is a lie.

> "It's real for us," said Snape. "Not for her. But we'll get the letter, you and me."
>
> "Really?" whispered Lily.
>
> "Definitely," said Snape, and even with his poorly cut hair and his odd clothes, he struck an oddly impressive figure sprawled in front of her, brimful of confidence in his destiny. (*HP/DH*, 666)

Even as a child, when Snape spoke of magic, he was spellbinding. He manifested magic so young, Snape didn't need wand-waving or spoken words to make it real. It was in his head, and in Lily's head, as well, and that made everything real enough. Rowling was careful to show the full intellectual range at Hogwarts, but at one level, her story is an allegory about giftedness. It's not a letter or a school that makes you magic; it's the way you encounter the world.

What the school does, though, is bring you together with like-minded others to raise greater magic than you could have alone, spurred by the joy of working with friends. Three first-years can tackle a mountain troll. Four Marauders can create a map. The pleasure of friendship makes magic stronger. Giftedness can be terribly lonely: Dumbledore, pacing in his office on sleepless nights, has no confidants. For the highly gifted Snape, meeting someone of equal aptitude was unlikely and miraculous. *She* was miraculous.

Lily worries about prejudice and her place in the wizarding world.

> "Does it make a difference, being Muggle-born?"
>
> Snape hesitated. His black eyes, eager in the greenish gloom, moved over the pale face, the dark red hair.
>
> "No," he said. "It doesn't make any difference." (*HP/DH*, 666)

In this protected space where a person's innate gifts matter more than beauty or status, child Snape can look at the evidence and speak the truth as it ought to be.

> "You've got loads of magic," said Snape. "I saw that. All the time I was watching you . . ."
>
> His voice trailed away; she was not listening, but had stretched out on the leafy ground and was looking up at the canopy of leaves overhead. He watched her as greedily as he had watched her in the playground. (*HP/DH*, 667)

Lily doesn't have the kind of neediness that drove Snape to spy on her. She has been raised securely enough for her to see the protection around them, currently embodied in the canopy of leaves overhead. This is something Snape can't see yet. She has received some kinds of nourishment that he craves but has never gotten, and this hunger leaves him unprotected. He is drawn to the wholeness of the love she has known and is too young to know the difference between wanting it, and wanting her, for himself. Too young to control the craving.

They have talked about this before. With delicate strokes, Rowling supports what readers have suspected, based on Snape's childhood memory of crying while a hook-nosed man shouted at a cowering woman. (*HP/OotP*, 591) Snape probably lives with domestic abuse as well as poverty and neglect and has confided in Lily.

"How are things at your house?" Lily asked.

A little crease appeared between his eyes.

"Fine," he said.

"They're not arguing anymore?"

"Oh yes, they're arguing," said Snape. He picked up a fistful of leaves and began tearing them apart, apparently unaware of what he was doing. "But it won't be that long and I'll be gone."

"Doesn't your dad like magic?"

"He doesn't like anything, much," said Snape. (*HP/DH*, 667)

Rowling carefully uses language that makes the argument sound equal: *they* are arguing, rather than one of them dominating the other. Lily asks if the argument is about magic. Maybe the Muggle father is threatened by the skill his wife and son share, the way Petunia is threatened by Lily. Certainly, judging from Snape's dismissive comment that he wouldn't spy on Petunia because she's a Muggle, Snape has associated the fact of being a Muggle with being lesser.

But Snape's reply makes clear that the issue lies with his father, not with the magic. He speaks with the terse grimness common to many children who live with explosive or abusive parents. The disparaging way he speaks of Muggles suggests that his Muggle parent is the more unreasonable or despicable of the two, and this has led Snape to associate feelings of contempt with Muggles.

The family is clearly poor, but Snape shows signs of neglect as well as poverty. By magic or by hand, his parents could have altered his odd garments or trimmed his hair, but they did not. Perhaps Snape's father is too hostile or his mother too depressed to groom what is, as far as we know, their only child. We see no evidence that Snape has companions other than Lily or that his parents track his whereabouts.

Snape clearly doesn't want to spend more time at home than he must. But it looks as though Eileen has given him a powerful gift: the encouragement to leave home without guilt. We know Snape came to Hogwarts with at least one of her books, already performing adult-level magic. We know he has broad and accurate knowledge of wizarding culture. Eileen has not neglected his education. She has promised him Hogwarts as his birthright. As a witch married to a Muggle, she would not have chosen Tobias Snape unless she wanted him; perhaps, despite their arguing, the couple wants to stay together. Perhaps Snape's eagerness to leave home means that he does not fear for Eileen's safety if he is not there to protect her. We know he returned to Spinner's End as a teen, so he remained in touch with his parents.

Lily asks Snape about dementors. He tells her they guard the wizard prison, Azkaban, using the words Petunia parrots the summer Harry turns 15 (HP/OotP, 31). Snape assures Lily, "You're not going to end up in Azkaban, you're too—" and then turns red. What was he about to say? Good? Pure? Beautiful? Loved? (HP/DH, 667)

We don't find out because they discover that Petunia has been spying on them. Petunia responds to Snape's outrage with an insult to Snape's masculinity: "What is that you're wearing, anyway?" she said, pointing at Snape's chest. "Your mum's blouse?" (HP/DH, 668)

Sexualized humiliation always enrages Snape. Perhaps Tobias Snape was disappointed in his bookish, unmanly son, and frequently said so. We have seen Snape's response to James revealing his underwear and to students laughing at the thought of him dressed as an old lady. We see now that Lily knew this about him, which means that when he called her a Mudblood, her rejoinder about washing his pants was a pointed renunciation of her steadfast defenses of his appearance. If he was going to see her as the outside world did, instead of for her true self, she would make sure he understood that he broke something with this betrayal.

When Petunia taunts Snape, he spontaneously breaks a tree branch so it hits her, hard. Lily asks angrily if he hurt Petunia on purpose and he lies in response, "defiant and scared." (HP/DH, 668) This outburst is not out of the ordinary for a magical child, but what makes it a problem is that Snape doesn't know how to forgive and apologize. His vengeful tendencies, his precocious mastery of curses, his "miserable and confused" response to Lily's anger all suggest that in his experience, slights are met with retaliation, not retracted with apology and forgiveness. The constant arguing in his home life makes him vulnerable to the appeal of Dark Magic: a cycle of vengeance that never ends but continues to do harm that intensifies over time.

No wonder Petunia was afraid of Harry's uncontrolled magic. She knew how frightening such outbursts could be.

This history puts a new angle on the heavy detentions that Snape administers to Harry for *Sectumsempra*. Yes, he misses an entire spring's worth of Quidditch and dating. But if things had gone differently, he could have killed someone, and "I didn't know what I was doing" is not a defense that can stand up to such guilt. The fact that *Sectumsempra* was punishable by detention means that Snape considers what Harry did to be *forgivable*. When Harry's detentions are complete, on an institutional level, it's an acceptance of Harry's apology. There's an end to it. There will be no further retaliation. Draco has no scars, and Harry is free to go. This is something that Snape did for them.

#3: Platform 9 ¾

The first time Harry went to Platform 9 ¾, the Dursleys dumped him in the bare space between Platforms 9 and 10 and drove off, all three of them laughing. (*HP/SS*, 91) But Petunia had been there before, on the magical side of the barrier. One of Snape's gifts to Harry was the sight of Lily, age 11, surrounded for the first time by a crowd of magical schoolmates.

> Harry looked around: He was on platform nine and three-quarters,
> and Snape stood beside him, slightly hunched, next to a thin,
> sallow-faced, sour-looking woman who greatly resembled him.
> Snape was staring at a family of four a short distance away. The
> two girls stood a little apart from their parents. Lily seemed to be
> pleading with her sister; Harry moved closer to listen. (*HP/DH*,
> 668)

Part of the magic of the Pensieve is that the viewer, by moving around, can feel more empathy. It's a literal version of a change in perspective. Harry is standing beside Snape, almost as though, via Time-Turner, he can be company for Snape on the platform.

Harry overhears Lily and Petunia arguing about Petunia's secret request to attend Hogwarts. Lily offers to ask Dumbledore again: so that's who came to the Evans home to invite Lily to Hogwarts. By showing Harry this memory of Petunia's poisonous envy, Snape is passing on the explanation for her cruelty to Harry—and an apology of sorts. All the time Snape was convincing himself that Harry enjoyed a celebrity childhood, he knew exactly who had raised Harry. He can't have been surprised by what he saw of adult Petunia during Occlumency lessons.

#4: The Hogwarts Express

On the Hogwarts Express, Lily has been crying over Petunia's anger. Snape doesn't understand Lily's distress.

"So what?"

She threw him a look of deep dislike.

"So she's my sister!"

"She's only a—" He caught himself quickly; Lily, too busy trying to wipe her eyes without being noticed, did not hear him. (*HP/DH*, 670-1)

Snape probably dismissed the opinions of Muggles as a matter of course, starting with his unimpressive father. The way his comment almost slipped out, it seems he has tried to curtail this habit only to please Lily without understanding her objection. Certainly, Petunia has never given Snape any reason to esteem her. Lily finds attachment to family members so self-evident she doesn't think it needs explaining, but Snape has not had enough experience with it to empathize. It's outside his understanding.

Unperturbed by leaving home, Snape exults that they are going to Hogwarts and tells Lily she'd better be in Slytherin, apparently certain that he is headed there himself. This gets the attention of 11-year-old James Potter, another child raised with the luxury of family love: "slight, black-haired like Snape, but with that indefinable air of having been well-cared-for, even adored, that Snape so conspicuously lacked." (*HP/DH*, 671)

Even adored. What a different life this is from the shouting that Snape has endured, the abuse of Harry's childhood, the alienation of Tom Riddle's. James Potter is not beautiful, but the glow of well-being that comes from a childhood of being cherished is as good as beauty. This is the sort of wealth that Snape craves. Harry has a look of neglect to him as well, but he is better off than Snape or Riddle were, with the magic protection of 15 months of parental adoration before he was orphaned.

Snape was always poorly groomed. Sirius mocked him for being "greasy" in his teens, and Fred Weasley cracked on *Potterwatch* that Voldemort "can move faster than Severus Snape confronted with shampoo when he wants to." (*HP/DH*, 444) Luna, too, unsettled people with her odd appearance, but at the Lovegood home, Harry noted a photo of her with her late mother: "Luna looked rather better-groomed in this picture than Harry had ever seen her in life." (*HP/DH*, 417)

Beauty, well-being, the habit and urge to groom the self that is instilled by years of care and grooming from others, the conviction of lovability that makes one feel worthy of grooming: these are inequalities that separate Snape from Lily, alongside class and blood status.

Sirius is in the train car as well, worried because his new friend James dislikes Slytherin, where his whole family has been sorted. Snape disparages Gryffindor, saying, "If you'd rather be brawny than brainy—" And Sirius fires back at Snape: "Where're you hoping to go, seeing as you're neither?" (HP/DH, 672) Snape is clearly not brawny, but Sirius has absolutely no reason to assume that Snape is not brainy. Given Sirius and James's later reputations as the top students in their year, it may be that Sirius is assuming himself the smartest person present, which has usually been a safe bet.

This first meeting puts a class difference angle on the academic rivalry between Snape and the two Gryffindors. Perhaps it wasn't just that Snape's brightness was overlooked due to anti-Slytherin bias or his creepy fixation with Dark Magic. Perhaps it was the common story of the poor student with second-hand books being overlooked while the wealthy purebloods got the credit, though they were all similar in talent.

Lily is unimpressed with James and Sirius picking on Snape and leads Snape to a different compartment. Lily saves the moment for Snape with her healthy emotions. It becomes a memory of her solidarity with him.

#5: The Sorting

Harry gets to watch his mother as a small girl being sorted into Gryffindor, giving Snape "a sad little smile" as they experience their first separation. (HP/DH, 672) Again, Harry walks with Snape, this time to the stool with the Sorting Hat: at least in memory, Snape doesn't have to make this walk alone. Snape is sorted into Slytherin and "moved off to the other side of the Hall, away from Lily, to where the Slytherins were cheering him, to where Lucius Malfoy, a prefect badge gleaming upon his chest, patted Snape on the back as he sat down beside him. . . ." (HP/DH, 673)

For all his attitudes about wealth and status, it is Lucius Malfoy who first makes Snape feel welcome at Hogwarts, in contrast to the eventual Gryffindors who picked on Snape before any of them had even been sorted into their desired houses.

#6: Snape and Lily arguing about Dark Magic

Fifth-year Snape and Lily are arguing about their growing rift.

"... thought we were supposed to be friends?" Snape was saying. "Best friends?"

"We *are*, Sev, but I don't like some of the people you're hanging round with! I'm sorry, but I detest Avery and Mulciber! *Mulciber!* What do you see in him, Sev, he's creepy! D'you know what he tried to do to Mary Macdonald the other day?"

Lily had reached a pillar and leaned against it, looking up into the thin, sallow face.

"That was nothing," said Snape. "It was a laugh, that's all—"

"It was Dark Magic, and if you think that's funny—" (*HP/DH*, 673)

So far, the argument is going predictably. The proto-Death Eater is minimizing Dark Magic and making a case against the people Lily knows and "the stuff Potter and his mates get up to." (*HP/DH*, 673) Snape hints at Lupin's lycanthropy, which strikes Lily as nosy, and he seethes about James fancying Lily. At first read, this looks like teen jealousy and rationalization. But then, we find out that this argument is taking place *after* Sirius lured Snape toward Lupin in werewolf form, though Lily doesn't know about that.

"They don't use Dark Magic, though." She dropped her voice. "And you're being really ungrateful. I heard what happened the other night. You went sneaking down that tunnel by the Whomping Willow, and James Potter saved you from whatever's down there—"

Snape's whole face contorted and he spluttered, "Saved? Saved? You think he was playing the hero? He was saving his neck and his friends' too! You're not going to—I won't let you—" (*HP/DH*, 674)

Dumbledore has forbidden Snape to tell anyone that Lupin is a werewolf. Snape has been nearly killed by Sirius, he believes James was in on the plot, he can't tell Lily what happened, and now James is trying to date her. Snape is trying to warn her away from befriending would-be murderers without disobeying Dumbledore. It makes sense that, at this point, he might not believe Dark Magic to be worse than what Sirius and his friends tried to do. Nothing that Avery and Mulciber have done yet has probably come as close to murder as Sirius's prank.

#7: Snape's Worst Memory

We've seen this memory before in *Order of the Phoenix*, the first of the three that Snape removed for Occlumency lessons because he didn't want Voldemort to see them in Harry's mind. Rowling wrote it carefully so it wasn't clear, in that volume, whether the worst aspect of this memory was Snape being bullied, Snape calling Lily "Mudblood," or something that happened after Harry stopped watching.

> But Harry kept his distance this time, because he knew what happened after James had hoisted Severus into the air and taunted him; he knew what had been done and said, and it gave him no pleasure to hear it again . . . He watched as Lily joined the group and went to Snape's defense. Distantly he heard Snape shout at her in his humiliation and his fury, the unforgivable word: *"Mudblood."* (*HP/DH*, 675)

Unforgivable. Rowling equates this name-calling with torture, abuse, and killing. It's worse than the *Sectumsempra* that Harry cast on Draco, which could be expiated with detention. Like the Imperius, Cruciatus, or Killing curses, it causes a deeper sort of destruction, including the destruction of any trust between victim and caster. The victim does not owe the caster forgiveness. Even if they did forgive, that would not settle the primary harm. As for the caster, the only way to reverse their internal damage from having cast an Unforgivable is remorse. As Hermione said, "You've got to really feel what you've done." (*HP/DH*, 103)

#8: Snape's apology to Lily

Teen Snape keeps a vigil outside the Gryffindor common room until Lily sends him away, ending their friendship. He is terribly sorry to have broken the rule about not calling her a Mudblood and begs her forgiveness. He doesn't even begin to understand what's wrong with apologizing for forgetting to exempt her from his general prejudice. She accuses him of planning to join the Death Eaters, and he can't deny it.

> "I can't pretend anymore. You've chosen your way, I've chosen mine."

"No—listen, I didn't mean—"

"—to call me Mudblood? But you call everyone of my birth Mudblood, Severus. Why should I be any different?" (*HP/DH*, 676)

It's not that he called her a Mudblood. It's that his increasing prejudice requires so much self-delusion on her part, if they are to remain friends, that she has to withdraw from him to protect herself. She cannot accept tokenism from an aspiring member of a group that wants to kill her kind.

What does Snape think will happen if he rises in Voldemort's ranks? Does he intend to keep Lily as a sort of concubine from the oppressed class, protected by his personal favor? If he cannot see that his plans and desires are mutually exclusive, there is nothing further Lily can do except save herself.

#9: Snape's request of Dumbledore

This is the second of the three memories Snape hid from Harry and Voldemort: the night he betrayed his master and pledged his life to Dumbledore in exchange for protection for Lily, James, and Harry.

Voldemort's plan to kill Lily, James, and baby Harry finally alerts Snape that he has pledged to follow a monster for life. He asks Voldemort to spare Lily and realizes he has made a terrible mistake: his request has exposed an amusing weakness to Voldemort and given Voldemort a tool for controlling him. Voldemort may spare Lily for the short term, but there is no protection in going to Voldemort with requests born out of love. It is not safe to let Voldemort see what one loves. We have seen Snape try frantically to impress upon Harry, during their Occlumency lessons, that those who cannot control their emotions around Voldemort are simply handing him weapons (*DH/OotP*, 536).

Young adult Snape's concern for the life of someone he loves is greater than concern for himself. At last, he begins to be able to see something that Lily's eyes have always seen: that attachment can lead to protection. She had already experienced this by the time they met, nourished by her family's love. Snape was born into a family where emotional resources were scarcer: it was not until he feared for Lily's life that this power in him came alive. Love for Lily made this magic manifest in him, relatively late in life.

Voldemort's response to this magic is greater destruction. At last, Snape sees the simplicity of the decision. He hadn't been sure enough of love before to see it, overwhelmed as he was by his dominant experiences of strife and the desire for vengeance. But seen from the perspective of the value of Lily's life, there is no argument. It is done: Snape will never be Voldemort's man again. With nothing to lose, he takes his case to Dumbledore, who understands love magic and may hear his plea.

Dumbledore arrives with terrible, Biblical magnificence on the appointed hilltop.

> Then a blinding, jagged jet of white light flew through the air: Harry thought of lightning, but Snape had dropped to his knees and his wand had flown out of his hand.
>
> "Don't kill me!"
>
> "That was not my intention." (HP/DH, 676)

Dumbledore begins as Draco began: not with an attack but with *Expelliarmus*. This is a time for talking, not for weapons.

Lily surely calls herself Lily Potter now that she's married, in accordance with wizarding culture, but Snape asks Dumbledore to protect her under her maiden name of Evans. Dumbledore sounds him out with a trick question: "Could you not ask for mercy for the mother, in exchange for the son?" (HP/DH, 677) He's not wrong to test this. Snape did, indeed, ask Voldemort for that inhumane bargain, earning him the harshest words Dumbledore speaks to anyone in the series:

> "You disgust me," said Dumbledore, and Harry had never heard so much contempt in his voice. Snape seemed to shrink a little. "You do not care, then, about the deaths of her husband and child? They can die, as long as you have what you want?" (HP/DH, 677)

Dumbledore's father died in prison for indulging his grief-mad desire for revenge and left Dumbledore's mother to raise three extremely high-needs children on her own. He will not countenance any discussion of love that misunderstands the nature of love so thoroughly. His coldness gets through to Snape where tenderness might not have. Snape is at his most raw. He is ready to learn and Dumbledore is willing to teach.

"Hide them all, then," he croaked. "Keep her—them—safe. Please."

"And what will you give me in return, Severus?"

"In—in return?" Snape gaped at Dumbledore, and Harry expected him to protest, but after a long moment he said, "Anything." (*HP/DH*, 678)

Snape throws himself on Dumbledore's mercy, and Dumbledore accepts the responsibility: the two of them have entered into a bond. Dumbledore's condition requires Snape to develop more understanding, more protectiveness, toward James and Harry as well as the person Snape loves: this is a magic spell. Snape has increased the range of his protectiveness because of an interaction with the man who accepted his plea for help. Snape is already more powerful than he was before.

Anything. Narcissa came to Snape for the Unbreakable Vow in the same state of absolute desperation, saying there was nothing anymore that she would not do. Snape is pledging himself to Dumbledore because the life of a loved one is more important to him; he is offering his life for Lily's. Dumbledore will use the new power he has just gained over Snape to continue to ask more love of Snape, more sacrifice, more protectiveness toward others. Not all of us are born into lives of love; not all of us receive the love we crave. That doesn't mean we are doomed to be loveless monsters. We can gain more love within ourselves by increasing our desire to protect others. If that sounds stark and unrewarding—well, it can be. But if there's someone we want to protect, we will make that bargain.

#10: Snape's second chance from Dumbledore

The third memory that Snape hid from Voldemort and Harry is the moment Dumbledore told Snape of Lily's death and offered him a second chance at life. Never in his life has Harry been better prepared to understand the emotion he sees in this memory. The howls of grief and guilt from Snape are like Harry's torment after seeing his friends' bodies in the Great Hall, dead, he feels, because of him. At a time like this, the griever needs something extreme, something they cannot imagine.

Something was making a terrible sound, like a wounded animal. Snape was slumped forward in a chair and Dumbledore was standing over him, looking grim. After a moment or two, Snape raised his face, and he looked like a man who had lived a hundred years of misery since leaving the wild hilltop.

> "I thought . . . you were going . . . to keep her . . . safe. . . ." (*HP/DH*, 678)

Snape shrugs when Dumbledore mentions that Harry survives, but Dumbledore is merciless in prodding at Snape's pain, hammering at the resemblance between Harry's eyes and Lily's, trying to reach into Snape's explosion of grief to connect it to something more.

He asks, "Is this remorse, Severus?" Snape doesn't reply. He doesn't understand yet what Dumbledore means. Instead, he says he wishes he were dead. (*HP/DH*, 678)

He is quite sincere. His life is over. From this point on, if Dumbledore intervenes and calls on the most vital thing remaining in Snape—his love for Lily—Snape can *start again*, from the beginning, and have a second chance to do right. It is too late to protect Lily, but if all goes well, Snape can help spare the innocent life of Lily's son, whom Voldemort will surely attack again. Snape cannot live for himself anymore; his heart is broken by guilt; he doesn't feel deserving. But he gave himself to Dumbledore when he pledged "anything" in exchange for Lily's protection, and Dumbledore sees a hope. If he calls on Snape to live *for Dumbledore* for the moment, to do as Dumbledore orders him, and *keeps* calling on the part of Snape that loves, keeps calling on Snape to do more and more for love and protect others for love, there's a chance that this love can grow strong enough to sustain Snape so that he can find his own reasons to live again.

> "I wish . . . I wish *I* were dead. . . ."
>
> "And what use would that be to anyone?" said Dumbledore coldly. "If you loved Lily Evans, if you truly loved her, then your way forward is clear. . . You know how and why she died. Make sure it was not in vain. Help me protect Lily's son." (*HP/DH*, 678-9)

For Snape to take on Lily's work, he will have to learn empathy. He will have to understand why she felt tender and protective toward her child. This is dangerous. Thinking about what she would have wanted goes directly into Snape's guilt for contributing to her death, and that may be too painful to tolerate.

But it's also undeniable that working against Voldemort from the inside to protect Lily's son is work that only one person in the world can do, and it will require all of Snape's genius. Finally, there is a good purpose for Snape's gifts, something that can unite his intelligence and his urge for vengeance with his newly awakened protectiveness.

Snape accepts Dumbledore's offer. This would not have been possible if he had not thrown himself upon Dumbledore's mercy and accepted an emotional connection, a sort of life debt, between them.

Snape's frantic urge to protect Lily drove him to ask Voldemort to spare her, leading to Voldemort offering Lily a choice. What Lily did with that choice would have killed Voldemort with jealousy if he had been mortal. He saw Lily care for her baby's life more than for her own, the kind of protection Voldemort lacked and craved even more than Snape did, so much so that he followed Harry Potter with greedy eyes for the rest of his life. He even stole Harry's blood, rich with the oxytocin of the love between child and mother, trying to gain some of that protection for himself. It may not feel like much to Snape at the moment. Lily is dead, after all. But there was protection in his request of Voldemort to spare her. Her boy still lives.

Snape's urge to protect Lily drove him to ask Dumbledore to protect her, and at Dumbledore's insistence, her husband and child as well. The debt he incurred to Dumbledore is an emotional connection: gratitude, a form of love. This gives Dumbledore the closeness to suggest to Snape that he begin a second chance at life. Without that closeness, nothing would have tethered Snape to life once Lily died. Everything Snape does in life after this moment is extra. It's a gift from Death. Snape is infinitely stronger because he doesn't fear Death after this. He was willing to meet Death at 21; at Dumbledore's offer, he goes under an invisibility cloak of sorts, takes on a life of double agency, to see what he can accomplish before he takes off the cloak and meets Death again. The two requests Snape made because of love for Lily are what created enough power to protect Harry Potter until Harry was strong enough to confront Voldemort himself.

> At last he said, "Very well. Very well. But never—never tell, Dumbledore! This must be between us! Swear it! I cannot bear . . . especially Potter's son . . . I want your word!"
>
> "My word, Severus, that I shall never reveal the best of you?" Dumbledore sighed, looking down into Snape's ferocious, anguished face. "If you insist . . ." (*HP/DH*, 679)

Snape's ferocious, anguished face. There is nothing ugly about Snape here. In these memories, Harry is seeing Snape through his mother's eyes, or through Dumbledore's. We see with Dumbledore's demeanor here that he regards Snape with more tenderness than we might have guessed, based on the harsh words of his earlier challenges to Snape. We know Dumbledore kept his word never to reveal the best of Snape. He left that choice to Snape.

#11: Harry's first year

This memory is an apology to Harry: 31-year-old Snape ranting to Dumbledore about his belief that Harry is "delighted to find himself famous, attention-seeking and impertinent." This is almost hilarious in its lack of self-awareness, considering that in reality, Snape picked on 11-year-old Harry repeatedly until Harry finally snapped. The inclusion of this memory is an admission that he had been wrong. Snape's rant is countered by Dumbledore's marvelously balanced assessment of Harry as "modest, likable, and reasonably talented."

Dumbledore dismisses Snape with the reminder, "Keep an eye on Quirrell, won't you?" (*HP/DH*, 679) Just in case Harry was still wondering, Snape has left him confirmation that Quirrell had never had them fooled. Whether he liked Harry or not, Snape's protection of him was well underway.

#12: The Yule Ball

Snape the spy reports to Dumbledore that Karkaroff intends to flee when Voldemort returns.

> "Does he?" said Dumbledore softly, as Fleur Delacour and Roger Davies came giggling in from the grounds. "And are you tempted to join him?"
>
> "No," said Snape, his black eyes on Fleur's and Roger's retreating figures. "I am not such a coward." (*HP/DH*, 680)

In this highly curated collection of memories, it's odd to see minor players Fleur and Roger featured so prominently, mentioned twice by name. Snape forfeited romance on his first chance in life and abstained on the second so he wouldn't jeopardize work dependent on constant secrecy. For this passionate man, that must have been a sacrifice. We know he did everything in his power to prevent Harry and Draco from making the kinds of mistakes that might require them, too, to close off the option of romance in their lives.

Dumbledore notes that Snape is braver than Karkaroff and muses, "I sometimes think we Sort too soon," leaving Snape "stricken." (*HP/DH*, 680) Was he disparaging the Slytherin capacity for bravery? Was he sorry that Sorting put distance between Snape and Lily so early, or that vulnerable young Snape was surrounded by peers who undervalued his bravery? It's an odd comment, but it does confirm that Dumbledore believes Snape is not the same person he was as a teen. He has changed, and Dumbledore sees this.

#13: Dumbledore's request of Snape

When Dumbledore is close to death, there is only one person he asks for.

> It was nighttime, and Dumbledore sagged sideways in the thronelike chair behind the desk, apparently semiconscious. His right hand dangled over the side, blackened and burned. Snape was muttering incantations, pointing his wand at the wrist of the hand, while with his left hand he tipped a goblet full of thick golden potion down Dumbledore's throat. After a moment or two, Dumbledore's eyelids fluttered and opened. (*HP/DH*, 680)

This is Snape at his most beautiful, understanding Dark Magic and reversing it as nobody else can. What potion was he administering? Probably not Elixir of Life; as mentioned earlier, nobody but the Flamels had the right to that potion. Voldemort thought he could steal the Stone and brew it himself, but Voldemort has been known to be mistaken. This potion is something that can counteract physical damage from Dark Magic: perhaps it contains phoenix tears. The golden color suggests Fawkes, who symbolizes second chances, and Rowling often uses the color gold to indicate love or the connection between people. Maybe this potion was something that had to be brewed by someone who had known Dark Magic and then renounced it for love.

Frequently, when Snape has been mean to Harry, it's because he was afraid for Harry's safety. His fear expresses itself as anger. It's rather fun to see Snape scold Dumbledore the exact same way.

> "Why," said Snape, without preamble, "*why* did you put on that ring? It carries a curse, surely you realized that. Why even touch

it?"

> Marvolo Gaunt's ring lay on the desk before Dumbledore. It was
> cracked; the sword of Gryffindor lay beside it. (*HP/DH*, 680)

Snape explains to Dumbledore that a curse of such extraordinary
power can be trapped, but "to contain it is all we can hope for." He
estimates that Dumbledore has, at most, a year to live: "There is no
halting such a spell forever. It will spread eventually, it is the sort of
curse that strengthens over time." (*HP/DH*, 681) This description of
Dark Magic recalls Machiavelli's statement: "Those cruelties are badly
used that, although few at the outset, increase with the passing of time
instead of disappearing" (Machiavelli, 34).

With this rescue, Snape has repaid his life debt from the turning
point when Dumbledore talked him out of suicide on the hilltop and
gave him a new reason to live. Snape is just as invested in their cause as
Dumbledore now. They must both stay alive long enough to protect
Harry and defeat Voldemort. With his life debt repaid, Snape could walk
away now; everything he does from this point is consciously chosen, of
his own volition, even if at Dumbledore's request. He is no longer
simply trusting in Dumbledore's guidance to fulfill his promise.

Dumbledore seems unafraid of death, only hoping to finish his work
before he dies. He and Snape have that in common. He will rely on
Snape to keep him alive until he's ready, the way the Flamels drank the
Elixir of Life until they set their affairs in order.

> "I am fortunate, extremely fortunate, that I have you, Severus."
>
> "If you had only summoned me a little earlier, I might have been
> able to do more, buy you more time!" said Snape furiously.
> (*HP/DH*, 681)

Dumbledore won't answer when Snape asks what tempted him to
put on the ring. Snape asks if Dumbledore was trying to break the curse
by breaking the ring with the sword and Dumbledore answers vaguely,
"Something like that. . . ." (*HP/DH*, 681)

Dumbledore won't tell Snape that the ring is set with the
Resurrection Stone or that there are such things as Horcruxes. He
doesn't want Voldemort to learn about the Deathly Hallows through
Legilimency on Snape, and he certainly wouldn't want to tell Snape
about Horcruxes and have Voldemort discover that Snape knows this

secret. The only thing Dumbledore can tell Snape about the ring without endangering his life is that there was, indeed, a curse upon it. Which makes this as good a time as any for Dumbledore to change the subject.

Dumbledore talks lightly of Voldemort ordering "the poor Malfoy boy" to murder him, and the backup plan to have Snape commit the murder when Draco fails. Judging from Snape's cautious replies, it seems that this is the first time the two have discussed this plan, which is unsurprising, since the conversation takes place quite early in the summer after Harry's fifth year. Snape probably didn't even realize that Dumbledore already knew about it. However Dumbledore found out, it wasn't through Snape.

Dumbledore sets the course for Snape's final two years. He secures Snape's promise to protect the students of Hogwarts if the school falls under Voldemort's control, although Snape probably would have chosen this course of action without prompting. He orders Snape to track Draco. Then he tells Snape that the only way to save Draco is for Snape to kill Dumbledore.

> There was a long silence, broken only by an odd clicking noise. Fawkes the phoenix was gnawing a bit of cuttlebone.
>
> "Would you like me to do it now?" asked Snape, his voice heavy with irony. "Or would you like a few moments to compose an epitaph?" (*HP/DH*, 683)

Every time Snape opens his mouth, he delivers. Yes, he certainly could feel like killing Dumbledore for this. The way Snape and Dumbledore talk to each other when no one else is listening is gorgeously tense, brusque, smart, rude. It's unlike any other conversations we've read in the series, especially unlike Snape's smooth subservience to Voldemort. They are a bit cutting with each other— perhaps close to the way they are with themselves.

> "Oh, not quite yet," said Dumbledore, smiling. "I daresay the moment will present itself in due course. Given what has happened tonight," he indicated his withered hand, "we can be sure that it will happen within a year." (*HP/DH*, 683)

Great. One of those deals, like working with a Time-Turner, where you have to be on a constant lookout, knowing there's something you must do but with no way to predict when or exactly how. Snape probably had very few nights of restful sleep for the remainder of his life. No wonder he was extra nasty, even by his own impressive standards, when Harry didn't make it off the Hogwarts Express at the beginning of sixth year. He was probably wondering if the moment to kill Dumbledore had arrived even before pudding at the Welcoming Feast.

We've seen it before with Snape: grief over a loss or imminent loss of a loved one raises powerful magic in him. Dumbledore wants him to *what?* Never mind, even, the aftermath of what Dumbledore is asking him to, the commitment to being hated and ostracized as never before. Never mind that Snape doesn't want to kill *anyone*, let alone his friend. It's that . . . Snape feels emotionally connected to Dumbledore. Does Dumbledore . . . not care? This surge of emotion makes Snape so much more powerful, so vulnerable, that he has the guts to cry out the thing he has so rarely asked of Dumbledore: *What about me?*

> "If you don't mind dying," said Snape roughly, "why not let Draco do it?"
>
> "That boy's soul is not yet so damaged," said Dumbledore. "I would not have it ripped apart on my account."
>
> "And my soul, Dumbledore? Mine?" (*HP/DH*, 683)

The last time we saw Snape ask in such a raw manner whether Dumbledore cared, it was the end of Harry's third year when Snape reminded Dumbledore that Sirius Black had once tried to kill him. Dumbledore's answer then—"My memory is as good as it ever was, Severus"—was hardly satisfactory at a time when it seemed that Snape ranked dead last in Dumbledore's favor, behind scores of Gryffindors living and dead. (*HP/PoA*, 391)

That took place only two years before this scene, but it feels like longer. Snape and Dumbledore have been through a great deal since then: the return of Voldemort, the resumption of Snape's double agency, the terrible year of Umbridge's rule. Has Dumbledore not found Snape more deserving of protection and care in that time?

> "You alone know whether it will harm your soul to help an old man avoid pain and humiliation," said Dumbledore. "I ask this one great favor of you, Severus, because death is coming for me as surely as the Chudley Cannons will finish bottom of this year's league. I confess I should prefer a quick, painless exit to the protracted and

messy affair it will be if, for instance, Greyback is involved—I hear Voldemort has recruited him? Or dear Bellatrix, who likes to play with her food before she eats it." (*HP/DH*, 683)

Dumbledore is not saying Snape's soul is disposable or less worthy than Draco's. He is throwing himself on Snape's mercy and asking if Snape thinks he might have what it takes to care for Dumbledore. Would he be able to kill for a protective reason, split his soul by killing, and then withstand the possibly fatal process of remorse that is the only way to reintegrate his soul? They can't let Draco kill Dumbledore. In the unlikely event that he succeeded, he wouldn't be able to recover.

Snape has never yet admitted remorse. That will make this more of a gamble, attempting it deliberately for the first time. Dumbledore suggests scenarios so Snape can imagine his own reactions: Greyback turning Dumbledore into a werewolf who would attack his own students, Bellatrix humiliating him with torture. These are realistic possibilities, and they trigger Snape's protectiveness. There is protection in Snape's attachment to Dumbledore. He knows he could die for another person or stay alive for another, but what about killing? Can he stretch to cover that, as well? Dumbledore watches as Snape considers.

> His tone was light, but his blue eyes pierced Snape as they had frequently pierced Harry, as though the soul they discussed was visible to him. At last Snape gave another curt nod.
>
> Dumbledore seemed satisfied.
>
> "Thank you, Severus. . ." (*HP/DH*, 683)

From this moment, Snape has the protection of knowing he is, if not the most important person in Dumbledore's life, at least the most important person in his death. It's not the same thing as being cherished, but it puts trust in Snape's formidable abilities. Nobody in the world but Snape could do this job. It is a way of being seen, of being known for his true and best self.

We don't see, in Snape's bequest to Harry, any reference to the Unbreakable Vow he took with Narcissa soon after this scene. Narcissa's request that Snape look after Draco and kill in Draco's stead dovetails perfectly with Dumbledore's; they are identical. There was no need for Snape to inform Dumbledore about it. It added nothing except further protection for Snape in being the most important person in the world to someone, selected for his gifts. Draco's attachment to him will provide protection.

#14: The argument in the forest

Partway through Harry's sixth year, Snape's protective magic grows so powerful from looking after Harry and Draco, so acute from worrying about life after Dumbledore, that he gains the strength to ask, painfully, for some affection and assurance from Dumbledore. Harry surely recognizes this feeling as he views the memory. It is exactly the same as the doubt that tormented Harry about Dumbledore's love, just before Snape heartened him with the sword and the silver doe.

The ensuing argument is fraught and bears close examination. Dumbledore is so accustomed to Snape being closed off, private about his feelings, that it takes him a long time to realize that this conversation isn't about Harry.

> "What are you doing with Potter, all these evenings you are closeted together?" Snape asked abruptly.
>
> Dumbledore looked weary.
>
> "Why? You aren't trying to give him *more* detentions, Severus? The boy will soon have spent more time in detention than out."
>
> "He is his father over again—"
>
> "In looks, perhaps, but his deepest nature is much more like his mother's." (*HP/DH*, 684)

Dumbledore doesn't understand yet. He thinks this is Snape's usual tiresome harping on Harry's shortcomings.

> "I spend time with Harry because I have things to discuss with him, information I must give him before it is too late."
>
> "Information," repeated Snape. "You trust him . . . you do not trust me."
>
> "It is not a question of trust. I have, as we both know, limited time. It is essential that I give the boy enough information for him to do what he needs to do." (*HP/DH*, 684)

Dumbledore still doesn't get it. He and Snape have spent years discussing dispassionate martial tactics. There is so little time left. There's no time for anyone to take things personally. He thinks it will be enough to tell Snape that it's not a question of trust.

> "And why may I not have the same information?"
>
> "I prefer not to put all of my secrets in one basket, particularly not a basket that spends so much time dangling on the arm of Lord Voldemort."
>
> "Which I do on your orders!" (*HP/DH*, 684)

Dumbledore is now irritated—and perhaps defensive, judging by the strangely belittling tone of his retort. Dumbledore is feeling the pressure as well, then. He has been walking the delicate line of telling Snape as much as possible while withholding the information about Horcruxes that would be Snape's death warrant if Voldemort saw it in Snape's mind. He has been protecting Snape, and protecting him further by not telling him about it. If Snape is aggrieved because he has no confidant but Dumbledore to see his exertions and be moved by them, well, Dumbledore has had no confidant at all since the death of Nicolas Flamel.

But his retort uses the language of sexual insult. It is both emasculating and dehumanizing, as though comparing Snape to something Augusta Longbottom would wear. It suggests that perhaps Dumbledore still feels disgusted by Snape, will never be able to stop seeing him as the unlovable, stunted boy who became a Death Eater. Little wonder that Snape responds with outrage. *I am what you made me.* Has Snape not done every near-impossible thing Dumbledore has asked of him?

Dumbledore backpedals with standard praise. The fears that keep him from divulging more to Snape are so current that he is unable to apologize.

> "And you do it extremely well. Do not think that I underestimate the constant danger in which you place yourself, Severus. To give Voldemort what appears to be valuable information while withholding the essentials is a job I would entrust to nobody but you." (*HP/DH*, 684)

There it is again: *entrust*. Has Snape not shown, time and again, that he has reformed? That he deserves Dumbledore's trust? Is there something further he must do to finish paying for his sins?

> "Yet you confide much more in a boy who is incapable of
> Occlumency, whose magic is mediocre, and who has a direct
> connection into the Dark Lord's mind!"

> "Voldemort fears that connection," said Dumbledore. "Not so long
> ago he had one small taste of what truly sharing Harry's mind
> means to him. It was pain such as he has never experienced. He will
> not try to possess Harry again, I am sure of it. Not in that way."
> (*HP/DH*, 684–5)

What Dumbledore is telling Snape is important, and indeed, Snape
will remember and use it. But Dumbledore still thinks this is about Harry.
Dumbledore is so enthralled with Harry's goodness that he forgets—
continually—that perhaps Snape does not gaze at Harry with the same
stars in his eyes.

> "I don't understand."

> "Lord Voldemort's soul, maimed as it is, cannot bear close contact
> with a soul like Harry's. Like a tongue on frozen steel, like flesh in
> flame—"

> "Souls? We were talking of minds!"

> "In the case of Harry and Lord Voldemort, to speak of one is to
> speak of the other." (*HP/DH*, 685)

This is difficult to watch. Snape is asking for love, and Dumbledore
waxes lyrical about Harry. Snape asks recognition for his extraordinary
mind, and Dumbledore changes the topic to souls, where Snape is at a
disadvantage, unsure still if Dumbledore even cares about the dirty soul
of a former Death Eater, if such things as *former* Death Eaters even exist.
Yes, yes, we know Harry is the issue—but how can Dumbledore not see
that Snape is simply jealous? *And my soul, Dumbledore? Mine?* Yes, only
Snape can know what his soul can handle, but sometimes, he would like
Dumbledore to simply *look* at him and recognize the sacrifices and
devotion.

> "After you have killed me, Severus—"

> "You refuse to tell me everything, yet you expect that small service

of me!" snarled Snape, and real anger flared in the thin face now. (*HP/DH*, 685)

Snape is snarling, and yet his face is described as thin, not sallow, hook-nosed, or sneering. He is not being ugly.

> "You take a great deal for granted, Dumbledore! Perhaps I have changed my mind!"
>
> "You gave me your word, Severus. And while we are talking about services you owe me, I thought you agreed to keep a close eye on our young Slytherin friend?" (*HP/DH*, 685)

Dumbledore is angry, now, as well. Now Snape is threatening the withdrawal of his help? Does he think that any of this is a game of power or favoritism? Of ego? It's about protecting everyone, including young Slytherin Death Eaters who have father issues and don't always know that their protectors are keeping secrets from them for their own good so Voldemort won't hurt them.

No one kept an eye on young Snape the way Snape is now watching Draco. After more than 20 years since Sirius nearly killed him, Snape is asking for proof of care from Dumbledore, one more time. It's brave. Dumbledore finally sees this.

> Snape looked angry, mutinous. Dumbledore sighed.
>
> "Come to my office tonight, Severus, at eleven, and you shall not complain that I have no confidence in you. . . ." (*HP/DH*, 685)

#15: The final message to Harry

At the eleventh hour, Dumbledore entrusts Snape with one last major burden, as he craves. Dumbledore was going to do this himself, even though he has proven a poor bearer of bad news to Harry in the past. But this is much better. Snape has no qualms about delivering bad news to Harry Potter. But even if he did, this would still be the best way. Dumbledore can tell Snape as many secrets as he dares without endangering Snape further, demonstrating that he has had a method in mind—it was truly not a matter of trust. Snape will see there is no need for jealousy: it is not true at all that Dumbledore confides more in Harry.

But those are just benefits for Dumbledore, and therefore of less import, as he would be the first to say.

Snape must be the one to deliver the final message to Harry that will result in the defeat of Voldemort because he was the one who set Voldemort to hunting Harry in the first place. We have seen, with Slughorn's release of guilt around the Horcrux conversation, that Dumbledore played a long game in engineering the one situation that could alleviate Slughorn's burden. To confess to Dumbledore or anyone else would have only increased Slughorn's shame, but to tell Harry, the one survivor among the people Slughorn most hurt with his mistake, made it possible for Slughorn to make reparations.

This is what the portrait of Phineas Nigellus Black didn't understand in Harry's sixth year:

> "I can't see why the boy should be able to do it better than you, Dumbledore."
>
> "I wouldn't expect you to, Phineas," replied Dumbledore, and Fawkes gave another low, musical cry. (HP/HBP 372)

This is one of Rowling's more cryptic passages and prone to misreading. Why wouldn't Dumbledore expect Phineas to understand? In a series that often demonizes Slytherins, could it mean that the unpopular Slytherin headmaster is simply not high-minded enough to think as Dumbledore does?

But the cry from Fawkes tells us that this is about healing and second chances. Slughorn once let his weakness cloud his judgment with fatal consequences he never intended. He enjoyed being flattered by a rising star and ignored the signs that he should have been more circumspect. Similarly, Dumbledore ignored signs of Grindelwald's evil and his sister died for it. Snape joined a hate group and Lily died for it.

Dumbledore is saying, then, that Phineas Nigellus Black has never been responsible for anyone's death and wouldn't understand the immobilizing shame.

Slughorn was intimidated by the risk in what Harry wanted: "But then . . . my dear boy . . . you're asking a great deal . . . you're asking me, in fact, to aid you in your attempt to destroy—" (HP/HBP 490)

But Snape will not be intimidated by bringing the final message to Harry. He already lives with that level of risk. Providing this vital service to Harry will only help relieve Snape of some of his debts, in the same way that Harry assured Slughorn, correctly, that it would benefit Slughorn to cooperate: "You'd cancel out anything you did by giving me the memory" (HP/HBP 490).

It won't be as simple as that, of course; Snape would never think he could cancel out his mistakes. But if he can confess to Harry the events that led to Lily's death, those memories can help Harry understand more about how to defeat Voldemort, and the peace of mind that this brings Snape will be greater than his shame.

By tasking Snape with this last-minute message, Dumbledore gives Snape an ally and companion in his otherwise solitary final year. Snape won't be able to pass Harry the message until the end, but he doesn't know when that end will be. At every moment, he will be conscious of Harry, knowing that Harry is outside of Hogwarts working toward Voldemort's end while Snape is inside Hogwarts, doing the same. Dumbledore gives Snape a reason to stay alive. It strengthens him.

> "Harry must not know, not until the last moment, not until it is necessary, otherwise how could he have the strength to do what must be done?"
>
> "But what must he do?"
>
> "That is between Harry and me. Now listen closely, Severus. There will come a time—after my death—do not argue, do not interrupt! There will come a time when Lord Voldemort will seem to fear for the life of his snake."
>
> "For Nagini?" Snape looked astonished. (*HP/DH*, 685-6)

This conversation starts out the same way as the argument. Dumbledore protects Snape from learning about the Horcruxes and Snape doesn't want to hear about Dumbledore's death. But then Dumbledore changes the conversation by telling Snape something new.

> "Precisely. If there comes a time when Lord Voldemort stops sending that snake forth to do his bidding, but keeps it safe beside him under magical protection, then, I think, it will be safe to tell Harry." (*HP/DH*, 686)

That's why Snape's eyes were fixed on Nagini in her enchanted sphere while Voldemort was going on about the Elder Wand. He was not afraid for his own life. He just knew the moment had come. He would have to put a stopper in death until he gave Harry his final message.

Dumbledore closes his eyes and tells Snape about the part of

Voldemort's soul that has taken refuge in Harry, "unmissed by Voldemort." (HP/DH, 686) He keeps his eyes closed the entire time as he tells Snape that Voldemort cannot die as long as this part of his soul lives on in Harry. He cannot risk Snape looking into his eyes and seeing anything about Horcruxes that Dumbledore is keeping secret for Snape's protection.

It is safe, however, to tell Snape about the fragment of soul in Harry. Voldemort has never guessed about the soul fragment. Dumbledore tells Snape that when Nagini is under magical protection, Harry "will have arranged matters so that when he sets out to meet his death, it will truly mean the end of Voldemort." (HP/DH, 687) Once Dumbledore is finished speaking, obliquely, about Horcruxes, he opens his eyes again.

Snape's response is stunned betrayal: "I thought . . . all these years . . . that we were protecting him for her. For Lily." (HP/DH, 686)

But Snape had never asked why *Dumbledore* was protecting Harry, a strange and youthful oversight similar to Harry realizing, after Dumbledore's death, that he had never asked Dumbledore anything about himself.

> Snape looked horrified.
>
> "You have kept him alive so that he can die at the right moment?"
>
> "Don't be shocked, Severus. How many men and women have you watched die?"
>
> "Lately, only those whom I could not save," said Snape. (HP/DH, 687)

Again, the way Dumbledore speaks to Snape is callous, one jaded soldier to another. He does not answer Snape's question; it is not safe to explain to Snape what he hopes will happen once Harry dies, since that answer would involve Horcruxes. He responds, instead, with another question, and Snape's answer shows more than anything else how profoundly he has changed. Snape has learned to calculate precisely which lives he cannot save and how to remain impassive when he must, a self-control he needs when witnessing the death of Charity Burbage. At all other times, he has been protecting others, feeling connected to them, increasing the potency of his magic with every life saved.

This change in him shows the importance of Snape and Harry disliking each other to the end. They may come to respect and understand each other, but neither feels affection, nor is that a requirement. Snape once protected Harry *only* because he loved Lily; Snape once protected *only* his Slytherins and was spiteful toward other students. Since then, his powers have grown. He protects friends and enemies alike, even if this means he wishes he could save their lives and then punch them in the mouth, as Ron does with Draco. (*HP/DH*, 645)

In his first flush of disillusionment, Snape misunderstands Dumbledore's intentions regarding Harry and feels deceived.

> He stood up. "You have used me."
>
> "Meaning?"
>
> "I have spied for you and lied for you, put myself in mortal danger for you. Everything was supposed to be to keep Lily Potter's son safe. Now you tell me you have been raising him like a pig for slaughter—" (*HP/DH*, 687)

Dumbledore could have explained. Or he could have noted Snape's unprecedented use of the name "Lily Potter." But he's too struck by the phenomenon of Snape being appalled on Harry's behalf.

> "But this is touching, Severus," said Dumbledore seriously. "Have you grown to care for the boy, after all?"
>
> "For *him*?" shouted Snape. "*Expecto Patronum!*"
>
> From the tip of his wand burst the silver doe: She landed on the office floor, bounded once across the office, and soared out of the window. (*HP/DH*, 687)

Confirmation, at last, that the silver doe Patronus was Snape's. She soared out the window, flying like Lily did, showing us what image Snape held in mind as he took his own last flight.

> Dumbledore watched her fly away, and as her silvery glow faded he turned back to Snape, and his eyes were full of tears.
>
> "After all this time?"
>
> "Always," said Snape. (*HP/DH*, 687)

If this came as a surprise to Dumbledore, then he hadn't seen Snape's doe Patronus for years, or perhaps ever before. As far as we know, the only people who ever saw the doe were Sirius, Dumbledore,

Harry, and Ron. Dumbledore worked with Snape, depended upon him, but never asked him the private source of his growing strength. Perhaps he assumed that with time, Snape's memories of Lily would have faded or been replaced. But Snape's Patronus is powerful and effortless: it must be never far from his mind that all his protective powers have grown from that one original source, the love for Lily that first made him feel that someone else's life was more important to him than his own.

Loving Lily is the best of Snape. It is not like Dumbledore's untrustworthy attraction to Grindelwald. She was the first to teach him empathy, standing up for others, and the equality of the oppressed. They played together and created magic of it. She showed him, too, the power of defending the self by walking away. These are good ideals for him to keep in mind when giving form to his truest, most protective magical self.

The magic of the silver doe stills the conflicts between Snape and Dumbledore. They speak no more of Snape's belief that Dumbledore protected Harry only so he could die at the most strategic moment. Snape is going to have to figure out on his own how to pass Harry a message that he believes to be so stark.

#16: Advice from Dumbledore's portrait

It would have been difficult indeed for Snape to spend a year in the headmaster's office, with Dumbledore's portrait behind his desk, if he had been the murderer he needed everyone to think he was. The portrait is the closest Snape has to a friend and confidant that year. Dumbledore's portrait advises Snape to maintain his cover by telling Voldemort the correct date of Harry's departure from Privet Drive and to maintain Harry's safety, or at least decrease the danger, by Confunding Mundungus Fletcher into suggesting the use of decoys. Harry sees the portrait reminding Snape "to act your part convincingly" in the chase (*HP/DH*, 688), confirming for Harry that Snape's participation was part of the plan.

Acting convincingly will require Snape to hurt someone or make a good attempt at it. Dumbledore's strategy is reminiscent of Ron's impatient explanation of strategy in Harry's first year: "'That's chess!' snapped Ron. 'You've got to make some sacrifices!'" (*HP/SS*, 283)

#17: Confunding Mundungus Fletcher

Snape Confunds Mundungus in an unfamiliar tavern. One wonders how he lured Mundungus there. Perhaps he offered a business opportunity concerning one of Dumbledore's silver instruments that would have betrayed that Snape was truly loyal to Dumbledore. (*HP/DH*, 688)

#18: The flight of the Seven Harrys

Snape's *Sectumsempra*, which severed George's ear, was originally meant for a Death Eater who was about to curse Lupin. Snape never liked or respected Lupin, but he's always protected him. His use of *Sectumsempra* gives the impression that he's returned to his Dark Magic ways, useful for convincing Death Eaters and the Order alike, but it's likely the last time he ever casts a Dark spell or even one meant to attack. This night falls between the time he killed Dumbledore and the time he purged his entire being with remorse. (*HP/DH* 688)

#19: Remorse

The most intricate magic that Snape ever casts takes place in the Grimmauld Place bedroom of the late Sirius Black, possibly the single place in the world most likely to fill Snape with loathing.

Rowling wrote this memory in careful layers. It requires more than one reading to understand what Snape was doing in his least favorite person's room, vandalizing property and weeping as we have never seen from him before.

Like many of the most significant moments in *Deathly Hallows*, this one goes by quickly, despite its import. The memory, in full:

> And next, Snape was kneeling in Sirius's old bedroom. Tears were dripping from the end of his hooked nose as he read the old letter from Lily. The second page carried only a few words:
>
> *could ever have been friends with Gellert Grindelwald. I think her mind's going, personally!*
>
> *Lots of love,*
>
> *Lily*
>
> Snape took the page bearing Lily's signature, and her love, and tucked it inside his robes. Then he ripped in two the photograph he was also holding, so that he kept the part from which Lily laughed, throwing the portion showing James and Harry back onto the floor, under the chest of drawers. . . . (*HP/DH*, 688-9)

A few reactions stand out on a first reading of this passage.

Confirmation: it was Snape who had ransacked Grimmauld Place, just as Harry and Hermione had guessed, although they never pursued that question since nothing dangerous came of it.

He must really be in an extreme state to be in Sirius Black's old room without his skin crawling with hatred. It's not an accident that the story put him here, of all places, right?

Tears were dripping from the end of his hooked nose. This is so hideous, so embarrassing, that one wants to look away. There are dignified ways to cry. Then there are blotchy, mucose breakdowns that turn the stomach to witness. Human dignity can be brought very low indeed. This is like the sight of Snape's bare bloodied leg, his trouser hem pulled up, that revolted Harry when he was 11. This is beyond pathetic; this feels indecent. Surely we aren't meant to see this.

The old letter from Lily. He broke into Grimmauld Place to find something of Lily's? Well, he has just killed Dumbledore and he's about to have the toughest year of his life. Perhaps it makes sense that he might want a talisman for private comfort. A bit like a courtly knight's favor from his lady. Except, of course, that this lady is dead, and he would be stealing.

At last, we see what was on the missing second page. Not much. She couldn't believe that a good man like Dumbledore could have been friends with the evil Grindelwald. And then—oh.

Her love. That's what was on the second page. He tucks it into his robes. Okay.

And then he does something so distasteful that many a reader might recoil. He tears the photo, takes the part with Lily and throws James and Harry away. What? Weren't we supposed to be seeing the complexity in this character? Are we meant to be reminded that Snape is nothing but a nasty, petty man, grudging to the end?

After the first reading, doubts form. Suppose Snape really is being obsessively creepy about a long-dead woman who was happy with someone else. This would be a cruel reminder, then, of Snape's failures, his loveless life, breaking into someone else's house at great risk to himself for the smallest of crumbs, stealing Lily's love that was *sisterly* love, not even romantic, and certainly not meant for him. This would be self-flagellating to an almost indulgent degree. Could someone with Snape's tasks ahead of him really afford this emotional path? Did Snape really need reminders of how badly he betrayed Lily? Didn't he already think about it every day?

Why Grimmauld Place? Did he even know what he was looking for when he went there?

Why did he leave a mess behind? Surely he must have been in a hurry before he was discovered, but a wizard of his powers would have needed no time at all to restore order before he left.

He's so ugly in this memory. He's uglier and more repellent than we have ever seen him. This is a memory he has died to give Harry. Why is he showing himself to Harry as so ugly? What's the point of drawing Harry's attention to this mid-battle, minutes before he must face Voldemort? If the point was to show Harry the other halves of the letter and photo, returning what Snape had taken, could Snape not have omitted the sight of his own hooked nose dripping with tears?

Like many of the other memories, this one adds Snape's perspective on something that Harry experienced. What did Harry remember from the day he found the first page of the letter and half the photo?

He, Ron, and Hermione had just escaped the Death Eaters in a Muggle café. They took refuge in Grimmauld Place and knew immediately that someone had searched the house. The troll's leg umbrella stand was overturned. (*HP/DH*, 169) Doors had been left open, possessions scattered. In his investigations, Harry had entered Sirius's bedroom for the first time, which was plastered with artifacts of his teen rebellion, items that surely reminded Snape of how much he had loathed Sirius: Gryffindor banners, posters of Muggle girls in bikinis, a photo of the Marauders. (*HP/DH*, 178-9)

With confirmation that the messy intruder was Snape, this line is much funnier: "Evidently Sirius's bedroom had been searched too, although its contents seemed to have been judged mostly, if not entirely, worthless." (*HP/DH*, 179) Even in the passive voice, the sentence resounds with Snape's disdain for everything to do with this room and its late owner.

Rereading this sentence in light of Snape's memory involves extraordinarily layered perspectives and time shifts. We readers are going back in our own time, looking at this sentence anew and remembering how we read it before. The narrator is showing Harry's perspective as he reads the evidence of the room, recognizing that someone had been there before him, reconstructing the probable process of that person's search and the probable conclusions they eventually reached, considering again how the room looks but from the point of view of the unknown intruder. This person had judged Sirius, and not favorably. Snape is not in the scene at all, yet we can imagine his presence vividly throughout.

Judged mostly, if not entirely, worthless. The reader reviewing this scene after reading "The Prince's Tale" is conscious of at least five viewpoints simultaneously: Snape living the scene, Harry the first time he saw the mess, Harry revisiting the scene through Snape's memory, the reader encountering this scene the first time, and the reader reviewing the scene with the new information from Snape's memory.

The first time around, Harry sees that the intruder judged Sirius's bedroom to be mostly worthless, but he doesn't know the identity of the intruder. Some readers would have guessed the intruder the first time, but most probably did not. The reader, the second time around, feels wry amusement at knowing something Harry originally did not know; we can picture Snape sneering at the room. And the reader, the second time around, considers Harry going back in his memory to this moment, filling in the identity of the intruder and making new connections. It's like going back to a moment repeatedly with a Time-Turner, but all taking place in our heads, all at once. We do so much work in our minds when we learn someone else's perspective on a shared history.

Snape curated these memories specifically for Harry. The memory showed Harry the second halves of the letter and photo—he must have intended to remind Harry of the experience of encountering the first halves.

Harry had picked up several pieces of paper before finding the crumpled letter that started, "Dear Padfoot." The letter was a combination report of quotidian and revolutionary life. Harry learned that his first-year flying lesson was not his first time on a broom, after all, and Sirius had given him his original broom when he was a baby. No wonder it meant so much to Sirius to give Harry the Firebolt. He learned that they had had a cat, that Petunia had sent a hideous vase, that James had been proud of his baby's ability on a broom . . . ordinary things that Harry would have given anything to have in his life growing up.

The letter was an "incredible treasure" to Harry, as it would have been to anyone: "He stood quite still, holding the miraculous paper in his nerveless fingers while inside him a kind of quiet eruption sent joy and grief thundering in equal measure through his veins." (*HP/DH*, 181) This is blood magic, this uncontrolled rush of painful love for and from his mother flooding all Harry's being, changing him, bathing him in the oxytocin that is the Muggle name for the magic of love flowing in the blood to create more love, to help infants grow, to hasten healing, to create empathy and protectiveness. This is what Harry craved, having known 15 months of it and then no more until he gained his friends at Hogwarts. This is what child Snape craved when he gazed greedily at Lily, who had been raised with such love. This is what Voldemort craved so badly that he didn't even know he craved it until he saw Lily's love for baby Harry and then the force of his craving sent him howling into nothingness, unable to regenerate a human body until he stole the oxytocin in Harry's blood with Lily's love still in it.

Harry searched wildly for the second half of the letter but found only the torn bit of photo.

Snape created this experience for Harry. Snape staged the clues, a treasure hunt from the overturned troll's leg to the scattered papers to the torn photo hidden under the chest of drawers, knowing it would raise urgency in Harry, showing him in inanimate objects what he could not tell Harry yet in words: *Look for your mother's story.* Snape knew the rush of hunger for more of Lily would be unstoppable for Harry, like the letters from Hogwarts pouring in when he turned 11, more and more, because the one thing Harry has ever wanted is his own story, his own family. Harry had been given back so much of his father through knowing Lupin and Sirius, through wearing his cloak and flying his Firebolt. But he was still starved for his mother, still had so little of his mother except for her eyes, and this was something Snape could give him.

Voldemort boasted to Snape that neither Snape nor Lucius knew Harry as Voldemort knew him. He was certain he did not need to seek Harry; Harry would come to him, unable to permit others to suffer for him. (*HP/DH*, 654) But Snape knew that the one thing that would compel Harry more than any other would be the knowledge that something of his mother's love remained at large, tangible and real. He ensured that Harry would find something—anything—whatever he could find among Sirius Black's possessions during the few moments he dared risk at Grimmauld Place—that would give Harry part of Lily's love. Snape would hold the other part, drawing Harry toward him so Snape could pass it to him along with Dumbledore's final message.

Blood magic, which works equally for wizards and Muggles. Delicate, mundane, invisible to Voldemort, and something that would have been utterly beyond Snape's understanding for the first part of his life.

That was the letter. Snape performed a different sort of magic, just as mundane and just as potent, with the photograph.

In the memory, Snape showed himself ripping in two the photograph of the family, keeping the part with Lily and throwing the part with James and Harry onto the floor.

In a crucial but easily missed passage of *Deathly Hallows*, Hermione discusses the process of making a Horcrux by "ripping" the soul through murder. Ron asks if there's any way to put yourself back together.

> "Yes," said Hermione with a hollow smile, "but it would be excruciatingly painful."
>
> "Why? How do you do it?" asked Harry.
>
> "Remorse," said Hermione. "You've got to really feel what you've done. There's a footnote. Apparently the pain of it can destroy you." (*HP/DH*, 103)

The concept of remorse is central to the seven-book series, but Rowling never shows us a character actually undergoing this painful process—except for one. Snape, fallen to his knees with tears dripping down his nose, is reintegrating his soul through remorse. This is how he recovers after splitting his soul through killing Dumbledore, as he implicitly told Dumbledore he would do when accepting their agreement. The process is so wrenching that a person cannot *choose* the areas in which to feel remorse. It must be total. This is how hideous we humans can feel when we finally face ourselves. And Snape cannot feel remorse for killing his friend without also facing his almost unbearably profound remorse for something he did years ago, forcing himself for the first time to truly feel what he had done.

All these years, he convinced himself of Harry's arrogance, of his resemblance to James and not Lily, of flaws that Harry did and did not have, because he couldn't endure the guilt of what he had taken from this child. Lily's baby showed up at Hogwarts ten years later, abused and half-starved, prone to headaches, constantly aware that the mass murderer who attacked him would return to finish the job. Snape had been terrified to let himself feel the life he had really given Harry. Better to believe that Harry didn't suffer. That Potter was so insulated by his arrogance, he could barely feel pain at all. That criticism would simply bounce off him without effect.

The ordinary things in Lily's letter, the garish bad taste of a godfather's room, the quiet birthday teas . . . these are the things that Snape took from Harry. By tearing the photo, he recreated what he had done to Harry's family when he asked Voldemort for the mother's life but not the father's or child's. There was no magic to this act, but it raised emotion and cast a spell nonetheless: a mundane spell for remorse. Snape showed Harry through the memory that he understood what he had done. This memory is an apology.

In asking for Lily's life alone, in feeling love for her yet thinking nothing of separating her from her husband and child, he was fatally greedy, wanting something that belonged to other people by rights. Snape had memories of Lily's love, but they wouldn't work for him as they would work for the person to whom they truly belonged. Snape thought that Dumbledore's final message meant Harry would die very soon. It was imperative to Snape that he return memories of Lily's love to Harry, their rightful owner, before Harry died. They would protect Harry. They would bathe him in love and courage on his walk to meet Voldemort.

Lily's love, her power of flight, her protectiveness, her ability to walk away rather than attack: all of these things were Harry's maternal inheritance. Snape held them in trust until it was safe for him to pass them on, as Dumbledore had done with Harry's paternal inheritance years ago (*HP/SS* 202), in such similar spirit that he could have written Harry nearly the same note:

Your mother left this in my possession before she died. It is time it was returned to you. Use it well.

#20: The sword of Gryffindor

Phineas Nigellus Black comes running into his portrait with news of Harry and Hermione's location. Snape has been looking for them for months to give them the sword of Gryffindor, but even so, there's something else so important that he interrupts this long-awaited announcement.

> And now Snape stood again in the headmaster's study as Phineas Nigellus came hurrying into his portrait.
>
> "Headmaster! They are camping in the Forest of Dean! The Mudblood—"
>
> "Do not use that word!" (*HP/DH*, 689)

In this final memory from Snape, Rowling is making a deliberate parallel to Dumbledore, letting us know without ambiguity that Snape is just as steadfast on issues that matter. When Draco had Dumbledore at wandpoint on top of the tower, he referred to Hermione with a slur.

> "Please do not use that offensive word in front of me," said Dumbledore.
>
> Malfoy gave a harsh laugh. "You care about me saying 'Mudblood' when I'm about to kill you?" (*HP/HBP*, 589)

Snape and Dumbledore are equally clear that they fight for the rights of Muggle-borns, just as Snape and Dumbledore both sacrificed the chance to save their own lives because they used their last moments to protect Harry instead.

The portrait of Dumbledore reminds Snape that the sword must be taken "under conditions of need and valor" (*HP/DH*, 689) and that he cannot let Harry see him, in case Voldemort reads Harry's mind. Snape asks, one last time, if Dumbledore is going to tell him why Harry needs the sword, and Dumbledore replies again, "No, I don't think so." (*HP/DH*, 690) Dumbledore is still protecting Snape from Voldemort, and Snape still misunderstands and resents this. He dies without full knowledge of Dumbledore's care. But he delivers Dumbledore's final message to Harry anyway, along with 19 other memories of his own selection, to strengthen Harry and ease his way.

> And Snape left the room. Harry rose up out of the Pensieve, and moments later he lay on the carpeted floor in exactly the same room: Snape might just have closed the door. (*HP/DH*, 690)

And then Harry returns to the battle to let Voldemort kill him, as he has just learned he must.

The Forest Again

Harry emerges from Snape's Pensieve memories with the mistaken thought, "Finally, the truth." (*HP/DH*, 691) Based on the incomplete information Dumbledore gave Snape, Harry believes Dumbledore did not intend Harry to survive the confrontation with Voldemort. Feeling somewhat betrayed and slightly bitter, Harry goes to his death of his own volition, knowing it's his nature to want to save others. The Snitch he inherited from Dumbledore cracks open to release the Resurrection Stone. Harry uses it to call dead loved ones to walk with him, providing comfort as he presents himself for attack without defending himself.

He has just seen Snape do the exact same thing. Cornered by the Heads of House, Snape crashed out the window rather than defending himself, letting McGonagall call him a coward without saying a word in his own defense, remembering Lily as his childhood friend and flying the way Lily flew.

Snape and Harry both chose this course of action, able to override their instincts for self-defense because of unwavering belief in their end goal. Both required strict discipline to shut down their extraordinarily strong defenses. Harry noted, "This cold-blooded walk to his own destruction would require a different kind of bravery," not like the adrenaline-fueled heroics that come naturally to him. (HP/DH, 692) Both Harry and Snape, when they committed to letting themselves be killed, focused by calling upon memories of loved ones who were dead rather than living people who might tether them to life.

King's Cross: Master of Death

In the moments after he receives Voldemort's Killing Curse without defending himself, Harry holds an illuminating conversation with Dumbledore, a Dumbledore who is at once real and imagined, part of himself. In the course of this conversation, Harry learns answers that he didn't realize he already knew.

For one thing, Harry isn't dead. For another, Dumbledore had expected and hoped as much. He hadn't betrayed Harry after all:

> "But I should have died—I didn't defend myself! I meant to let him kill me!"
>
> "And that," said Dumbledore, "will, I think, have made all the difference." (HP/DH, 708)

The sight of Harry choosing to die without defending himself made an impact on Voldemort, just as the sight of Snape taking his hands off his wound convinced Harry to pay attention to the message Snape delivered. Harry and Snape both had something they valued more than their own survival.

Dumbledore acknowledges Harry as a Master of Death, powerful enough to unite the three Hallows by using them all for their proper purpose. Even Dumbledore, in his greatness, could only master one of the Deathly Hallows: the Elder Wand, the urge to dominate. His greed for the Resurrection Stone showed that he had not accepted the finality of death for his loved ones:

> "I was fit only to possess the meanest of them, the least
> extraordinary. I was fit to own the Elder Wand, and not to boast of
> it, and not to kill with it. I was permitted to tame and to use it,
> because I took it, not for gain, but to save others from it.
>
> "But the Cloak, I took out of vain curiosity, and so it could never
> have worked for me as it works for you, its true owner. The stone I
> would have used in an attempt to drag back those who are at peace,
> rather than to enable my self-sacrifice, as you did." (*HP/DH*, 720)

Harry is unusual in that he can work with all three Hallows properly, without greed. Not everyone is interested in all three. Voldemort did not recognize the Resurrection Stone and wouldn't have found it compelling in any case, nor would he have felt the need for the cloak. (*HP/DH*, 721) Dumbledore and Grindelwald rarely thought about the cloak and wanted to use the stone to bring back the dead, albeit in very different ways. (*HP/DH*, 716)

Snape is a different case. He is also a Master of Death, unafraid and accepting of death but barely interested in any of the Hallows at all. He is the anti-Voldemort. Whereas Voldemort is obsessed with material objects, stealing cups and rings and lockets to house shreds of his soul, Snape depends on very little outside his own mind. His greatest specialties, potions and Occlumency, are even performed without wands or incantations. Unlike Voldemort, Snape's discoveries led him further *away* from relying on dangerously uncontrollable artifacts.

The Dumbledore of King's Cross points out that Voldemort gambled everything on the Elder Wand rather than self-reflection:

> "At first, he was afraid that you had conquered him by superior
> skill. Once he had kidnapped Ollivander, however, he discovered
> the existence of the twin cores. He thought that explained
> everything. Yet the borrowed wand did no better against yours! So
> Voldemort, instead of asking himself what quality it was in you
> that had made your wand so strong, what gift you possessed that
> he did not, naturally set out to find the one wand that, they said,
> would beat any other." (*HP/DH*, 721)

Snape's thinking has always gone in the opposite direction. His style of self-sufficient magic is accessible to almost anyone. A child can win a duel with *Expelliarmus*. Anyone who wants to protect a loved one can learn to fend off dementors. Magical artifacts pass through Snape's hands, work properly for him, and move on, like Potter's Invisibility Cloak or the Elder Wand that Dumbledore knew would have recognized Snape as its master without Snape even knowing it.

In King's Cross, Dumbledore leaves Harry with this joyous tribute to the mundane human power of changing ourselves simply by *thinking*:

> "Tell me one last thing," said Harry. "Is this real? Or has this been happening inside my head?"
>
> Dumbledore beamed at him, and his voice sounded loud and strong in Harry's ears even though the bright mist was descending again, obscuring his figure.
>
> "Of course it is happening inside your head, Harry, but why on earth should that mean that it is not real?" (*HP/DH*, 723)

Snape's signature magic is magic that happens inside the mind. He was a Master of Death without needing any of the Deathly Hallows at all.

He did not need the Elder Wand. He authored the ownership of the Elder Wand by training two of its young adult owners to come into possession simply by being worthy, without ever seeking it.

He did not need the Resurrection Stone. He could recall the love in his interactions with Lily Evans as powerfully as the Resurrection Stone recalled Lily, James, Lupin, and Sirius for Harry. His Patronus was just an outward manifestation of this steadfast source of strength, usually visible to himself alone, the way Harry's loved ones were invisible to everyone else. This protection was powerful enough for Snape to block out dementors or the world's self-proclaimed greatest Legilimens. This ability to connect to that feeling of love kept him airborne when he leaped.

He did not need a cloak to become invisible. Going undercover as the right-hand man of the tyrant he brought down was the same magic on a grander scale. Like the brother in the story who asked for Death's cloak, Snape walked away from death, for a while, on the night he pledged to protect Harry rather than end his life. Harry will always understand this about Snape after his own decision, during this conversation with the imaginary Dumbledore, to return to battle rather than board a train to go on:

> "By returning, you may ensure that fewer souls are maimed, fewer

families are torn apart. If that seems to you a worthy goal, then we say good-bye for the present."

Harry nodded and sighed. Leaving this place would not be nearly as hard as walking into the forest had been, but it was warm and light and peaceful here, and he knew that he was heading back to pain and the fear of more loss. (*HP/DH*, 722)

Dumbledore withheld information about Hallows from Snape, but it was not information that would have interested him or helped his work. According to Dumbledore, "Maybe a man in a million could unite the Hallows"—a rare quality, then, but not unique. In every way, on his second chance in life, Snape proved himself a worthy Master of Death.

The Flaw in the Plan: Invisible to Voldemort

Now that Harry, like Snape, has chosen to live for others rather than die, he has gained the same magical power to fend off dementors without a Patronus. He knows his purpose and that strengthens him. When he feigns death and Voldemort forces Hagrid to carry him back to the castle, he senses dementors through his closed eyes, but they do not attack him: "They would not affect him now. The fact of his own survival burned inside him, a talisman against them, as though his father's stag kept guardian in his heart." (*HP/DH*, 728)

Snape lived and died assuming that his true efforts would never be known, his true self never exonerated. But in the final duel with Voldemort, Harry reveals Snape's true work to all assembled at the Battle of Hogwarts, firing their imaginations with the wonder and enormity of Snape's achievement, strengthening them more when they realize what he sacrificed to protect them all. He tells Voldemort of the pact between Snape and Dumbledore, which started "from the moment you started hunting down my mother." (*HP/DH*, 740)

Voldemort's response is in keeping with his insistence that human sentiment can be broken down into nothing but weaknesses that can be exploited. His stance looks brittle, embarrassing, next to the simplicity of what Harry is saying about Snape.

"Snape's Patronus was a doe," said Harry, "the same as my mother's, because he loved her for nearly all of his life, from the time when they were children. You should have realized," he said as he saw Voldemort's nostrils flare, "he asked you to spare her life, didn't he?"

"He desired her, that was all," sneered Voldemort, "but when she had gone, he agreed that there were other women, and of purer blood, worthier of him—" (*HP/DH*, 740)

Snape was truly an Occlumency master if he was able to keep up his end of a conversation in which Voldemort offered him dating advice.

Harry's dialogue with Voldemort shows that Snape's strategy to evade Voldemort's understanding took a clear path. Voldemort couldn't understand that Snape could be sorry enough for his betrayal of Lily to forswear romance for the life of a double agent. He couldn't understand Dumbledore's faith in Snape or how Snape felt such loyalty to Dumbledore that he would agree to kill and die for their shared cause. There was no chance that he could understand how Snape took the Elder Wand out of his reach by teaching Harry and Draco to defend, to disarm, and to walk away.

Voldemort dies when Harry offers him a chance to feel remorse for everything he's done. Harry, Ron, and Hermione go to the headmaster's office, where all the former heads give Harry an ovation and Dumbledore weeps with pride.

There is no portrait of Snape.

Readers questioned whether the absence of a portrait meant that Snape was not truly dead, or perhaps that he hadn't had a chance to sit for a portrait, or that Rowling had simply overlooked that detail. Rowling confirmed in a web chat shortly after publication of *Harry Potter and the Deathly Hallows* that the omission was intentional.

> Laura Trego: Was the absence of snapes (*sic*) portrait in the headmasters (*sic*) office in the last scene innocent or deliberate
>
> J.K. Rowling: It was deliberate. Snape had effectively abandoned his post before dying, so he had not merited inclusion in these august circles.
>
> J.K. Rowling: However, I like to think that Harry would be instrumental in ensuring that Snape's portrait would appear there in due course. (The Leaky Cauldron 2007)

The headmaster's office casts its own magic. In Harry's fifth year, it sealed itself against Dolores Umbridge, refusing to recognize her as headmistress. The office remained faithful to Dumbledore even though he was gone. After Dumbledore's death, the office recognized both McGonagall and Snape. That the magical castle itself thought Snape had abandoned his post shows that when he leaped through the window, that was the moment he could no longer both protect Harry and remain headmaster, and he chose with his full heart to protect Harry. But it also shows that Snape Occluded himself so profoundly that not even the sentient castle, which is a sort of mirror, could detect his unwavering loyalty to the school. He managed to fool powerful sentient objects as well as wizards and witches. He knew that sometimes, fleeing to protect others is more important even than being known.

When Harry buried Dobby, he almost broke down contrasting Dobby's humble burial with Dumbledore's funeral: "He felt that Dobby deserved just as grand a funeral, and yet here the elf lay between bushes in a roughly dug hole." (HP/DH, 480) When Harry was applauded by the headmasters' portraits, Phineas Nigellus Black had his say: "And let it be noted that Slytherin House played its part! Let our contribution not be forgotten!" (HP/DH, 747)

Harry's fiercest desire has always been to know the full story, to have the truth be known, especially about those, like his parents, who died protecting others. The urge that led him to commemorate Dobby is the same one that makes him sympathetic to Phineas Nigellus Black's plea to credit the profound but necessarily covert work that Slytherins did to bring down Voldemort. Snape will be an interesting addition to that cacophonous portrait gallery, the very young protégé hand-selected by the great Albus Dumbledore to see Hogwarts through one grim, pivotal year.

Snape died believing that Dumbledore meant to sacrifice Harry. Perhaps, once his portrait is installed, his portrait can talk to Dumbledore's and understand better that Dumbledore meant to help Harry free himself of Voldemort. Perhaps Dumbledore's portrait can finally explain that he withheld information about Horcruxes not for lack of trust but because he cared about Snape enough to protect his life. Perhaps, when she moves into the headmistress's office, Professor McGonagall will get to speak to Snape's portrait about the heartbreak of his apparent betrayal and her even greater heartbreak when she realized everything he endured while she attacked him. Whatever Snape's portrait tells her, the other portraits can back up his story. They were witnesses to his final year.

Epilogue

Nineteen years later, Draco and Harry see each other on Platform 9 ¾. They are nearly the age that Snape was when he died, but unlike Snape, they have wives and school-aged children—the kind of family life that Snape forfeited as a teen but fought for others to have.

Harry's middle child, Albus Severus Potter, is off to Hogwarts for the first time. He is afraid he might get Sorted into Slytherin.

The middle name suggests a hidden core, a secondary trait that complements and strengthens a person's dominant traits. So much of what helped Harry survive in his 18th year was the Slytherin strategy, patience, and self-control that he learned from Snape. He would not have survived if he'd retained the abhorrence of Slytherin that led him to repudiate parts of his own nature when he was younger.

Harry tells Albus that he was named for two Hogwarts headmasters: "One of them was a Slytherin and he was probably the bravest man I ever knew." (*HP/DH*, 758)

Through Harry's words, Rowling is equating Snape not only with Dumbledore but with a literary figure from a different novel: Atticus Finch from Harper Lee's *To Kill a Mockingbird*, which Rowling once named as one of her top 10 recommended books for young readers. (Higgins, 2006) Scout, the narrator, remembers Atticus as "the bravest man who ever lived." (Lee, 100)

Albus is still anxious.

> "But just say—"
>
> "—then Slytherin House will have gained an excellent student, won't it? It doesn't matter to us, Al. But if it matters to you, you'll be able to choose Gryffindor over Slytherin. The Sorting Hat takes your choice into account."
>
> "Really?"
>
> "It did for me," said Harry.
>
> He had never told any of his children that before, and he saw the wonder in Albus's face when he said it. (*HP/DH*, 758)

As a child, Harry had vehemently rejected the Sorting Hat's assertion that he could do well in Slytherin. He was terrified to think that he had anything in common with Voldemort or that the attack might have made him more like Voldemort. If Harry can tell his child he was once considered for Slytherin, he must be healed from his old trauma. But it also means that he has accepted his true nature as genuinely Slytherin enough to be considered for that house, independent of and outlasting his trauma from Voldemort.

If his child is Sorted into Slytherin, Harry will be prepared to tell him how Slytherin can help him on his way to greatness. His image of the quintessential Slytherin is no longer Voldemort but Snape. His image of bravery, that quintessential Gryffindor trait, is not any of the Gryffindor loved ones for whom he has named his children. In Harry's story as he tells it, Severus Snape is the name he passes to his children to define bravery.

WORKS CITED

John Granger, *The Deathly Hallows Lectures* (Allentown, PA: Zossima Press, 2008)

Charlotte Higgins, "From Beatrix Potter to Ulysses...What the top writers say every child should read," *The Guardian* (January 31, 2006) http://www.theguardian.com/uk/2006/jan/31/buildingachildrensli brary.guardianchildrensfictionprize2005

Hilary Kovar Justice, "Mind the Gap: Severus Snape and the Final Imperative," *Terminus*, Ed. Sharon K. Goetz (Sedalia, CO: Narrate, Inc., 2010)

The Leaky Cauldron, "J.K. Rowling Web Chat Transcript" (July 30, 2007) http://www.the-leaky-cauldron.org/2007/07/30/j-k-rowling-web-chat-transcript/

Harper Lee, *To Kill a Mockingbird* (New York: Warner Books, 1960)

Niccolò Machiavelli, *The Prince*, trans. Peter Bondanella (New York: Oxford University Press Inc, 2005)

Stephen McGinty, "The JK Rowling Story," *The Scotsman* (June 18, 2003) http://www.scotsman.com/lifestyle/culture/books/the-jk-rowling-story-1-652114

J.K. Rowling, "Gilderoy Lockhart," *Pottermore* (October 3, 2013) https://www.pottermore.com/writing-by-jk-rowling/gilderoy-lockhart

J.K. Rowling, *Harry Potter and the Chamber of Secrets* (New York: Scholastic Inc, 1998)

J.K. Rowling, *Harry Potter and the Deathly Hallows* (New York: Scholastic Inc, 2007)

J.K. Rowling, *Harry Potter and the Goblet of Fire* (New York: Scholastic Inc, 2000)

J.K. Rowling, *Harry Potter and the Half-Blood Prince* (New York: Scholastic Inc, 2005)

J.K. Rowling, *Harry Potter and the Order of the Phoenix* (New York: Scholastic Inc, 2003)

J.K. Rowling, *Harry Potter and the Prisoner of Azkaban* (New York: Scholastic Inc, 1999)

J.K. Rowling, *Harry Potter and the Sorcerer's Stone* (New York: Scholastic Inc, 1997)

INDEX

antidotes, 101–2, 121, 182, 244, 267
Arthurian legend, 216, 236–37, 238
Avada Kedavra, 201, 228
Azkaban, 43, 44

Beatrice, 245
beauty, 257–58
bezoars, 183
Binns, Cuthbert, 36
Black, Phineas Nigellus, 229–30, 276, 294
Black, Sirius
    altercations with Snape, 70–71, 120–21, 141, 142, 257–58
    appearance vs reality, 105–6
    in Azkaban, 43–44, 84
    bedroom at Grimmauld Place, 283
    death, 151–52
    friendship with Lupin, 67
    innocence of, 72–73
    letter from Lily, 284
    parallels with Snape, 111
    as protector of Harry, 119–20, 233
    revealed as Animagus, 80
    shame at past behavior, 148
    Snape nearly killed by, 69–70
    Snape's suspicions of, 59, 60
blood magic, 8, 158, 284–85
boggarts, 53, 54
Buckbeak, 66–67, 75–76, 205
bullying, 12, 44, 51–54, 93–94
Bulstrode, Millicent, 32, 33
Burbage, Charity, 215, 220–21

Carrow, Alecto, 217–18
Carrow, Amycus, 217–18
Chang, Cho, 118
chivalry, 237, 238
class differences, 258
combat, as teaching tool, 33, 40
courtly love, 236–37
Crabbe, Vincent, 189
Crookshanks, 67

Crouch, Jr., Barty, 85, 87–88, 89–90, 103
Cruciatus Curse, 114, 194, 202, 217, 223, 228
Dante, 245
Dark Arts, 177–78, 211–12, 258–59
Dark Mark, 85, 90, 96, 104, 240–41
Davies, Roger, 266
Death Eaters, 85, 97, 100–101, 105, 133, 170, 213. *see also* names of individual DEs
Deathly Hallows, 219–20, 265, 289–91
defensive magic, 31, 226–27
Delacour, Fleur, 266
dementors, 44–45, 110, 181, 232–34
Department of Mysteries, 130–31, 137
Devil's Snare, 18
Dippet, Armando, 229
disarmament, 41–42. *see also* *Expelliarmus*
Dobby, 230–31, 294
Dolohov, Anton, 154
Dueling Club, 29–30, 31–34, 101
Dumbledore, Albus
    agrees to protect Lily, 262–63
    argues with Snape, 193, 272–75
    asks Snape to kill him, 269–72
    avoids Harry, 109–10, 119
    death, 201–2
    defends Snape to Harry, 197–98
    disarmed by Draco, 41
    Elder Wand and, 225, 226–27
    favoritism towards Gryffindor, 22–23, 34–35, 36, 51, 73–74
    final plan for Harry, 275–80
    healed by Snape, 267–69
    hires Lockhart, 26–27
    in Horcrux cave, 198–99
    King's Cross conversation, 289–92
    mistakes of, 152–53
    offers Snape second chance, 91, 263–66
    reconciles Snape and Sirius, 105–6
    rescue of Buckbeak, 74–76

response to Lupin's deceptions, 80–82

sets Snape to watch over Draco, 192–93

silences Snape, 44, 50–51, 78–79

trusts Snape, 96, 98–99, 161–63

use of DADA professor jinx, 160

use of gossip, 68

withholds information about Hallows, 219–20

Dumbledore, Albus (portrait), 280

Dumbledore's Army (D.A.), 113

Dursley, Dudley, 110

Dursley, Marge, 48–49

Dursley, Petunia, 118, 249–50, 251, 255, 256–57

Elder Wand, 219, 224–28, 231, 289–90

emotion, influence on magic, 39

empathy, 39, 128, 145, 146–47, 230, 256

Evans, Lily. see Potter, Lily Evans

Excalibur, 238

Expelliarmus, 31, 40–42, 72, 101, 112, 199–200, 212–13, 223–28, 262

extremists, 88

eye contact, 122, 245–46

the Fates, 166

Fawkes, 238

Felix Felicis, 198

Filch, Argus, 13, 38–39, 95–96, 185

Finch, Atticus, 295

Finite Incantatem, 32

Fletcher, Mundungus, 280–81

flight, 210–11, 241, 250

flight of Seven Harrys, 281

Flitwick, Filius, 18

flow state, 8

Fluffy, 13–14

Foe-Glass, 90

Fudge, Cornelius, 79, 104

gold (color), 267

Golden Snitch, 215, 288

Goyle, Gregory, 28, 93, 189

Granger, Hermione

ability to learn from mistakes, 19–20

blames self for not watching Snape, 206

boggarts and, 55, 65–66

brews Polyjuice Potion, 27–29

concern for Snape, 77

connection with Snape, 229–30, 245

defends Snape, 14, 49, 89, 118

duels Millicent Bulstrode, 32, 33

faith in Snape, 99, 218–19

helps Buckbeak, 66, 75–76

helps Neville, 51

injured by Dolohov, 154

nonverbal spells, 178–80

opinion of Half-Blood Prince, 182, 207, 209–10

proposes Harry teach DADA, 111–12

reveals Lupin is werewolf, 67–68

sets Snape's robes on fire, 14–15

similarities to Snape, 59, 68

Snape's disregard of, 9–10, 17, 28, 36–37, 58, 66, 93–95, 94

solves Snape's puzzle, 18–19

Time-Turner, 45–46, 65–66

Granger, John, 245

Grimmauld Place, 110, 119, 166, 216, 218, 281–82, 283

Grindelwald, Gellert, 219, 224, 281

Gryffindor House, 34–35, 36, 52

guilt, 64–65, 191–92, 193, 199, 204–5

Hagrid, Rubeus, 12, 30, 148–49, 193, 205, 217–18

Half-Blood Prince, 181–88, 203, 207–12

Headmaster's office, 229, 280, 293, 294–95

Heir of Slytherin, 27, 39

Hogwarts Express, 256–57

Horcruxes, 157, 238, 268–69, 278, 286

Imperius Curse, 222, 228

innocence, 66, 71, 72, 74–75, 83

Inquisitorial Squad, 138–39

Invisibility Cloak

Harry's use of, 66, 96–97

Moody's ability to penetrate, 95

Snape's use of, 68, 70, 76, 219, 227

jealousy, 158

Jordan, Lee, 35–36

Justice, Hilary K., 246

Karkaroff, Igor, 91–92

Killing Curse, 201

Kreacher, 221

Krum, Viktor, 93

Legilimency, 13, 15, 121–22, 149–50, 222
Lestrange, Bellatrix, 166–67, 168–72, 174
Levicorpus, 185–86
Liberacorpus, 185
life debts, 61–62, 70, 72, 268
Lockhart, Gilderoy, 25–27, 29–34, 38
loneliness, 8, 253
Longbottom, Neville, 11, 18, 51–55, 57, 150–51, 217
"Look at me," 245–46, 250
Lovegood, Luna, 257
Lovegood, Xenophilius, 222
Lupin, Remus
    boggart class, 53–55
    confrontation in Shrieking Shack, 67–71
    criticizes use of *Expelliarmus*, 223–24
    departure of, 80–82
    guilt for misleading Dumbledore, 64–65
    Harry's bond with, 55–56
    Marauder's Map and, 63–64
    as minority, 47
    opinion of Snape, 162
    reasons for hire, 44
    shame at inaction, 141, 147, 148
    Snape's dislike of, 48, 259
    Snape's mixed motives towards, 49–51, 55–57
    Snape's protection of, 281
    Snape's suspicions of, 50–51, 59–60

Machiavelli, Niccolò, 211–12, 220–21, 222, 268
Malfoy, Draco
    attempts to kill Dumbledore, 164
    attitude towards Muggle-borns, 27, 37
    becomes Death Eater, 158–59
    duels Harry, 32–34, 193–95
    Elder Wand and, 227–28
    Expelliarmus usage, 40, 41–42, 199–200, 225
    ferret punishment, 87–88
    rejects Snape's help, 188–89, 200
    relationship with father, 35
    Sectumsempra injury, 193–95
    Snape's attempts to reach, 190–93
    Snape's protection of, 154, 159, 212–13
    Voldemort's treatment of, 223
Malfoy, Lucius, 34–35, 103, 258
Malfoy, Narcissa, 157, 166–67
Marauders, 43–44, 55–58, 62–64, 69–70. *see also* Black, Sirius; Lupin, Remus; Potter, James
Marauders' Map, 58, 63–65, 70, 82, 97
McGonagall, Minerva
    advises Harry re: Umbridge, 110–11
    defends Hagrid, 148–49
    gives Time-Turner to Hermione, 45–46, 65–66
    rescues Draco, 88
    as Snape's ally, 13, 38, 154–55, 190, 205
    as Snape's enemy, 240–41
Mirror of Erised, 18, 19
Montague, Graham, 139, 140, 147
Moody, Alastor "Mad-Eye," 87–88, 95–97
Moseley, Clare, 18
Mrs. Norris, 38–39
Mudbloods, 27, 35, 36, 37, 143

Nagini, 242, 243, 277–78
nonverbal spells, 178–80, 185

Occlumency, 109, 121–22, 188–89, 231–32, 243
Occlumency lessons
    Harry's failures, 126–32
    Harry's success, 135–37
    need for, 121–25
    reasons for ending, 145–46
    reasons for failure of, 153–54
    reasons for Snape to teach, 119–20
    results of, 132–33

Parseltongue, 34, 39–40
Patronuses
    as defense, 181, 232–34
    as method of communication, 152
    Snape's, 216, 218–19, 234–37, 279–80, 292
    Tonks', 163
Peeves, 57
Pettigrew, Peter, 43–44, 57, 141, 167–68, 225
Platform 9¾, 256, 295

Polyjuice Potion, 27–29
portraits, 229–30
possession, 120
post-traumatic flashbacks, 46–47, 71–72, 73–74, 199
Potions class
　first year, 6–12
　second year, 29
　third year, 47–48, 51–52
　fourth year, 101–2
　fifth year, 116–17
　sixth year, 157, 181–84, 188
Potter, Albus Severus, 295
Potter, Harry
　acceptance of Slytherin-ness, 295–96
　blames Snape for parents' death, 197–98
　casts Unforgivable, 222–23
　defeats Voldemort, 292–93
　Dobby and, 230–31, 294
　doubts of Sirius, 146–47, 148
　Draco and, 32–34, 164–65, 176–77, 194, 213, 223, 255–56
　duels Voldemort, 101
　Elder Wand and, 228, 231
　empathizes with Snape, 146–47, 223
　Expelliarmus usage, 40–43, 223–26, 228
　fights Snape, 202–5
　first encounter with Snape, 5–6
　in Horcrux cave, 198–99
　King's Cross conversation, 226–27, 289–92
　Legilimency attempt, 149–50
　Lupin's bond with, 55–56
　mother's eyes, 145
　parallels with Snape, 48–49, 139–40, 155–56, 181, 221–22
　parents, 142, 146–47, 233, 284–85
　Parseltongue, 39–40
　refuses to kill Pettigrew, 70, 72
　refuses to listen to Snape, 60–62
　self-sacrifice, 288–89
　Snape's apology to, 266
　Snape's dislike of, 6–7, 25, 47–48, 86–87, 113–14, 159, 278–79
　Snape's praise of, 128, 136
　suspicions of Snape, 14–16, 49, 56–57, 107
　teaches fellow students, 111–13
　Voldemort's mental link with, 122–25, 130–33, 230–32, 242–43, 274

Potter, James
　bullies teenage Snape, 141–43
　Harry's doubts about, 146–47
　Harry's resemblance to, 56, 61
　as loved child, 257
　Marauder, 43–44
　protects Harry, 233
　saves Snape's life, 62–63, 69–70
　as Seeker, 21
Potter, Lily Evans
　falling-out with Snape, 142–43, 258–60
　protects Harry, 233
　skill at Potions, 182, 186–87
　Snape's apology to, 260–61
　Snape's first meeting with, 249–52
　Snape's friendship with, 252–56
　Snape's love for, 237, 246, 261–63
Prince, Eileen, 158, 207–8, 210, 254–55
privilege, 46
prophecy, 197–98
protectiveness
　Harry's of Dudley, 110
　James' of Harry, 233
　James' of Snape, 62–63, 69–70
　Lily's of Harry, 233
　Lily's of Snape, 141–42
　McGonagall's of Draco, 88
　McGonagall's of Hagrid, 148–49
　power of, 153–54, 230–31, 234, 263, 264
　Sirius' of Harry, 119–20
　Snape's of Draco, 158–59, 174–75, 188–95, 202, 212–13
　Snape's of Dumbledore, 271
　Snape's of Harry, 14–16, 19–20, 89–90, 147–48, 202–3, 212–13
　Snape's of Lupin, 56, 281
　Snape's of Narcissa, 172, 175
　Snape's of Neville, 149–51
　Snape's of students, 154, 217–18

Quibbler, 133
Quidditch matches, 14–16, 44–45
Quirrell, Quirinus, 5, 13, 16, 19–20, 21, 26

remorse, 192, 286, 293
Resurrection Stone, 219, 233–34, 288, 290
Riddle, Merope, 158
Riddle, Tom Marvolo, 158, 192–93

ring, cursed, 268–69
Rowling, J. K., 210–11, 250, 293

scar, Harry's, 90–91, 119, 130, 131,
    132, 133, 230
Sectumsempra, 164, 193–96, 255–56,
    281
Serpensortia, 34
sexual humiliation, 53, 142, 255, 273
shame, 141, 144–45, 147, 148, 276
Shrieking Shack, 67, 242
Shunpike, Stan, 223–24
silver doe, 216, 218–19, 234–37, 279–
    80, 292
Skeeter, Rita, 93
Slughorn, Horace, 157, 159–60, 181–
    84, 186–87, 276
Slytherin, Salazar, 36
Slytherin House, 7, 22–23, 34–36, 52,
    88, 133–34, 295–96
Smith, Zacharias, 112
Snape, Severus
    ambiguity of, 1–2, 5, 15
    anger with Harry, 60–62
    as anti-Voldemort, 290–91
    attitude towards Muggle-borns, 36–
        37, 143, 253, 260
    beauty of, 213
    captures Sirius, 70–72
    childhood, 136, 253–55
    colleagues' view of, 12–13, 206–7,
        218
    death, 226, 242–46
    as Death Eater, 97, 215–16
    Death Eaters' opinion of, 163–64,
        213
    desire for DADA position, 160–61
    dislike of Harry, 6–7, 9–12, 25, 47–
        48, 85–87, 89, 99, 113–14, 159,
        217, 266, 278–79
    as double agent, 105–8, 134–35, 212
    Dumbledore's request of, 267–72
    entrusted with final message to
        Harry, 275–80
    flees Hogwarts, 202–5, 239–42
    guilt, 204–5
    as Half-Blood Prince, 208–12
    as Headmaster, 242
    as Head of Slytherin, 23, 140, 154,
        189
    as hero, 213

hostility towards new teachers, 16,
    27, 47, 48, 49–50, 87–88, 114–15,
    159–60, 217–18
immaturity of, 90, 94
as Master of Death, 290–91
motives of, 20–22, 37–42, 49–51,
    89–90, 117–18, 164–65, 218
as Order of Phoenix member, 109,
    110, 151–52
passion for Potions, 7–8
post-traumatic flashbacks, 73–74,
    77–79
as protector (see protectiveness)
readers' opinion of, 164, 201–2
reliance on Dumbledore's trust, 96,
    98–99, 162–63, 270–71
remorse, 192, 281–87
reputation of, 20–21, 36–37, 48–49,
    79, 88–89, 115–16, 155–56, 160–
    64, 206–7, 218
reveals Dark Mark, 104
romance, absence of, 92–95, 141,
    236–37, 266
shame, 144–45
as teacher, 58–60, 177–81, 184, 187,
    212–13, 220–23 (see also Potions
    class)
as teenager, 140–44
ugliness of, 38, 92, 100, 104, 140–41,
    213, 217, 240, 257–58, 283
Snape, Severus (portrait), 293–94
Snape, Tobias, 208, 209, 211, 254–55
Snape-shaped hole, 241–42
Sorceror's Stone, 18–19
Sorting, 258, 267
Sorting Hat, 238, 295
spiders, 141, 166
Spinner's End, 165–67
Sprout, Pomona, 18, 30
Squibs, 39
Sword of Gryffindor, 227, 235, 237–39,
    287–88

The Prince (Machiavelli), 211–12, 220–
    21, 222, 268
Time-Turners, 45–46, 78, 83
To Kill a Mockingbird (Lee), 295
Tonks, Nymphadora, 163, 206
trauma, 44–45, 82, 128, 129, 232–33
troll in the dungeon, 13
trust, 96, 98–99

ugliness, 38, 92, 100, 104, 140–41, 213, 217, 240, 257–58, 283
Umbridge, Dolores, 110–11, 114–16, 138–39, 149–50, 232
Unbreakable Vow, 174–75, 200, 271
Unforgivable curses, 173–74, 222–23, 228, 260

Vanishing Cabinet, 139
Veritaserum, 103, 114–15
Volant, Ann, 210–11
Voldemort
    Bellatrix's relationship with, 169–70
    death, 292–93
    duels Harry, 101, 227–28
    Dumbledore's awareness of, 26
    Elder Wand and, 224–25, 226, 290
    enters Hogwarts, 231–32
    kills Snape, 243
    lures Harry to Department of
        Mysteries, 149
    mental link with Harry, 122–25, 130–31, 132, 133, 230–32, 242–43, 274
    murders Charity Burbage, 220–21
    possession of Harry, 119, 120
    resurrection of, 85
    Snape's reassurance of, 107–8
    as threat to Lily, 261–62
    treatment of Draco, 157, 158–59

Weasley, Arthur, 119, 121
Weasley, Fred, 139, 257
Weasley, George, 15, 138–39
Weasley, Ginny, 182
Weasley, Molly, 121
Weasley, Percy, 50
Weasley, Ron
    on difficulty of lying, 222
    dislike of Draco, 37
    Levicorpused by Harry, 185–86
    non-verbal spells, 180
    opinion of Half-Blood Prince, 165
    rescues Harry, 238–39
    suspicions of Snape, 89, 118, 161–62
    treatment of Hermione, 55, 93, 94
werewolves, 58–59, 59–60
Wolfsbane, 50
Wormtail. see Pettigrew, Peter

Yule Ball, 86, 92–93, 94, 266–67

ABOUT THE AUTHOR

Lorrie Kim lives in Philadelphia, PA with her clever, grumpy, magical spouse and their Harry Potter-reading offspring, one born between *Order of the Phoenix* and *Half-Blood Prince* and one in gestation during the publication of *Deathly Hallows*.

CPSIA information can be obtained
at www.ICGtesting.com
Printed in the USA
LVHW040404240120
644559LV00010B/72